FOREST LIFE AND SPORT IN INDIA

FOREST LIFE AND SPORT IN INDIA

S. EARDLEY-WILMOT

GYAN

Published by

Gyan Publishing House
5, Ansari Road
Daryaganj, New Delhi-110002
Phone: 011-47034999, 9811692060
E-mail: books@gyanbooks.com

Distribution Network
gyanbooks.com
India, USA, Canada, UK, Australia

ISBN: 978-93-6433-120-3 (HB)

First Published, 1910

2nd Impression 2024

Printed at: Gyan Press, Delhi.

FOREST LIFE AND SPORT IN INDIA
Author: S. EARDLEY-WILMOT

A FOREST ROAD IN BENGAL

London, Edward Arnold

TO

THEODORE ROOSEVELT

FORESTER AND NATURALIST

IN ADMIRATION OF HIS SUCCESS IN THE CONSERVATION

OF THE

NATURAL RESOURCES OF HIS COUNTRY

PREFACE

A NATIONAL interest in forestry is necessary to its success as a permanent industry. Such an interest has been long existent in Europe with beneficial results; in the United States of America it has conduced to much good work during the past decade; in the United Kingdom it is a growing force.

If this narrative arouses some interest in the forests of India it will have served a useful purpose; for there State Forestry is still in the beginning, and its results are all in the future.

S. E.-W.

CONTENTS

LIST OF ILLUSTRATIONS

FOREST LIFE AND SPORT IN INDIA

CHAPTER I

INTRODUCTORY

THE India of to-day lies like an open book before the world, yet it is but comparatively recently that the nation who first won an Empire, and now governs it by the strenuous exertions of her sons, has taken more than a passing interest in the country and in its inhabitants. Only a generation ago the ships passing to and from the East carried few save those who were occupied in administration or trade, or were returning home to recruit their strength, or to rest after the work of a lifetime was over. To-day the pleasures of a winter trip to India are known and enjoyed; visitors arrive in their hundreds from Europe, from America, from Australia, and for three or four months they delight in the climate and in the beauties of scenery and architecture; they pass in comfort from one centre of attraction to the next, travelling luxuriously and receiving the unstinted hospitality of Indian Princes and English officials, and they leave with regret, for to them has been presented the bright side of the shield, and there has been no leisure to study the reverse, save perhaps in the case of a few who recognize that relaxation is the smallest part of life in the East, and that there are many to whom the performance of social duties comes as an added burden to responsibilities already almost intolerable.

Amongst the pages of the book of India which are seldom turned are those that tell of its forest wealth and of the manner of its disposal. To the majority of visitors the forests are of no importance, except that they serve to enhance the beauties of the passing landscape, and are perhaps reported to contain some interesting animals; and even should there be opportunities of so-called "camping out," the charms of the free life and the chances of sport afford the sole emotions which remain in the memory. In these circumstances even a slight acquaintance with the Indian forests may add to the delights of a rapid tour, by indicating a new field for knowledgeable observation; so that, as the traveller is hurried by mail-trains through the vast jungles of the Peninsula, he will be better able to comprehend the mysteries they hide, and what manner of man and beast inhabit them; he will have opened up a new field of surmise and interest; he will better understand what Hindustan was like in the days when the temples, palaces and forts that hitherto have received all his attention were in building; he may even enter in imagination into the struggle of primeval man against the overwhelming forces of Nature.

The remains of the great forests of India still

extend in broken sequence from the south of the Peninsula, to cease in the north at that point where elevation is prohibitive of tree growth; and they still exist in large or small patches from Kashmir in the west to the border of Siam; they cover an area of one fourth of the Empire, and some 240,000 square miles are, in British India, the property of the State, the remainder being within the boundaries of native principalities. As might be expected in a country that extends from the region of perpetual snow to within 8 degrees of the Equator, the variations in forest growth are as great as those of temperature; but there are other conditions which exert even a greater influence than temperature, the chief of these being the average amount of rainfall that is annually received. It would be possible to divide the whole of India into numerous zones dependent on the amount of rainfall each enjoys, but this is not a botanical treatise, and for general purposes it will suffice to say that where the rainfall is below 20 inches the dry forests can alone exist, that from 20 to 70 inches suits the deciduous forests, and that where more than 70 inches of rain falls the evergreen forests flourish. Thus, in Sindh and Rajputana the first type may be observed; the second occupies nearly the whole of the central portion of the Peninsula; while the third is found in the West Coast of Madras and in Burma. The hill, tidal and riparian forests possess characteristics governed, in the one case, by elevation, and, in the others, by the tides and river floods that nourish them, and they are to be seen at their best respectively in the outer ranges of the Himalaya, on the coasts of Bengal and Burma, and in the Panjab.

In England there is, save amongst specialists, small knowledge of the greater number of the Indian timbers and other forest products, for the reason that only few of these reach the West, the great bulk of the forest crop being utilized in the country. Teak, which is largely exported from Burma, is familiar, and so is the sandal from Mysore; rose-wood, ebony, and black-wood, are not unknown, while lac and various dyes and tanning materials come into evidence in many occasions of our daily life; but these exports, important as they are, do not account for the million and three-quarters sterling which represents the income from the Indian forests, nor for the five million tons of timber and fuel and the two hundred millions of bamboos they annually yield; by far the largest proportion of this harvest is absorbed by the population, whose houses and whose agricultural and domestic implements are almost entirely manufactured from forest products, and who thus depend upon the forest, not only for the grazing of some fourteen million head of cattle each year, but for many other articles both of food and of general utility—in short, for luxuries as well as necessities.

But not only may the forests of India be looked upon as necessary to the daily welfare of an agricultural population in supplying at a cheap rate, or often free, the requirements of their simple existence, but they present yet another aspect which is of even greater importance. In India, speaking generally, the rainfall of the year occurs at two seasons known

The Sinthan Pass, Kashmir.

as the North-East and South-West Monsoons; in some parts of the country the former is most important, in others the latter, but in both cases not only is the amount of precipitation of vital importance, but also the time of its delivery. Either a delay in the rainfall or its unseasonable occurrence may, by preventing ploughing or the ripening of the harvest, cause widespread disaster amongst a people who have few resources at their disposal when their food-supply fails, and thus it is that the question of the storage of water and of the regulation of its off-flow becomes of vital importance. Much has doubtless been done by the construction of tanks, wells and canals to hold up the water on the surface of the ground or to utilize the subterranean moisture, and such works are indeed a marked feature of the winter landscape in India; yet it is to the forests that we must look for wider results in restraining the surface flow after heavy rain; it is by their agency that the water level is maintained at such a height that it can be reached by the primitive methods of the East; that the springs are kept supplied; and that perennial streams may be made to flow in the place of those watercourses trickling through dreary beds of sand, that would hardly be suspected of becoming later on in the summer turbulent and muddy torrents, often carrying devastation instead of blessing.

When it is once recognized that the forests of India are more important in their effect on the general welfare of the people than merely by reason of the material they supply to the industries of the West, they will assume quite a different aspect to him who visits them. Whether he stands on the upland meadows and looks down through forests of birch, cedar, fir, and pine, to where, clad in lighter green, the less hardy species flourish; or wanders through the damp forests of the Tarai, or amongst the burning hills of Central India, or in the gloomy shades of the evergreen forests, he will realize that this is all part of the vastest sylvan property ever set apart by any Government in the interests of the people, and he will be glad that, while its utility is indisputable, it renders yet another service to man in delighting his eye and in imparting a feeling of rest and calm.

An explanation of the system of management of these great forest areas will afford further insight into their national importance.

In former days the forester, when on furlough from India in England, was frequently asked the question, "What do you do in the forests?" And as a rule, being unprepared to explain his multifarious duties in few words, he commenced a hesitating reply, and was relieved when the subject was dismissed by the remark, "Oh, you plant trees, I suppose." At the present time the number of those with a knowledge of, or an interest in, forestry has vastly increased; but the large majority still naturally base their ideas of Indian State Forestry on what they see around them in the British Isles, and they cannot be expected to realize the fundamental differences which exist between forests at home and those in our distant Empire in the East. Here there may still be some remnants of the primeval forests which once covered the land, but even these have lost most of their distinctive characteristics during the centuries in which they have been under the fostering care of man or suffered his neglect or ill-treatment; but the larger areas of our English woodlands are probably at this time of artificial origin, and have been planted and managed with other designs than the production of marketable timber. There the forests are almost invariably the remains of the "shadowy desert" that in some places still retains the mastership of the soil; they depend on natural regeneration for their maintenance, and their management is conducted, not with a view to increasing the facilities for sport, not to enhance the beauties of the surrounding landscape, or for other such private reasons, but, as has been said, solely for the public benefit, whether that demands the supply of timber, fuel, grazing or other forest produce to the people or to the markets of the world, or whether it necessitates the protection of the soil in the hills or plains against the various climatic influences which are in India so drastic in their effects.

Thus, the planting of trees, which in England is synonymous with afforestation, is in India one of the least frequent duties of the Forest Officer, and when now undertaken is mostly for experimental purposes, with a view to study the habits of some valuable species. As a commercial speculation, with the object of growing timber, plantations cannot compete with the practice of forestry in natural forests, nor has the small staff of the Indian Forest Service the leisure from more important work to attend to the detailed treatment over a long period that comparatively small plantations require to make them successful.

The word "comparatively" is used advertently, for in India there were in 1907 over two hundred square miles of plantation, some of them, as at Nilambur, already more than paying their way; but when the extent of the Indian State Forests is recalled, and also the fact that the present strength of the staff would give to each block of 1,200 square miles only one English officer, one Indian officer, and seventy-five native subordinates and clerks, it may be considered fortunate that Nature in the East is in herself sufficiently prolific to insure the reproduction of forest vegetation, provided that no hindrance is opposed to her efforts.

Afforestation in India therefore does not mean, as in England, the creation of forests. It implies rather that a certain area has been set apart for the practice of forestry, and the inference is, not that this area is to be sown or planted by artificial means, but that Nature will be aided in her work of covering the soil with woody growth, and of ultimately yielding a harvest for the use of man. Such, indeed, are the present conditions in which forestry is practised in India; what the future may bring forth it is impossible to predict, but it is quite probable that it may be found later on necessary, and even remunerative, to stock the waste places of the earth artificially with tree growth, in order either to protect the water-supply or to supply timber and fuel to a growing population. When this time arrives, both the personnel and the expenditure of the Forest Department will have to be very largely increased if work on a large scale is to be undertaken.

It has been said that the continuance of the forests in India depends as a rule upon natural regeneration, and this process may be seen in all its profusion in those areas unfrequented by man. But Nature's forces cannot be expected to contend against cattle that destroy the seedlings, against fires that kill the saplings, and against the axe that removes the seed-bearers. Persistent attacks by these enemies, ever increasing in strength with the increase of population, must result in the deterioration and ultimate disappearance of the forest, and these are just those forces which have been active ever since the time when men were few and forests overwhelming. And now that the position is reversed, and forests are restricted while men are all-powerful, yet so strong are inherited instincts that it is difficult for the victors to understand that it was but the supremacy of the forest that was a danger to their existence, and that when trained to their service it becomes of importance to the welfare of their daily life, and sometimes even necessary to their progress. A frequent custom of the East was to slay the defeated enemy, and so avoid further trouble. In this instance the Forest Officer intervenes with his Western conviction that defeated enemies are useful as future allies, and introduces forest protection as the first step in the new policy.

The incidence of his work is, roughly, as follows : He first explores forest areas, which may be but little known even to the neighbouring inhabitants, and decides on their value to the State, not only on account of the timber they do or may hold, but also having regard to their utility in furnishing forest produce to a present or prospective population, or in protecting the cultivation which already exists in the vicinity or may be created in the future. The assumption of the right of ownership by the State is then notified to all whom it may concern, and, after a detailed inquiry, the claims of successful applicants to timber, fuel, produce, grazing, etc., are duly recorded. The area is then gazetted as State Forest, and comes under the Forest Law. But though afforestation is then complete, the work of the forester has but commenced. He has to demarcate the newly-created forest and arrange for its survey. Next he must draw up a plan for its working which will define the silvicultural treatment it is to receive during a period of years, and afford an estimate of its yield and of its revenue and expenditure. The plan will, moreover, suggest the staff that it will be necessary to maintain, and the roads, houses, and bridges, that may be suitably constructed. Finally it will provide a scheme for protection from fire, from cattle, and from men, which must be both effective and workable in conditions which, at first, are almost always unfavourable.

With this plan as his guide for the next ten, twenty, or more years, the forester will proceed to work by endeavouring to secure the good-will of the wild tribes of the forest or of those, more civilized, who live on its outskirts. He will probably find them indignant at the restriction of the full liberties previously enjoyed, and suspicious of any innovation which limits their destructive habits. He will find them reluctant to afford aid in the introduction of any novelty that appears to them to threaten their prescriptive rights to an area which they have up till now looked upon as their exclusive property. It will need much tact to remove that active opposition which is prohibitive of any success, and it will take much patient teaching before eager help will be afforded; but when that is forthcoming it will provide the proof that the people have recognized the fact, that though under the new régime the wanton destruction of the forest wealth is prohibited, yet they enjoy, even as before, all the advantages of its products, while at the same time they are able to earn good wages when employed in carrying out the works incidental to a regulated management.

As a general rule the forester spends more than one-half of the income of the forest on its improvement and management, while the greater portion of that income is paid in, not by those who live in the vicinity of the forest, but by purchasers from a distance. Thus, the work of the Indian Forester provides a considerable sum of money to the State, and distributes a large proportion of it locally; and this tends towards creating a population who, in the course of time, learn to take a personal interest in the welfare of the forest.

When the population in the vicinity have ceased to be actively hostile, or have even shown in practice their concurrence in forest conservancy, there still remains the vital question of successful finance, which is based on the proper exploitation of the forest crop. It is easy with forestry to pay dividends out of capital, and it is in order to prevent such illicit operations that the working plan is framed in such detail. It is possible, even with a carefully-devised plan, to do such injuries to the stock that many years are required to rectify them, and it is for this reason that professional experts are required to administer the plan so far as its silvicultural prescriptions are concerned; but even given the amount of the various kinds of produce to be removed, there remains the problem of how this shall be brought to market in the most effective manner. It may be possible to obtain purchasers who will themselves cut and remove the timber and other produce, and this is, of course, the most satisfactory manner of working; it may be incumbent on the Forest Officer to arrange for the felling, and then to sell the outturn in the forest; or, lastly, everything, including the felling, carting to depot, sale, and delivery, may be duties imposed on him in order to convert his harvest into money; and under such conditions much of the time is occupied that would more profitably be spent in other works of which the large area under his charge is so badly in need.

The winter and early spring is generally the most busy time during the year, for then the forests are least unhealthy, and work is not so much hampered by malaria and epidemics. With the withdrawal of the labour gangs and the cessation of road-making and building the forester's work is, however, not complete; he has to watch through the dry season till his forests have become green from the monsoon rains, and not till then can he return to headquarters, after eight months or more of jungle life.

Fire conservancy is in India carried to a fine art in those deciduous forests where natural regeneration is often dependent on its success. First a trace is cut along the boundary, and from thence, as good opportunity offers, the surrounding forest and grass-lands are burnt to insure isolation; next the inside area is divided into blocks by rides varying from a few to one hundred or more feet in breadth, and these are kept clear of vegetation by burning carefully at night-time; finally, watchmen are stationed at short distances apart, who control the traffic and give notice when any fire occurs. These men are recruited from the surrounding villages, and not infrequently go in danger of their lives from wild beasts, often sleeping in perches placed in high trees, so as to be out of reach of tigers and elephants.

Then, all his arrangements complete, the forester sits lonely, as in the centre of a gigantic web covering an area of several hundred square miles, waiting for a summons for help from a distance, or locating any column of smoke that may be observed by day or fiery glow by night, always on the alert to save the State property entrusted to him. When the call comes, he has no body of disciplined athletes, equipped with all modern appliances, at his orders; he hurriedly collects as many men as may be present, and leads the unwilling troop to battle, their only arms the green boughs hastily torn from the nearest tree, and their only desire to flee as soon as possible from the heat and thirst of the distasteful work. Probably it will be found impossible to check the flames advancing on a front of miles in length, and then counter-firing is resorted to from one of the many drives through the forest; but even if this operation is successful, the work is not yet over, and it may be still the labour of days to extinguish the timber smouldering on the burnt area, which may at any time, in the high winds, again cause conflagrations to break out in the area that has been saved. Some 4,500 fires are reported yearly in the Indian forests, and it is certain that each of these caused anguish and trepidation to one or more Forest Officers; and thus the dry season is often a period of mental and physical strain that is liable to undermine both health and energy in a most marked degree.

The executive Forest Officer is therefore not a planter of trees by profession; he is rather the land-agent for a vast estate that is chiefly concerned with forestry. If his only accomplishment is a knowledge of silviculture, he cannot efficiently carry out the duties entrusted to him. He requires besides some knowledge of botany, and of chemistry and zoology; he must be an engineer to align his roads and design and build his bridges and houses; he must be familiar with the timber and fuel trade, and possess commercial information with regard to other products of the forest, such as lac, myrabolams, wax, hides, spices, dyes, and roots; he must be ready to afford facilities for railway construction, and know all about the rafting, sledging, and sliding of timber; he must be an adept at the vernacular languages, and be able to influence the people; he may, indeed, be a magistrate, and be authorized to punish their offences; and if to these accomplishments he can add some hobby which has its foundation in a love

A "Fire Line" in Garhwál.

of Nature, and at the same time succeed in keeping his health, he has the certainty of contentment, so far as that can be secured by constant occupation, for he will never have an idle hour.

He need not, however, always remain with none but executive duties; he may look forward to rising to administrative rank. The constitution of the Indian Forest Department comprises three great branches: first, the Imperial Service, recruited in England, consisting of an Inspector-General of Forests at the headquarters of the Government of India, of two Chief Conservators in charge of the extensive forests in Burma and the Central Provinces, and of fourteen Conservators in charge of Circles, and below these, again, Deputy and Assistant Conservators in charge of districts; next, the Provincial Service, whose members are statutory natives recruited in India, comprising Extra-Deputy and Extra-Assistant Conservators, who are either in charge of or attached to districts; and, lastly, the Subordinate Service, which consists of Rangers, Foresters, and Forest Guards, in order of rank, and of clerks and others, such as messengers, treasure-guards, or orderlies. The strength of the Imperial and Provincial Services is about 200 officers in each branch, and that of the Subordinate Service about 15,000 or 16,000 men. The Conservator is an administrating officer who has territorial charge, and who, under the orders of the Provincial Government, conducts the forest policy of a province; the Inspector-General is an advising officer, who is consulted by the Supreme Government in all forest questions that come before it.

The Conservator is held responsible for the finance of his Circle, and for due progress being made in the protection, improvement, and outturn, of his forests. During eight months of the year he is occupied in tours of inspection in the forest; during the remaining four he remains in his office preparing his annual report and his budget estimate, disposing of the returns from existing working plans and scrutinizing new proposals, and arranging for next season's work —in fact, in the labours incidental to an agent who has under his control from five to nine great estates, each with separate interests, but all belonging to one owner.

The foregoing brief sketch of the forests of India and the duties of those who have them in their charge is intended to present without unnecessary detail such information as may serve to obviate frequent explanations in future chapters.

CHAPTER II

EARLY DAYS IN OUDH

I JOINED the Indian Forest Service on December 3, 1873, at Lucknow. At that time the bridge over the Ganges at Cawnpore was not completed, and Oudh was a non-regulation Province; that is to say, it was administered by a Commission whose members had been recruited chiefly from military officers—men who were here, as in the Panjab, in the Central Provinces, and in Burma, preparing the way for more settled rule, and, their work accomplished, were being replaced by members of the Indian Civil Service, men who had no experience of the sword, which in the East has inevitably preceded the more mighty pen. It was but fifteen years since the great Mutiny had been quelled, and our companions were, some of them, men who had taken part in it; its memory had not been forgotten by the people, who could tell more than they cared to of the pacification of Oudh. The numerous extensions of the Oudh and Rohilkhand Railway were at that time not opened, and the Rohilkhand and Kumaon line was not commenced; the Bengal and North-Western Railway had not extended its operations towards the northern districts of the Province.

But good-fellowship resulted from isolation; the

officials of the Province were all known to each other, and hospitality was the custom of the day. The "dâk-bungalow," or travellers' rest-house, at the headquarters station of the district would not have paid its way had it been dependent on the visits of Government officials, who went as a matter of course to the houses of their colleagues. The military outpost of Sitapur, held then by Queen's troops and native cavalry, was reached by posting along the now nearly deserted highway. The traveller was offered a police escort, and his refusal was committed to writing, for the justification of the authorities in case of outrage: for as a rule one preferred to run the risk of robbery-under-arms to loading the wretchedly horsed box-on-wheels in which one travelled with the weight of two policemen, who might perhaps be the friends or relatives of the dacoits; but one went armed with a serviceable revolver. Northwards from Sitapur, Kheri lay twenty-eight miles away, and it took seven hours to reach it in a dooli; beyond was the unknown, and again the dooli, with its band of "kahars" of "banghiwálas," and of "masálchis," was requisitioned to bear the traveller through the misty night, through jungle and grass, across the great Sarda River, and so on to the Government forests on the confines of Nepal.

Once arrived, the forester would probably not see a white face—save occasionally that of a fellow-officer—until the return to headquarters eight months later through the monsoon floods, unless happily he encountered a shooting-party on its way to Nepal, or persuaded some friends to aid for a time in dispelling the loneliness of his life. At present, Lucknow is only separated by about thirty hours' journey from Bombay, and this time may be spent commodiously in an express train with restaurant accommodation; while from Lucknow one may nowadays enter the saloons of the Rohilkhand and Kumaon Railway one evening, and the next be at the railhead on the Nepal frontier. Running train thefts have replaced highway robbery, and political unrest, punctuated by bombs, the display of the more warlike tastes of the population of that period, while hotels constructed on European designs have taken the place of the genial hospitality of the past.

The Trans-Sarda Forest, where I first was posted as assistant, comprises an area of about 300 square miles abutting on the Nepal border, and on its outskirts were numerous small villages, struggling against malaria and against the disadvantages of the jungle and the raids of its wild beasts; there were then probably few populous and wealthy villages within a distance of five miles of the State Reserves. Inside these the aboriginal Thárus were settlers, and they, on an area of about 30,000 acres, enjoyed what the peasant of the plains considered to be the greatest drawbacks to the locality. They were proof against malaria, and mighty hunters and fishermen; they fed on rice, flesh, and fish, distilling their own liquor, and, like the Burmans in the north-east of India, tattooed themselves with indigo, were adepts at the manufacture of artistic baskets, and answered no call to work for others when they could otherwise live in comfort. The forests even then were recognized as being amongst the most valuable of Upper India; they were composed almost entirely of *Shorea robusta*, or "sâl," with a mixture of *Terminalia tomentosa*, or "sain," and other valuable species standing on the high alluvial land. Lower down, the "Shisham" and the "Khair" formed pure forests, water-sown by the floods sent down from the Nepal hills.

The whole area had been devastated by fire and by unregulated felling. The forest was burnt over every year by the Thárus to clear the undergrowth for hunting, and by the graziers to obtain a crop of young grass; while anyone might in former days have felled half a dozen trees of six-foot girth for a rupee, and have selected one of the best for removal without further payment. The best had thus disappeared, and the forest was full of fallen timber and of trees tapped either for the extraction of resin or to verify their soundness. Beyond a two-roomed shanty at Duduaghat, now a station on the railway, there were no houses in the forest, and tents were the only shelter against the frosts of winter, the heats of summer, and the breaking of the monsoon. Once a week a runner arrived from headquarters with news from the outer world and with a small stock of its luxuries; a bullock-cart took three weeks or more to reach the nearest railway-line, and to return with a load of the more bulky necessaries of life.

Within the forest and on its borders game literally swarmed. The most common was the spotted-deer, and of these there were often to be seen herds of hundreds on the open plains in the morning or evening. Shooting did not appear either to diminish their numbers or to appease the appetites of the staff or of the workmen in the forest; to these they formed a valuable addition to an otherwise meagre diet, and no doubt helped to ward off the attacks of malaria, a disease to which all were liable. Next to the spotted-deer in frequency came the parha, or hog-deer; every patch of grass seemed to hold some of these animals, although both they and the pig were commonly netted by the Thárus. Shooting hog-deer from an elephant is perhaps the best training for one who wishes to become an expert with the rifle at running game. It was seldom that a long run in the open was risked—short rushes through the burnt grass from cover to cover was the order of the day; it was, in fact, like rabbit-shooting on a gigantic scale without the advantage to the sportsman of the spread of the shot. Swamp-deer were then not uncommon in the lowlands in the winter, and in the tree-forest in the summer, and good heads of twelve and even sixteen points were not rare. The stag afforded an easy target when he rose, often with his massive antlers covered with dry grass; but if he kept to the bogs covered with high reeds, where the elephant could not follow, only occasional glimpses of his retreating form could be secured. Sámbhar were frequent throughout the Tarai, but here a head of even 36 inches was rare, for these deer are at their best in the mountains, and thrive in the climate of the hills or in the dry plateaux of Central India; the damp of the submontane areas seems to reduce the size of the antlers, while causing the body to grow unwieldy both in size and weight. Of other deer, the kákár, or barking-deer, was often heard, but seldom seen; they are timid beasts, and shy of appearing in the open, but both they and the monkeys give the surest warning of the whereabouts of the great carnivora.

Amongst this profusion of animal life it was inevitable that the tiger and panther should lead a regal existence, and at this time it was only by the young tiger, killing for the love of slaughter in the joyous strength of his youth, or by those past their prime who found it less trouble, that the cattle of the graziers or the buffaloes from the timber-carts were molested.

Outside the forest, the nilgai, the wild-boar, and the Indian antelope, were in such numbers that they disputed the harvest with the cultivators. On the lowlands duck abounded in the numerous shallow lakes, so that often the sound of the rising wild-fowl resembled the rumbling of distant thunder through the still night; while of other game there were two kinds of florican; the black, the grey, and the swamp partridge; peafowl, hares, and red jungle-fowl, innumerable; and occasionally, especially in areas affected by the four-horned antelope, spur-fowl were seen. Wild-elephants had ceased to cross from Nepal, though the frequency of abandoned pitfalls in the forest testified to their recent presence; it is probable that they deserted these forests as soon as the tree-jungle had, by its shade-giving properties, ousted the bamboo, and thus deprived these animals of a favourite kind of fodder.

It was natural that a youth, fresh from the pursuit of the red-deer, roe, and wild-boar in the Hartz Mountains, where a part of the professional training of those days was passed, and imbued with the cult of sport learnt in the severe school of German hunting etiquette, should be happy in his new surroundings. The work was congenial enough, though consisting chiefly of the exploitation of the forest by selection fellings, the logs being either brought to depot and sawn on indent, or floated down the rivers, to arrive months later at Bahrámghát, then a railway terminus on the Gogra River. There was also some road- and bridge-making to be carried out, and the forest was being cut up into blocks by straight rides of from 15 to 100 feet in breadth, while buildings had to be constructed which necessitated the burning of bricks and lime. To one who had three years' practical training amongst the forests of Germany, all this was easy; and in those days, when the organization of the forest areas was still incomplete, silviculture took a minor part, for the area had first to be opened out, and its produce made accessible to a distant market. Thus the Forest Officer spent the whole day in the jungle either on the works in progress or in exploring the forest in order to acquire an intimate local knowledge of his charge; he was supplied with one elephant, so that it might be possible to do this satisfactorily; he kept ponies for use where paths or tracks happened to be in existence, but once off these tracks riding was impossible.

My first introduction to the wild tiger was not long delayed. I possessed what was then termed an Express rifle of ·577 bore, which fired a light hollow bullet with a medium charge of black powder, and also a 12-bore double gun, which was used with spherical bullets as well as with shot, these two weapons completing a battery that in these days would be considered quite inadequate for the solitary hunter of big game. It is partly to this inadequacy, partly to an absolute inexperience in shooting from an elephant, that the signal defeat suffered in the first encounter may be traced. The camp at Sathiána, a depot seven miles from Dudua, was, and still is, an ideal headquarters for general shooting, being within reach of the haunts of all the various fauna of the district; and it was here that one morning a Gujar arrived and squatted on the ground in front of my tent, patiently awaiting an audience.

The Gujars are a tribe apart, who keep herds of buffaloes, and make a living by the sale of milk and butter. They dwell in the forest, selecting a place for their huts in the vicinity of grazing and water, moving on as these become scarce, and roaming far into the Himalaya in the summer. Their buffaloes return to the cattle-station twice a day, morning and evening, and after being milked wander off again into the forest, sometimes alone, at others accompanied by a youthful Gujar, who often reclines on the broad back of one of the cows. The Gujars know no fear; they were in the past a martial race, and to-day they show no subservience, and present picturesque figures as they stand on their high wooden sandals, robed in black blankets and armed with formidable six-foot bamboos. They are one of the numerous forest tribes with whom the Forest Officer comes into frequent contact, and from whom he learns the characteristics and habits of an uncivilized Eastern population—habits which he may condemn, but which he must acknowledge to have good reasons for their origin.

The story of my visitor was related in a voice trembling with rage, and in few words. A tiger had attacked the buffaloes as they were returning in single file from grazing, and had wantonly killed three cows near to the cattle-station. As a rule the jungle tribes will not readily give information as to the whereabouts of a tiger, and it is not till he passes the bounds of neighbourly acquaintance that they ask for help or set to work to remove him; thus, the killing of plough or milch cattle destroys at once the neutrality which is the etiquette of forest life, while the tiger that contents himself with hunting game may live unmolested. The latter goes and comes amongst the herdsmen and their cattle, and is sometimes even seen by the night watchmen as he prowls around the fields in the hope of seizing a meal from amongst the trespassing herds of deer.

On our arrival at the cattle-station the dead buffaloes were visited; each had fallen on the narrow homeward track, and there was no sign of a struggle. None had been dragged or eaten; it was evidently the work of a powerful tiger, dealing death for the love of sport. The Gujar was asked if he knew where the tiger was, and we followed as he strode gloomily through the forest leading to the banks of a stream lying to the north-west of Sathiána. On the edge of a patch of grass, nowhere more than breast-high and not a quarter of an acre in extent, the Gujar halted, and announced that the tiger was there. The stream meandered through an open plain, and a few score yards below there was a track which crossed at a shallow ford. Here some cartmen had halted to eat their midday meal, and were sitting over their little fires cooking their cakes of meal and water, while their bullocks grazed around in the vicinity, so that it was but natural to remark that no tiger would lie in such a spot during the day; but the Gujar, still furious, replied that if desired he would go in and turn the beast out with his staff; so, leaving him standing, we drove the elephant onwards.

The tiger, when we suddenly became aware of his presence, was crouching directly to the side of the elephant, and the bullet intended for his brain passed through a fore-paw. In an instant he stood erect and struck at the side of the howdah, ripping the cane-work next my leg; then, turning, leapt the stream and trotted down the opposite bank, his departure hastened by a shot from the second barrel. The cartmen and their bullocks scattered, the men with most sense jumping into their empty carts; but the tiger took no notice, and disappeared round a bend in the stream, and here we found him ensconced in a patch of heavy reeds, and growling ferociously. He could not be seen, and, after trying vainly to force him into the open by firing charges of shot into the cover, we retraced our steps, crossed the ford, and approached him from the other side. This, apparently, was what the tiger was waiting for, for he suddenly bounded towards us, undeterred by two shots fired at close quarters, and the next instant the elephant was careering across the plain, hotly followed by the triumphant tiger. Yet before the angry brute could make good his hold the elephant took charge of the affray, and, turning with a snort, he rushed upon his pursuer, who in turn retreated as fast as he could run. The tide of battle was now in our favour, but just as the victory was within reach the howdah struck the horizontal branch of a tree, and was flattened on the elephant's back; and seizing this bough as we passed beneath, I speedily ascended to a more convenient elevation.

The scene was somewhat comical. At a short distance the tiger, once more invisible, was growling fiercely, and the elephant, surmounted by a heap of broken wood and twisted iron, from which protruded the head of my orderly, was shamefacedly listening to the abuse of his driver, while turbans and pieces of guns bestrewed the ground. It took some time to remove the ruin of the howdah, and longer to bring back the elephant, still excited from the fight, and to induce him to hand up the property lying about; then, as he came under my perch, I gladly leapt on his back, and we left for camp, having saved our lives and our baggage, but gained no glory. The lesson learnt was, however, worth the risk—in the first place, to have no standing backsight on a weapon used for quick shooting at short range; and, secondly, to distrust the elephant as a platform from whence accurate shooting can be assured.

I have nothing but praise for the elephant after my long, intimate connection with the animal. He is intelligent to a degree, and therefore all the more dangerous when viciously inclined; he is clever and courageous; and, what is most endearing, he will do everything for a rider he is fond of, and nothing for one he dislikes. His confidence in carrying out orders that must be intensely distasteful to his natural instincts is based on his trust in his rider, and his gratitude for kindly words or actions is almost pathetic. He will suffer severe surgical operations with groans, and even tears, but will carefully refrain from injuring the operators, whose lives are at his mercy. But the momentum of a walking elephant is not to be stayed instantaneously, and often the supreme moment passes before the rifle can be steadied; while when he is standing there is a constant movement of the body in brushing flies from the sensitive skin, or in shifting the weight from foot to foot, so that often one delays in firing a shot for fear that the bullet will pass harmlessly away. The large majority of Indian elephants have been born in the wild state, and the wild-elephant is never still save during a moment of intense listening to detect danger, so much so that when this occurs the sportsman may know that his presence is suspected. Such inbred habits cannot be overcome save in generations of elephants bred in confinement, and at that stage we shall probably never arrive. Meanwhile in dense jungle we can hardly spare their services either when at work or at play, and thus to the Forest Officer they become, not only necessities in his outfit, but friends whose capabilities are known and trusted.

There are, of course, some exceptional men whose quickness in shooting obviates to a great extent the disadvantages of not standing on firm ground. With a shot-gun such instances are, in fact, not un-

"PAD" ELEPHANT ENTERING HIGH GRASS.

common, though with a rifle they are rare. There are, too, some elephants reserved for the use of the mighty, who have reduced to a minimum the faults of their species, but I write of the animal that most of us could expect to procure and improve with daily intercourse and practice. The officer under whom I worked in Kheri was a gentleman of the name of Dodsworth, and as a shot I have never seen him equalled. Using an antiquated pinfire 12-bore gun, and reloading his cartridges till they would no longer hold the charge, he never seemed to miss. For winged game he did not take the trouble to stop the elephant, and his shooting with a spherical ball from the same weapon was almost miraculous, for he frequently killed running hares and flying peafowl with a bullet; but this skill was acquired by passing many hours daily on his elephant, so that with the superior weapons of the present time it seems probable that nothing would have escaped him.

In those days we were in the habit of spending a fortnight of the month of May in Nepal, more for the sake of good-fellowship and a change than because we expected better sport there than in the Government forest. The average bag, with fifteen or twenty elephants, was about twenty tigers, panthers, and bears, and as many deer as one cared to shoot. But these trips never afforded me much satisfaction, for I felt that the tiger had seldom any chance against so many rifles, while as a trophy his skin during the summer months was at its worst; moreover, the old rule of first shot to confer ownership was not conducive to good sport, for it led to overeagerness in firing, and sometimes to subseqnent loss of interest in the hunt; and, lastly, all the woodcraft, which is the chief pleasure in big-game shooting, was in the hands of the leader, and his companions had nothing to do but to profit by his astuteness, as the marshalling of elephants in line and their advance and retreat was frequently directed by signalling, as in a military review. The Forest Officer will indeed find that he has little time to spare for organized shooting trips, and that he can obtain such sport as he desires when following his daily avocations.

After a few years in Kheri as assistant, I was sent across the Sarda to the charge of the Bhira forests, of which Mailáni, now on the Rohilkhand and Kumaon Railway, was the headquarters. This area of about 150 square miles is outside the Tarai, and is surrounded and intersected by the wheat, barley, and rice fields of many populous villages; there was, thus, never much game in it. Panthers, of course, lived and bred there, and tigers crossed from the main forests that lay to the north during the autumn months, but the deer were much harried by incessant poaching; and though even now a pleasant time can be spent in Bhira by the observant sportsman, it was not, nor is it even now, a place one would visit were the denser forests farther north available. Being nearer civilization, however, the work in the forests was incessant; there were roads to be aligned and houses to be built, while the marking of areas for felling took up much time, so I was glad when I was transferred to the charge of the forest division in the Bahraich district.

The forests here consisted of four separate blocks

—that to the west named Motipur, now a station on the Bengal and North-Western Railway, whose line runs through the whole area; then followed eastwards Chakkia, Charda, and Bhinga, the Nepal frontier forming the northern boundary of each forest. In those days the Motipur sâl forests on the high ground were full of game, and the lowlands, stretching away to the Sarda River in the west, and the Girwa River in the north, were called by the natives the "home of the wild beasts." Nishangara stood on a bluff in the centre of this sportsman's paradise, overlooking the plains, and a snug double-storied house that I erected now replaces the grass shanty found on my arrival there. Cultivation has since spread up to the forest boundary, and the rumble of the locomotive is now heard throughout the day; and listening to it, it is curious to reflect that not so long ago the wild-buffalo was seen in these swamps. Yet even now one may find panthers at almost every camp, and at Murtihá there are always at the beginning of the winter one or more tigers in residence in the bamboo thickets near the Mohán River. In the time of which I write the forests were not frequently visited even by the civil officers, and the solitary European fond of sport had a pleasant time.

The forests of Chakkia and Charda, now reached by road from stations on the Bengal and North-Western Railway, also contained a good head of game. It is true that tigers were always scarce, being generally visitors from Nepal, and staying only a few days; but the panthers were numerous and sly, and there was thus much sport—indeed, some is still to be had in shooting these, by using a live goat as bait. To be successful in this form of shooting, it is essential that neither the goat nor the panther should see the ambushed sportsman, and that there should not be the slightest sound or movement during the vigil; for if the goat is aware of the presence of man it will not bleat for help, and if the panther, himself semi-arboreal, detects any movement in the foliage above him, he too will not approach. The sportsman therefore first settles himself in his leafy perch with loaded rifle, and then the goat is tethered to a wooden peg a few yards to his front, and the "shikaris" retire.

To be absolutely alone in an Indian forest produces an indefinable impression, due perhaps to a remnant of the instincts of primeval man when he went daily in danger of his life. There is a charm in the knowledge that wild life is all around, though unseen by the intruder; for the animals are always watching, day and night they are on the alert to evade danger by timely knowledge. To them all noises of the jungle are signals; they detect the difference between the sound of the dry twig breaking in the breeze or accidentally under the careful foot of the intruder, and the alarm note of the largest beast or of the smallest bird uttered for the benefit of its kind conveys its warning; while in addition to these safeguards there are the senses of sight and scent, which rouse suspicion at any unusual shape, such as an unnatural disposition of the foliage, or recognize friend or foe in the eddying currents. So that the human being, even when trained by long years of experience, must remain heavily handicapped by his sluggish senses, and even his weapons could never save him from the stealthy attack of the man-eating tiger or from the sudden onslaught of an animal awaiting the approach of a trespasser in his domain.

The shrill bleating of the goat conveys to all within half a mile or more that an animal is in distress, and perhaps reaches the panther just aroused from his afternoon sleep. First the crows come to discover whether or not there is a chance for them to fall on a helpless victim, and, disappointed, they sit in neighbouring trees and add their clamour to the uproar. In the silences you feel as if you could no longer bear the cramp and strain of your position, were it not for the interest in some insect or bird in the vicinity, who, unaware of the presence of man, is affording a new insight into its natural history. Then, as the twilight falls and the jungle becomes still, you are nervous lest the panther should kill the goat, and so spoil your enjoyment of the sport. You recall that, fortunately, the carnivora rarely spring on a tethered animal, suspicious perhaps in virtue of the plots they lay for others; and while comforting yourself thus there is a rush, as with a bound the panther alights, not on, but a yard in front of, his victim. His fore-paws plough up the ground as he stops, and the goat stands feebly presenting her horns at the apparition; and then the rifle rings out, and the panther disappears in the undergrowth: the two crowded seconds for which you have waited for an hour are passed, and you descend, to be greeted by the friendly bleating of your ally. There is blood along the trail, and you follow for, say, 60 or 80 yards, knowing that within that distance a well-directed bullet would have proved fatal; and, if you find nothing and are wise, you will return for your trackers and proceed warily, for a wounded panther is a terror; he can conceal himself in the smallest hollow or patch of grass, and he charges home without a premonitory roar such as the tiger gives, so that he is on you almost before you can raise rifle to shoulder.

In the Bhinga forests surrounded by cultivation, a source of great interest used to be in the herds of wild-cattle which frequented them—the cows pure white with inky muzzles, and the bulls shading to grey on the shoulders, and with black humps, both beautiful animals, but untamable when caught. On account of the damage done to the crops on the border of the forest, the order went forth later for their removal, and as they could not be shot, by reason of the religious objection of the Hindu peasantry of the neighbourhood, many hundreds were caught alive by means of driving them into enclosures, and were then sold into a captivity which meant either a sudden or a lingering death. It is doubtful if any are now left in these forests.

To the north of Bhinga, the headquarters of a Raja of that name, and connected by a good road with the railway-station at Bahraich, lies a camp called Sohelwa, in which many pleasant days may be spent; for the country lies in the foot-hills of Nepal, and from thence great sámbhar stags descend in the early autumn to mix with the herds below, later again betaking themselves to their mountain fastnesses. The stalking of these stags is one of the pleasantest forms of shooting, and with a knowledge of the ground a few good heads can be obtained;

while beating with coolies can also be resorted to by those who find pleasure in assassinating a noble stag when his attention is diverted by an imaginary foe. But the pleasure of being awake before the dawn, and of wandering cautiously in the dewy grass before the fallen leaves are dry, of sighting, perhaps, at a distance a shadowy form stealing towards the broken ground in the north, of hurrying to intercept it, and then the careful shot and the slow return to camp, gaining as you go some new knowledge of the jungle—these are the joys of the wanderer who has worked with mind and body to overcome the skill and strength of the wild animal, and has succeeded without outside aid.

The sámbhar stag browses during the night on leaves and fruits, and does not ordinarily graze, but at dawn he resorts to a favourite spot, where he sits chewing the cud until the sun warns him to retreat to cover; and thus it is that one may notice small heaps of the rejected stones of jungle fruits, such as "bahera" and "ber," which are foolishly left to fix a location that may be occupied for several days. On misty and frosty nights in the winter the stags visit muddy pools, where they wallow in the icy water, standing afterwards in the moonlight and shaking showers from their shaggy hides; then, rubbing their horns on the neighbouring trees, they depart, with fierce grunts, to adventures of love and war. It is a pernicious taste which leads men, chiefly natives, to lie in wait for the lives of these noble beasts at these wallows; yet in the daytime one may visit them with profit to measure the footprints and the distance above your head that the horns have reached, to notice the direction the trail has taken, and to judge, if possible, where the retreat of the daytime has been selected, and the way that has been taken to reach it.

It was when I was in the Bahraich forests that I commenced to keep dogs for hunting, and to carry a rifle on horseback. I found for killing foxes, hares, and jackals in the open, or deer on the borders of the forest, that English greyhounds were too speedy, also that they would not tackle; moreover, they were too delicate to stand the damp cold of the Tarai, and were more often than not laid up with broken nails from the hard, rough ground. I, however, got good serviceable lurchers by crossing a Persian greyhound with a pointer slut, and these dogs would hunt by scent, run to sight, and occasionally of their own free will retrieve such small game as hares. They would also pull down any deer, generally an easy matter, for, as far as my experience goes, a stag when run into and thrown without coming to bay rarely attempts to rise, though when bayed it is only too ready with hoofs and horns. As a rule the stags of the Oudh forests were tackled on the run, and at once thrown, the dogs immediately attacking the groin-pits of the unfortunate animals. Pigs, too, they would run and bring to bay; but though they on more than one occasion treed a panther, they would not tackle a wild-dog, but sat round him growling. It seems at first curious that a panther should run from dogs, when it is remembered that he is inordinately fond of their flesh, and will take risks to make a meal of it; but he has a well-reasoned horror of the wild-dogs, who would tear him to pieces if opportunity offered, and who frequently drive him off, and themselves appropriate the animal he has killed. There are, it is true, fables that the wild-dog treats the tiger in the same disrespectful manner, but they are not borne out by my observations. It is a fact that as a rule tigers and wild-dogs are not found in the same forest at the same time, but the reason of this appears to be that the latter disturb the ground to such an extent that a quiet hunter like the tiger leaves in disgust.

I hunted with my lurchers for some time, then added to their number a formidable dog, the offspring of a deerhound and foxhound, to whom nothing came amiss. He would run a deer by scent, forcing him into the open and then killing him single-handed, and when no other sport was available would slay the village dogs around. One of his last exploits before we parted was to slaughter an inoffensive donkey whose braying annoyed him. Later on I was given by Mr. F. B. Bryant, now Inspector-General of Forests in India, a puppy whose father was a bull-terrier and his mother a smooth fox-terrier, and this dog remained with me for thirteen years, never leaving my side by day or night. No doubt Pickles was a mongrel, no doubt he was hideous with his stump tail and one ear cocked; but he had the nose of a retriever, the courage of a lion, and the grip of a bulldog. He was the only dog of a more blue-blooded crowd who would enter a box-trap, emerging clinging and being clung to by that furry fiend known as a wild-cat; and when he yielded up his honest little life I buried his body, scarred with a hundred fights, in the jungles he loved so well, and felt that I had lost one of the truest companions that a man could have. None other could take his place—neither Victor, the pure-bred bull-mastiff, who was killed in single combat with a panther; nor Punch, the cocker spaniel, who would retrieve any game though he had painfully to drag it along the ground; nor Grip, the Irish terrier, pacific only by training, yet longing to be bitten, so that he could conscientiously enjoy a real fight; hardly even Puggles, the Thibet terrier, whose eyes flashed red with the excitement of the hunt as he charged into a herd of astonished deer, they evidently thinking him to be a fox cub who had lost his way, or an outrageous squirrel, and treating him accordingly. The solitary Englishman without a dog is surely a pitiable spectacle, and when his loneliness is amongst those who cannot speak his mother-tongue nor think his English thoughts, he will appreciate the worth of a companion who understands both language and thoughts, and, understanding, will join in his amusements or silently show sympathetic affection, as may befit the passing mood.

With horses I found, as with elephants, that they were entirely dependent on their confidence in their rider. Most horses on first introduction to jungle life were exceedingly timid at finding themselves walled in by vegetation; they were prepared to fly from the slightest rustle, and hated narrow paths through heavy grass. In a short time, with careful handling, they were at home. Standing unstabled day and night, they became accustomed to elephants, to camels, to the wild beasts of the forest, and ceased to object to guns being fired from the saddle, some developing great courage in moments of real danger. An Australian mare bought in 1890 was still alive in honourable retreat in 1909, and, could she speak, could tell many a tale of the tigers, panthers, and elephants, she had met; and a white hill-pony I possessed took me within five yards of a tiger crouching by a buffalo he had just killed. It is true that neither the pony nor myself knew that the tiger was so close to us till he rose and glared at his visitors, but all the more credit to the pony in standing his ground when a hasty retreat through the dense undergrowth could but have led to pursuit and disaster. I trust that that tiger lived to a good old age and died in peace, for he had us both at his mercy and took no advantage.

One might write of other horses which in their time enjoyed the headlong rush after the pursuing dogs, or swiftly pulled the light dogcart along the jungle tracks when returning to the welcoming camp, while the lamps lit up the dim forms of the wild beasts, vague and fearful in the darkness; but while recording the loyal aid of elephant, horse, or dog, the natives of India must not be forgotten, those who were lovers of sport for sport's sake—not professional shikaris who adapted their work to the price it commanded, but those who enjoyed the success of the hunt after sharing its toil and danger; for them there is always grateful remembrance for unselfish service, for cheerful courage, which would, if necessary, save the master's life at the risk of their own. There is pleasure, too, in the knowledge that the devotion of man or beast, of orderly and mahout, of elephant, of horse, or of dog, can only be won by personal influence and kindness, and that without these neither the forester nor the solitary sportsman could hope to be successful.

One of the most charming spots in the Bahraich forests is on the Girwa River, which can now be reached by train from Motipur. A widespreading, swift and clear stream runs over boulders, and it is not for a mile or more below Katenia Ghat that sand-banks make their appearance. This is a great river for mahseer, which here attain their largest size; but on account of the swiftness and depth of the current it is difficult to fish, and almost impossible without the aid of a boat with skilled paddlers. The natives, however, succeed in catching mahseer from the bank, using chiefly a large prawn as a bait, with a weight tied some three feet above the hook. They hurl this apparatus far into the stream, and when in luck play the fish by hand, a long line being necessary on account of the strength of the fish when aided by the heavy water. It is, however, better to proceed upstream, where the river passes from Nepal and flows between wooded islands in various smaller channels which can be negotiated from their banks. Success in any case depends on clear water and skies, and even more so on the absence of poachers, who in these days do not tolerate the delay incidental to poisoning the pools, but use dynamite cartridges to produce an immediate result.

At the foot of the hills is a lake called Shishapani,

or the Mirror Water, and the lover of the beauties of Nature would be well repaid by a visit to this spot, even if he obtains no sport with gun or rod. The clear, still lake is bounded by precipitous rocks, and the strong river flowing from it is broken into waves as it passes over the boulders below. After a short rapid, across which neither elephant nor boat can cross, there is formed a triangular island with its apex to the stream, and this divides the waters of the Koriala River in the west from those of the Girwa River in the east. Thus accident determines the supply of water to each stream; a log adrift in the floods may alter in a day the volume of these rivers, and it is not till the monsoon is over that any estimate of the size of the watercourses during the coming winter can be made. Below Shishapani the forests of "shisham" and "khair" extend to the south. The rising waters bear the floating seeds of these species over the submerged islands, and as the floods subside germination follows and the islands are covered with the tender green of the seedling foliage; then, favoured by the absence of abnormal water-levels for a few years, a forest is formed which can withstand all but the fiercest inundations. And thus the scenery presents a peculiarly artificial appearance of groups and patches of trees, each such group being of one age, while no two groups may be of the same year of origin. In the spring the brilliant verdure of the foliage and the delicate yet intoxicating scent of the "shisham" flower will always be remembered in its associations with forest life in Northern India. At the present time permits to enter Nepal for tiger-shooting are mostly reserved for high officials and their guests, but a fishing pass can be obtained from the Durbar without trouble, and this will insure ingress to the country, which is well worth a visit even though the shooting of tigers is barred.

After a time spent in the forests of Bahraich and Gonda, I returned to the charge of the Kheri forests. There was an immense amount of work in progress, and at this time the protection of the forest from fire was giving much trouble. The people did not understand why they should abandon the immemorial custom of firing the forest in order to obtain a new growth of grass, or to make hunting and netting easier, or to restrict the raids of wild beasts on their crops or on their domestic animals. A system of broad "fire-lines," or cleared rides, had been devised in order to locate any fire that might break out, and so permit of counter-firing, but the task at that time seemed almost hopeless; fires occurred almost every year, and their intensity and the consequent damage were in proportion to the period of successful protection that had preceded them; and, moreover, each such catastrophe cast a slur on the Forest Officer's administration, often undeservedly, for it was not sufficiently recognized that in the East education can but slowly affect the habits of the people. They had to be taught in practice the difference between the value of a burnt and an unburnt forest, and, as the population increased, it had to learn how the forest could be of importance to the community, where before it was an enemy to be fought by a few opponents who regarded fire as their strongest weapon. With patience and perseverance this lesson has long since been learnt in the Oudh forests, and the struggle is now transferred to other Provinces where the Forest Officer is working as a pioneer in the van of civilization, securing for the State a property which, when the country is settled, when landownership, so dear to the Eastern heart, is assured, and when the benefits of a regulated forest to an agricultural population are understood, will be perhaps more valued by the people themselves than even by their rulers; for the first have a personal and practical experience that forest products are indispensable to their welfare, while the others can only form an estimate of the inconveniences of strict forest conservancy.

Besides the protection of the forest there was its exploitation by means of departmental operations, a now antiquated system, which afforded to the subordinates unlimited opportunity for bribery and oppression, and occupied the whole time of the Forest Officer in detailed accounts which were impossible to check in the field. In those days the forester was beyond everything a timber-merchant and a revenue-collector, and this state of affairs naturally hindered silvicultural progress, for no time was left for the higher professional duties of the staff. After the "Holi" festival, which takes place about the end of March or beginning of April, the workmen left the forest, where malaria again began to be prevalent, and returned to their homes to reap their crops or to revert to the urban occupations of the next seven months; and the forester was then left to watch through the fire season, till the first burst of the monsoon should cause the jungle to be again clad in greenery. It was, fortunately, just at this time that big-game shooting was at its best, or his solitude might have become unbearable. It is true that the sámbhar, swamp-deer, and hog-deer, have then thrown their horns, for their rutting season is in October or November; but the spotted-deer are bellowing throughout the forest, and assuming their handsome coats of chestnut flecked with white, while the white gorget and the black tracery over the face mark the stag at this season with peculiarly beautiful colouring. No Indian stag, probably, carries a head so large in proportion to his size or so graceful in its sweep, for the weight of a good stag will only be about 170 pounds unbroken, while the record horn is about 38 inches long on the outside of the curve.

The spotted-deer is a thirsty soul, and is never found far from water; in the summer he will come to drink at midday, and in the evening nothing will keep him from rushing to the water-supply. They may then be heard advancing towards the edge of the forest, rustling through the dead leaves, till a hind appears in the open and stands sniffing in all directions, with ears twitching, seeking for the slightest scent or sound of danger; then, pushed on by those behind, the whole herd—maybe a hundred or more strong—emerge from the shadows of the great trees, and eagerly crop the grass on the open plain, at the same time steadily and hurriedly moving towards the nearest tank or stream. From your hiding-place you can note the stalks of the burnt grass striped with black from the charring of the softer sheaths between the nodes, and at once you see how easily one tiger, or indeed twenty, could crouch invisible in this scanty shelter—how the ringed spots of the panther or the dark stripes of the tiger would assimilate with their surroundings; and then, looking across the grey-green of the plain dotted with the earthen hillocks of the white ants, you realize how easily an enemy could approach from behind their shelter, and you understand why between each few bites the heads are raised with twitching ears and nostrils, and you are in sympathy with the constant alertness of the moving animals. They are far safer when they lie quiet in the forest and let movement and sound inform them of danger, as the sportsman will discover in practice when he himself is either the hunter or the hunted.

Meanwhile the herd is increasing its distance, carrying with it the young males, and perhaps a few almost mature stags, but none with heads that make the blood tingle with the lust of possession, till suddenly at a distance more horns moving within the forest become visible. Very cautiously they approach, and two or more stags stand alone on the plain; their animosities are forgotten in this strenuous moment when they feel exposed to unknown enemies, or perhaps the series of duels, common in the springtime with these deer, are over, and an armed truce prevails amongst the leaders of the herd. Slowly they walk forward, and now, if you wish to destroy the harmony of the scene and put terror into a hundred innocent hearts, the time has arrived; for unless you fire, and that quickly, they will lightly gallop after the retreating herd, to resume mastership and to check the amorous pranks of the youngsters. They are gone, and you are perhaps happier that you have for a time been a partner in the intimate life of the forest, and maybe you will not regret your reticence; for when the stillness of the forest night broods over your tent you may hear the danger-cries of the herd, the sharp whistle of the doe and the hoarser alarm-cry of the stag, and next morning, visiting the spot, you may perhaps trace out on the ground the history of a jungle outrage, and set yourself to the more difficult task of meeting the midnight assassin face to face.

When in charge of the Kheri Division, I once shot in the six weeks preceding the middle of June forty stags with heads that no sportsman need be ashamed of—the largest being 38 inches in length—all by fair stalking, unattended and on foot, in the forest near Duduaghát. The bag might have been quadrupled if trophies had been no object. In these days the sportsman would be fortunate if he got four really good heads in the same time; for, in the first place, the deer have been decimated by the ever-increasing population, so that now it has become necessary to limit on a licence the number that may be shot in one area; and, secondly, they have become much more nocturnal in their habits: they leave the tree-forest after dark, and re-enter it before dawn, and a noiseless approach in the forest is impossible to man or elephant. A curious shot made at this time remains in my memory. I pulled the trigger just as a fine stag was scratching his face with a hind-hoof; the bullet passed through his fetlock, through his ear, chipped his brow antler, and struck him high in the shoulder.

The spotted-deer passes much of his time in the spring fighting with other members of the herd, the light sparring with an opponent soon changing to deadly earnest. The object of the attack seems to be to get the frontal tines under the chest of the adversary; the stronger stag is thus generally he who has his head lower. They push savagely with interlocked horns, till one, seeing an opening, falls suddenly on his knees, and then, rising, endeavours to impale his adversary, and with such force is this done that the frontal tine is sometimes broken off, and remains embedded in the chest of the opponent. Meanwhile the does stand around placidly chewing the cud and regarding the combatants with an air of indifference, and the young stags make the most of the opportunities afforded by the forgetfulness of their seniors. But that affection exists between the sexes there can be no doubt, for on more than one occasion I have seen a doe detach herself from the startled herd and return to where the dying stag lay, though it will be understood that on such occasions the sportsman was not visible. The stag is not without courage, and when calling in the rutting season—provided he neither scents nor sees the hunter—will stand his ground, and even approach to investigate any rustling amongst the leaves and bushes which he suspects to herald the approach of an intruder; and I have, but only on one occasion, known a wounded stag charge with lowered antlers across the open, to fall almost at the hunter's feet with a bullet through the spine.

The chief enemies of the spotted-deer are the tiger, the panther, and the wild-dog, and the two former appear to prefer the doe to the stag. It would not, perhaps, be correct to attribute to the carnivora any choice in flavour resulting from sex, but it may be remarked, apart from the facts that the females are more numerous, and amongst the deer tribe are forced by the males to occupy the posts of danger, that the large carnivora appear to be nervous of attacking antlered prey, probably because of the danger they run from wounds accidentally inflicted in a tussle ending with a headlong fall. It is not, perhaps, sufficiently recognized that a slight injury may have very serious results to an animal who is dependent for his livelihood on the perfect condition both of his muscles and of the weapons provided by Nature, and that there would naturally be great repugnance to incur any risk of even temporary disablement. The tiger whose victory I recorded in a previous page, when killed some three weeks later, had evidently suffered much from hunger, although the wound in his fore-paw was rather inconvenient than severe; and in the same way a porcupine quill in a fore-leg, or a gash on the pad of the foot from a sharp stone or stake, may temporarily change a well-fed, good-tempered tiger or panther into a starving, morose, and dangerous brute.

Neither the spotted-deer nor sámbhar flee when the great carnivora are in their vicinity. They wisely endeavour to keep the foe in view, and will stand around in a wide circle uttering their alarm cries. It is easy for the hunter then to join the audience, for his presence will not readily be noticed. I once watched a tiger in grass about three feet high, which therefore concealed him when he crouched, endeavouring to secure one of a herd of spotted-deer around him. The tiger repeatedly charged, bounding above the grass in the direction of any rustling made by the wary deer, who at once scattered in every direction, to re-form the circle later on. The whole performance, which seemed more like a friendly game of blind-man's buff than deadly earnest, lasted for some twenty minutes, until the tiger wandered away and the deer resumed their feeding. There is evidently no perpetual dread of death accompanying the natural nervousness of wild beasts. They recognize the vicinity of an unpleasant neighbour by scent, by sight, and by hearing, and take steps to avoid him, and when death comes there is in most cases no painful struggle. It is rare that one hears such heart-rending cries as may be uttered when the hunter approaches a disabled animal, cries that extort a hasty vow that there shall be no more hunting, and have at least the practical effect of in future staying the hand until there is a certainty that the shot will be fatal.

I look upon the spotted-deer as one of, if not quite, the most sporting deer in India. His beauty, the ground he frequents, and the caution he displays, all conduce to render stalking a pleasure. In certain localities he may be speared from horseback, and many were thus killed by Captain Greig and his brother when Forest Officers in the Pátli Dun of Gurhwal; but the locality was exceptional, the deer were gross with feeding in the lush grass of the banks of the Ramganga River, and the result might be different if a stag were in hard training by having to go ten or twelve miles each day to water. In the Pátli Dun it sometimes happened that deer would fall and die during a short burst without being touched by the spear, showing that they were quite unfit to undertake a sharp gallop at full speed for even a distance of a mile or so.

Wild-dogs appear to kill a large number of spotted-deer, but exactly how they do so it is difficult to understand. In the frequent hunts I have witnessed, there seemed to be no great appreciation of danger on the one hand, or undue hurry on the other; rather, a feeling of annoyance was caused that the deer should bound lightly at half-speed, and that the dog should keep a distance of from twenty to thirty yards in the rear. One would also expect a burst to be made as the latter ran from scent to view, for probably the speed is with the dog for a short distance. But the leisurely procession passes, and leaves you with mixed feelings of anger and pity. I have never seen more than two or three dogs on the trail of a deer, though when not hunting packs of fifteen or twenty are not uncommon. I incline, therefore, to think that wild-dogs trust much to driving their prey into an ambush, and that this accounts for the slow pace of the run. The deer always make for water, and if they cross out of sight of the pursuers the hunt is often abandoned; while the fact that often deer are found lying in water where the kill has taken place seems to point to the inference that the ambush is fre-

In the Pátli Doon.

quently laid by the banks of a stream, and that if this is crossed at a distance from the waiting dogs further pursuit is abandoned. At any rate, the wild-dog is a spoiler of the jungle and a cruel fiend. He alone proceeds to eat an animal before life is extinct, tearing lumps of flesh from the quivering body; and though it may be said in his excuse that he has no means of otherwise killing the larger deer, yet the long-drawn anguish which surely in some degree, in spite of appearances, precedes the capture and the lingering death which follows it, seems to jar on the sportsman's desire that a sudden, painless death should conclude the triumph over the fleetness, cunning, or ferocity, of an opponent.

From the Kheri forests I made yearly a short trip into Nepal, crossing the boundary at the ford on the Mohán River north of Duduaghát, and here my attention was attracted to an aspect of forest life which afforded much interest in future travels. I allude to the superstitions of the forest people, to their firm belief in the spirits of the jungle, in the transmigration of the souls of bad men to the bodies of tigers and other animals, and to their conviction that the hunter might be seriously influenced in his life and welfare by interference with these dreaded powers.

My friend and I had on one occasion halted beyond the border at a Tháru village, and, as usual, we went amongst the inhabitants to have a friendly chat, and to discover, if possible, the whereabouts of any tiger that might be in the vicinity. We experienced the usual reticence to afford any information, and were not surprised, knowing already that a native does not so much mind betraying the tiger if he is certain that it will be killed, but dreads the vengeance that the beast will take if allowed to escape. Thus, the hunter who is known to be expert and fortunate will naturally have more opportunity than one whose capabilities are unknown. On this occasion we were referred finally to the village wizard, who was paid for protecting the village cattle by means of his potent charms, and the gift of a kid and a bottle of rum, combined with a promise of large reward, decided him that he could spare a few tigers from his stock in trade. So next morning, mounted on the largest elephant we possessed, murmuring various incantations, and ringing a small bell, he led us to a miserable patch of grass that might have held a brace of partridges or a hare, but seemed quite unsuitable as cover for a tiger. It was not till our five elephants were sweeping this area for the second time that my mahout pointed to a tiger crouching below us. This grand beast slowly arose and walked majestically away, till on the edge of the grass he turned, standing broadside to the elephant, and in an instant he lay prone on the earth, dying without a struggle. The wizard was begged to repeat the experiment, and once more leading the way we arrived at a more hopeful-looking spot, and here a similar scene was enacted with as little trouble.

Bewildered, we returned to camp. I forget at this distance of time the number of tigers this peculiar man presented to us in this manner; they were but few, as he explained that if there were no tigers there would be no fees for preserving the cattle, but they were sufficient to fill us with astonishment, and also with faith in his power. The curious sequel to this story is that on our return to Duduaghát we tried an incantation taught to my Brahmin orderly, consisting chiefly in lighting oil-lamps and in arranging grains of rice and spices, with the object of slaying an old tiger that had long lived near the bungalow, and had evaded all our skill by his cunning. Suffice it to say that we found this beast; that he strolled, as if dazed, in front of the elephants, and, while crossing the shallow river Soheli to gain the tree-forest, was fired at three times, and escaped unscathed. The charm as we had prepared it was evidently potent enough to bewilder the tiger, but not sufficiently so to insure good shooting.

In after years I often questioned wandering "fakirs," holy hermits and other individuals leading the simple and solitary life in wild places in the forests, as to their attitude to the animal life around them; and they gave me to understand that power over the beasts of the field was one of the earliest results of their self-imposed austerities. None expressed any fear of attack from their wild neighbours, and one even offered to call them up if I would promise not to shoot them on arrival; and I have personally no reason to doubt the authority claimed by some over wild beasts, whether this power is conferred by a holy life, or, as in the case of our Tháru, is accompanied by the fleshly lusts of gluttony and drunkenness. The Thárus certainly have a great name for witchcraft amongst the plains-folk, but as this is also the case in regard to many jungle tribes from Kashmir to Burma, the reputation in itself is not convincing. It is true that all these simple people themselves live in fear of the evil powers, and propitiate them by offerings on many occasions during the year, but I have seen no proof that they can, as they assert, transfer the ill-will of the demons from themselves to others. Often, indeed, the attempt is made in India to pass on plague and pestilence to birds and animals by exposing food on public highways, and copper coins are sometimes added, which can be no good save to needy men; but I never tested the efficacy of these somewhat selfish attempts, as the sum offered never covered even the smallest risk of their success.

CHAPTER III

WORK AND SPORT IN THE NORTH-WESTERN PROVINCES

In 1880 I was transferred from Oudh to the Ganges forests of the North-Western Provinces, and proceeded in July from Naini Tal to the Bhagarathi Valley. It was seven years since I had seen the mountains save at a distance, when the snow-peaks of Nepal were lighted up with the rosy tints of evening or stood deathly white when touched by the dawn. From Naini Tal to Srinagar, and thence onwards to Tehri and Gangotri, is an arduous march of over a fortnight, and intensely hot and damp in the valleys, where alone there are conveniences for pitching camp. Speaking generally, the Himalaya present a configuration of parallel mountain ranges running north-east and south-west, each range increasing in height till the Thibet plateau is reached; but the immensity and grandeur implied by the imposing statistics of their elevation are discounted by the fact that in order to see a high mountain from close at hand the spectator stands at a considerable height above the sea. There are, indeed, exceptions to this rule, one being where the traveller views Kinchinjunga from Darjeeling, but such advantageous positions are, I think, rare. The Bhagarathi River is held to be the main stream of the Ganges, and its sacred water flows from the "Gaumukh," or Cow's Mouth, a cavern of misty blue ice at the snout of a large glacier.

Here in the hills the life and work of the forester is different from that he has experienced in the plains. He passes abruptly from the bamboo-covered slopes of the foot-hills, with their burning rocks, into the forests of long-leaved pine, thence into the shady, damp recesses of the cedar, spruce, and fir trees; he rejoices in seeing again old friends of the West, such as the yew, the horse-chestnut, and the maple, and the familiar fruit, such as strawberries, gooseberries, and currants, here growing wild; and when he arrives at the forest limit, and looks back on the birch, the juniper, and the alpine-rose, and forward to the great flower-bedecked grasslands leading up to the eternal snows, he comes once more under the influence of the pure, keen air, and is happy to be free of the dust, of the noise, and of the clinging scents of the East. Not that he can do what he thinks he will be able to, judging by his first feelings of vigour and energy; he will soon find, when the barometer marks in the neighbourhood of 17 inches, that severe gradients are trying, and that there are other inconveniences to be endured; but, in spite of all, the changes in climate, in temperature, and in surroundings, are beneficial: they soothe the jaded nerves, and enable the relative importance of things to be better realized than when in the depression of sea-level on the plains. Our rulers acquiesce in these sentiments, as bear witness Simla, Naini Tal, Darjeeling, Pachmarhi, Ootacamund, and Maymyo, all centres of the Government of the Empire during the greater part of the year.

Of large game the Bhagarathi Valley did not contain many species; below, the "gural" and the "thar," both mountain goats, were not uncommon; and higher up, the "barhel," or mountain sheep, were to be found. Small game, especially the "chikor" partridge, was plentiful, and the "khalij," the "koklass," and the "monal" pheasant were also frequent. Black and red bear were also to be met, the former being much dreaded by the people, for they ravage the crops and willingly assault any intruder, inflicting terrible wounds in head and face that are followed by disfigurement, often grotesque in its horror. October is the month for hunting the "barhel," for then the rams descend from the precipices and join the flocks; and in the years of which I write there was excellent shooting to be obtained in the valley above Gangotri and at Rudagaira, on the left bank of the river. The forests have since been handed back to the Raja of Tehri, but there should be no difficulty in making a pilgrimage from Mussoorie to the Cow's Mouth, if beautiful scenery is held to be a reward for the trouble entailed. Of fishing there is none in these icy waters.

The inhabitants of the Bhagarathi Valley say that they expect a snowfall in each month of the year, and at Hirsil—formerly the residence of "Shikari" Wilson, the first European to settle here—19 feet of snow have been recorded in the winter; while above, at the higher villages of Mukba and Dharáli, the people leave their houses in charge of the old and decrepit, and spend the cold weather at lower elevations. The flat-roofed stone houses are then obliterated in the masses of snow, and when the return is made in the spring, it must be somewhat thrilling before it is ascertained whether avalanches have spared the village site, and whether any relatives have passed during the gloomy winter, and are waiting obsequies by sons or grandsons.

In the autumn of 1880 the great landslip at Naini Tal hurled to swift destruction many unfortunates, both English and Indian, and overwhelmed a band of devoted rescuers when engaged in their work of mercy. This cyclonic disturbance gave 40 inches of rain in twenty-four hours on the outer slopes of the Himalaya, and passed slowly up to the roof of the world. Warned by the threatening of the weather, I hurriedly descended from above the forest limit, where, with a few native companions, I was hunting "barhel" on the rocks below the snow-line, and succeeded in reaching Dharáli before the storm broke; and here, in a little tent 8 feet square, for three days, the first of rain, the second of sleet, and the third of snow, we awaited what the future might bring. No fires could be lit, no dry clothes were to be had. We watched with intense interest the rising of the river and the crumbling of the hills, till in desperation the villagers appealed to their gods, and brought the "Deota," with his silver face and crimson robes, from his snug temple to witness the devastation around. The climax arrived when from the top of the opposite ridge a great rock was seen to be slowly moving; it was poised above the village of Mukba, as large as two or three of the houses below; and on the roofs of these houses stood a gesticulating crowd of men, women, and children, helplessly awaiting their fate. This mighty rock, first sliding, then bounding, passed with a roar of thunder down a ravine to one side of the village, to come to rest in the bed of the river; so huge was it that for a few seconds the waters were dammed up, and then, accumulating, passed over the obstacle. We retreated after two days' clear weather, to find roads and bridges swept away, and had to ford the streams in companies of six to ten men, with arms interlaced over each other's shoulders. The country-side was full of stories of disaster, from which recovery was long.

In this part of the world the stalwart women were a valuable asset in the homestead, and gave great assistance in the fields. They commanded prices up to £30 or £40, paid not so much in cash to the parents as in rough jewellery to the bride, and domestic tragedies were not infrequent. On one occasion the newly-married wife of a Forest Guard committed suicide by leaping to instant death in the Bhagarathi River, for the rapid stream rolls huge boulders along its bed, and grinds to powder everything that cannot float lightly on the surface. To the new-comer the unseen passing of these rocks, with the gradually increasing rumble and tremor, is strangely reminiscent of the sound and feeling of the frequent earth-movement in the Garo Hills of Assam; in each case habit brings indifference. The husband on this occasion asked for ten days' leave, as he wished to examine the river-banks for some distance below, in the hope of recovering some of the jewellery that had purchased his wife, but failed to buy her affection; but of course he was unsuccessful in his search.

At Tehri, the headquarters of the native State of that name, the arm of justice was not in those days always long enough to reach men who had made themselves liable to punishment, and, moreover, the boundary of Thibet was near and not very clearly defined. In one village on or over the border the inhabitants turned out and massacred two out of three Chinese tax-collectors, by the well-known method of firing through the flimsy tent till the occupants were forced to take the open and meet their fate, the third escaping, after weary hiding in the hills, into British territory. The Raja's police, who later were sent to apprehend the offenders, were glad to be allowed to return with the promise that these would present themselves in the winter. The true hillman hates the heat and the level ground; he sits naked in the cold wind of the plains, and his muscles swell painfully when there are no slopes to climb or descend; so it was that these men deferred their trial till the winter, and then of their own accord went to receive punishment. In those days it would have been unwise to press matters to extremity, and the short time of imprisonment in the Tehri gaol, where all were under parole to return at night after spending the day in earning their food, was not so irksome as would be inferred from the wording of the sentence.

The people of the upper hills are wonderful on bad ground and in precipices. To follow a coolie hampered with his load would often tax the inexperienced mountaineer; and when these men take off their grass shoes and tuck up the skirts of their long coats, you may know that some balancing feat is to be accomplished that justifies caution even on the part of these acrobats. Many dangers, too, exist for him who, unaccustomed to these wild mountains, would leave the known tracks in pursuit of game or other interest. The streams, that are crossed almost dryshod at dawn, are from noon to evening, when the snow is melting, almost impassable torrents, where the water seems to grip your feet and tear them from under you; while the sand and gravel cuts into the flesh, and if happily you emerge, bleeding and breathless, from such an unexpected struggle, you will not again repeat the mistake that might have cost you your life.

Shooting in the hills has, I confess, never had much charm for me, save that of climate and scenery, and both of these are, needless to say, superb; but the scarcity of animal life removes one special interest in forest work, while modern arms of precision render the shooting of a "gural," a "thar," or a "barhel," chiefly a question of skill at a target; the quarry is in the open, and the difficulty lies in getting within a range, now in practice much shortened by the introduction of small-bore rifles of remarkable accuracy. To be successful, a man must enjoy walking on ground where a false step may mean extinction; and accomplished as he may be in this art, his companions are infinitely more so, and their verdict upon the performances will always take into consideration that they are criticizing a "sahib," and not a hillman. But the question of comparative joys of sport in the hills or plains of India must be decided by the tastes of the individual; it is well that there should always be some risk to season the zest for sport of all kinds, and the various forms in which this risk may be taken remain open to choice.

There can, however, be no question as to the exhilaration of camping at high elevations, of the beauties of the white outlines cut sharply against the indigo blue of the passing darkness, of the rosy tints of dawn, of the keen sunlight of midday, of the shadowy lights of evening, and of the intense brilliance of the night; they are each and all incomparable, so that whether you wander beneath the great trees clothed with banners of moss waving to the chilly north, or lie in the meadows where the spring flowers crowd against the edge of the retreating snows, or stand on the snow bridges while the grey water rushes loudly beneath your feet, you will be receiving and storing impressions that may years hence fill you with longings for the mountains that fascinate, perhaps because they seem so superior and so indifferent to man.

Or is there, perhaps, another and more powerful influence at work? Shall we say that those of old who, completing their lesson of self-abandonment by a period of solitude in the hills of Hindustan, descended to impart a superior knowledge to its people, were all self-deceived when they fancied that at the birthplace of the sacred river they were most receptive of its influence; and that the millions who live in this faith, and dying commend their ashes to the holy water, are all under the bane of a deadly error? Does our knowledge of things unseen justify us in referring all the physical and mental benefits

A PEASANT'S HOUSE AT SÁNGLA.

the mountains confer to barometric and thermometric scales? Those who hold other tenets than our own, based even more firmly on faith than on science, are not so decided in their views or so drastic in their anticipation of the result of a difference in opinion. I asked a Brahmin of the highest caste in Southern India what might be the effect of a visit to the "Cow's Mouth" on a Christian who entered unconvinced, but reverent of the feeling of others. The man remained for some time in deep thought, and then asked whether a good medicine was hindered in its action by the creed of the patient. My two visits to the source of the sacred stream had in his opinion evidently been in some way beneficial, and without further inquiry I was content to have it so, and pleased that there should be a religion which, in the opinion of a member of its priesthood, is potent enough to benefit even the unbeliever.

Before November the lowland forest of the Ganges Forest Division claimed attention, and I descended to the plains, passing through Mussoorie and Dehra Dun, to cross the Ganges at the head-works of the great canal below Hardwar. The scenery here will be well known to most of those who have visited India. The chief product of these rugged hills is bamboos, which are cut in millions for export to the plains; and here were for me two novelties, namely, man-eating tigers and wild-elephants; both were fairly common in those days, and both caused considerable danger or annoyance to the forester and his staff.

The man-eater of that time began her depredations in September, and up to the day of her death, in the end of the following March, was credited with destroying some seventy human beings. She was terrible chiefly because of her extreme cunning in capturing her prey, and because of her caution in evading reprisals; and so wary was she that I never saw her but once, and that when she lay dead, though often she had been within a short distance when living. A reward of Rs. 500 was on her head, and there could be no sort of error as to her identity, for on each track a transverse groove in the soil showed where the pad of the right fore-foot had been cut across in some former accident, and had healed unevenly. It is not improbable that this scar indicated the reason why the beast had taken to evil habits during a period of painful lameness; at least, the mark was sufficient, and with good cause, to strike terror in the hearts of those defenceless natives who observed it. There was little forest work done that season, and even field cultivation in some of the hill villages was abandoned; for the brute roamed over an area of about sixty square miles, and the kill of one day was as often as not a long march from the scene of the last tragedy. As usual, the women were the chief sufferers, for on them fell the duty of cutting fodder for the cattle, and of bringing in head-loads of fuel for the winter fires, and well was it for them not to stray far from their party when in the forest, or to lag behind when taking the homeward path. Nor were the men safe from attacks, the more appalling from their suddenness, and the more nerve-destroying because of their daring, till at last the sound of the axe in the forest was held to serve as a call to the tigress which none but the most courageous would dare to give.

During weary months every endeavour was made to rid the country of this pest, but without success. She would not return to a poisoned corpse, when a man of high caste was killed, the relatives would indeed follow the trail under my protection, but they would insist on removing the body for the funeral rites; while if the victim were of low caste none would give me assistance. The ground was extremely unfavourable, consisting of steep slopes densely covered with undergrowth and cut up with deep ravines; and thus for one or even two men to follow the trail fully exposed to the wiles of a silently watching tiger, while attention was concentrated on the track, was to run fearful risks without the smallest chance of success; moreover, the country was impossible for an elephant save in the wider valleys, and when roaming on foot with one orderly over the forest it was necessary to be perpetually on the lookout, so that, when halted to rest or to eat a frugal meal, we sat facing each other, our backs against trees, to prevent the possibility of an onslaught from the rear.

Some occurrences there were to relieve the gloom of the country-side, notably when a woman heroically saved her husband from death. The couple were cutting rice in their terraced fields, when the tigress, approaching from above, suddenly pounced on the man; his wife instantly attacked the animal, and drove her off with the heavy sickle she was using. I went to see this courageous couple, and found the man with five distinct claw marks on the scalp, and others on the chest; he had bandaged his wounds, and sat over the fire in his bloody clothes. The woman took the affair with an air as if she had done nothing remarkable; it was the second occasion on which I had known a woman of the people in India show a calm front in the presence of almost inevitable death. Shortly afterwards the village grocer was carried off when nearing my camp with supplies; his pony galloped into safety, with its load trailing on the ground, leaving a track of various comestibles leading up to the scene of the onslaught. Then the approach of the hot weather, when I was to leave the forest, and an incident which brought home to me the futility of further efforts, forced me at last to apply for outside help.

I was sitting in my tent one afternoon, when a hillman burst rudely upon me, almost speechless with emotion, yet stuttering that his brother had been killed by the tiger. In answer to hurried questions, he had not seen the beast, his brother was cutting bamboos about twenty yards away, he had heard a blow and a groan and a dragging through the leaves; the forest was extremely dense, and the affair was not five minutes old: he could lead us to the spot. In less than that time we two, with an orderly carrying a spare gun, had set out, and ten minutes later had reached the scene. On the swaying bamboos there was blood as far as a man might reach; on the ground was a billhook and torn pieces of cotton cloth; a sinister-looking trail led towards the higher ground above. It was easy to follow, with its fresh blood and fresh footmarks, and we hurried along for about two hundred yards till we entered the bed of a dry watercourse where there was even less need for tracking. Judging from the marks, the tigress was evidently just ahead of us, when our way was barred by a wall of dry rock, a waterfall in the rainy season. This was about eight feet high, and my companions pushed me up and handed the rifle. The man lay some twenty yards farther on, probably abandoned at the sound of our pursuing steps; he had no face, his skull had been flattened on his neck by a blow from above, and he had been gripped in the loins when carried away; the eight-foot obstacle had apparently been negotiated at a bound, for there was no mark of dragging up the face of the rock.

The tigress, I thought, was certain to return, and I proposed to go back to camp and bring the necessary materials to fix up a seat in an adjoining tree; the brother followed wailing and weeping, but immediately on his arrival, collecting friends from the neighbouring bamboo-cutters' huts, he set out to retrieve and burn his brother's corpse. They were a party of twenty or more, making sufficient uproar to communicate to the tigress the fear they themselves felt. The next day I wrote to the officer commanding a Gurkha regiment at Dehra Dun, for the loan of a non-commissioned officer and ten or twelve men to try their luck; and fortune was with them even on their arrival at Chila, opposite Hardwar, a few days later, for almost simultaneously came a report that a woman had been killed some miles from the camp, and they at once started in pursuit. They formed, with the neighbouring villagers, a wide circle in the forest, and advanced towards the spot where the corpse was supposed to be lying, and soon in the centre of this ring of rifles and bayonets the tigress leapt on to a rock to determine her line of retreat. She fell with her back broken by a lucky shot fired by the son of the "havildar," a lad of about fifteen years old, and the little Gurkhas, closing in, soon despatched her. They brought down a tigress of under eight feet long in the prime of life, and vouched for her identity by some poor bones taken from her stomach; but I only looked at the pad of the right fore-paw, and paid the reward with a thankful heart.

Rid of this pest, there was more zest for the work of the forest, and more delight in roaming in its solitudes. I was interested in studying the habits and disposition of the wild-elephants—how during the winter the chief food was found in the bamboo-forests, and, when the foliage fell, how the herds resorted to the swamps or shady ravines where green grass was still to be had; how the shelter and shade of the forest was sought by day, and how darkness heralded the luxuries of bathing and drinking.

The wild-elephant when in a herd is perhaps the noisiest of the jungle animals, for the reason, probably, that he has no fear of other beasts and little of man; and so it is that, when the mothers cease from trumpeting and gurgling, and the calves from squealing and squeaking, there is yet the constant sound of the breaking of bamboos or of the overturning of the clumps in order that the youngsters may reach the leaves. The unsafest way to approach a herd is to ride up to it on a tame elephant, unless this be a very speedy one ; the safest is to go on foot, if the ground is at all steep, for an elephant cannot run quickly across a slope, nor can he climb a perpendicular bank of six feet high without breaking for himself an easier gradient ; but he can come downhill like a tornado, and will slide down a bank that a man would have to be careful in negotiating, by the simple method of kneeling on his hind-legs and letting himself go. The large males are nearly always some distance behind the herd, but keep to its track ; they frequently use the main roads at night, possibly to shorten the longer route taken more leisurely by the mothers and young ones to their new feeding-ground, and this habit is often a source of trouble to the forester's camp when marching at night. For three or four days the new-born calf cannot walk, nor can he rise without help ; his mother stands over him, waving a foot or trunk within a fraction of an inch of his body to keep off the flies, and from time to time she kicks the ground with her fore-foot, so that a shower of soil flies over the prostrate calf ; then when he grunts, to express his hunger or desire for a change, she places her trunk on the farther side of his body, and heaves him with her fore-foot to an upright position. Once on his feet, he staggers about trying to find the pendent udders, and waves his fore-feet in the air in futile endeavour to obtain nourishment ; having secured the teat, he seems to be careless of any pain or inconvenience he may cause. He speedily picks up strength and wickedness with his sturdy growth.

The mode of catching elephants in Upper India

is by noosing from trained animals; and to do this the herd is marked down and surrounded by men on foot, who endeavour, by firing guns if necessary, to prevent it breaking through till the hunters arrive. On each trained elephant is a small "pad," or stiff, thick mattress, and on this is carefully coiled a stout noosed rope; in front sits the mahout, or driver, armed with his iron hook, and behind stands his assistant with a wooden club faced with iron spikes. This club is an implement much dreaded by domestic elephants. It is vigorously applied at the root of the tail, and soon produces an open sore many inches in length; it is a spur to induce the greatest possible exertion, and most elephants will respond to the memory of the punishment of the club, even if not used in recent years, when a smart blow is struck by the hand or foot of the rider on the pad. The trained elephants dash into the herd at speed, and uproar and confusion are paramount; for each driver, incited by the reward paid for capture, selects a victim, and pursues it with shouts while seeking to throw the noose around its neck. This the wild-elephant endeavours to prevent with his trunk, but is not always quick enough; and as soon as the snare is over the head the tame elephant is stopped, and strangulation would soon ensue were not the rope loosened and secured from again slipping. The application of a second rope is then easier, and the unhappy captive stands with its captors fore and aft, with hawsers tight to prevent drifting in either direction.

The mahouts naturally select from the herd young females of a manageable size; the largest animals are left to those last in the field, and so frequently escape, and are none the less morose after the experience they have gone through. Sometimes as a *tour de force* the tusker of the herd is run to a standstill by the trained elephants, who are both lighter and faster, and then the fighting males are brought up to secure him; but often the injuries inflicted on the captive are so severe that he succumbs to them shortly after, or, if uninjured, he remains untamable, and it is seldom that a really useful full-grown male is secured. In all cases the sight is somewhat sad; one sympathizes with the loss of dignity and freedom in so noble a beast, though perhaps resentful of the manner in which he has dominated the forest.

The females and the calves show little opposition when caught. I once saw twenty-one elephants captured during the afternoon, and led into camp the same evening over seven miles of a difficult path. When first captured, they are dangerous to approach except on a tame elephant, and the females often refuse to allow their own calves to touch them, so that the sad sight of an orphan wandering round many mothers is sometimes witnessed; but the tame elephants take kindly to such waifs, and, if they are old enough to browse, will carefully look after them. There is no difficulty in leading the newly captured animals to water twice a day, or in marching them slowly to headquarters, and in about a year they are fit to be driven alone; though it not infrequently happens that one escapes and joins the wild herd, even after years of domesticity, and in such circumstances the animal becomes specially dangerous, for it has lost its unreasoning fear of man, and promptly resents his approach. Elephants are fit for light work at fifteen years of age, are mature at about forty, and continue to work till seventy years of age or older; but they are delicate creatures, suffering much from sun and heat, and from lameness. In Burma they are let loose in the forest with a forty-foot tracking chain attached to one leg, and thus it is that there the young are frequently born in confinement; but in India elephants are stall-fed, and therefore the more enjoy being ridden slowly through the forest, when each mouthful plucked may be a *bonne bouche* of excellent flavour.

The wild tusker is dangerous or harmless according to the humour he is in. For instance, when he occupies his leisure in tearing the bark off the "sál" tree and consuming strips of many feet in length, he is taking his spring tonic, and is not bad-tempered; but when he is heard smashing trees and uprooting saplings, it may be inferred that he is venting his seasonal fury on inanimate objects for want of better sport, and on such occasions he is to be avoided. Many foresters have had narrow escapes from wild-elephants. For instance, Colonel Campbell had the animal he was riding upset and deeply gored, his orderly being killed, and he himself escaping up a stout tree; and as the Colonel was one of the best shots in India, it seems certain that he was unable to stop or turn the charge with the weapons at his disposal.

The elephant stands very silently on the approach of man, and to turn suddenly round a clump of bamboos and see a monstrous and expectant form in waiting on the other side is startling. The invisibility of so large an animal is due somewhat to the dust and mud plastered on their bodies, and this protection is in the hot weather often supplemented by covering the head with dry grass. An 8-bore rifle or paradox gun with a heavy charge is a suitable weapon for surprise visits from elephants; but if a steady shot at a longer distance is possible, any of the high-velocity rifles of the present day, with nickel-covered bullets, is preferable. The old-fashioned steel-capped bullets appear to be useless. I once watched Mr. Greig, then Conservator of Forests in the North-Western Provinces, place three of these bullets behind the shoulders of a tusker at twenty-five yards' distance. He then followed up and fired four more shots into his head; but the elephant went off at his best speed, and my trackers, on their return in three days, reported him to be twenty miles away, eating bamboo, and his wounds stopped with clay. Mr. Osmaston, also a noted sportsman in the Forest Department, has killed two or three tuskers, in particular a rogue elephant that had been proclaimed; and he, I believe, at least on one occasion, used a 12-bore rifle at close quarters. But the long bullet of the old Martini-Henry military rifle will easily reach an elephant's brain, and perhaps the best weapon for all emergencies would be the high-velocity rifle of the same or somewhat smaller bore.

The male elephant possesses formidable weapons—in his trunk, for the demolition of small, light objects such as a man; in his fore-feet, which he uses with force and accuracy against a tiger, pig, or bear;

and in his tusks, which are useful in his duels or to hurl aside any intruder. They fight by pushing forehead to forehead till one gives way and falls or flees, when he may be severely gored, or at the least have his tail torn out, by his pursuer; for many wild-elephants are tailless, or possess only sorry stumps, the males bearing this disfigurement as a token of defeat, and the females probably as a proof of their resistance to the advances of the male. To be pursued in the open, when unarmed, by a tusker is a most exhausting experience. I was surprised by one when fishing in the Ramganga River, and only reached safety on the rocks of the farther bank by exerting all my agility both on land and water, leaving the rod and tackle as the spoils of the intruder.

As to the enemies of wild-elephants, they have none save man and those of their own household. An animal that with one kick can send a boar staggering to his death ten yards away, and can throw a bear violently on to the ground and then stamp him to a pulp, need not fear to be assaulted when roaming through the forest. It is only when furious with pain that a tiger will dare to attack the elephant, and no animal but the rhinoceros cares to measure strength with him. Yet some are killed in fighting; others meet their death by accidentally falling on precipitous ground in the rainy season, or even by being carried away in the monsoon floods; and I have seen instances of each. Perhaps no animal is so useless in the wild state, and so indispensable in captivity, as the elephant. I have already sung his praises in the realm of sport; it is sufficient to add that without his help the supply of teak timber to the world would almost cease. He it is who drags the logs to the floating streams in readiness for the next flood; who guides them in their passage to the main river, releasing jams at the peril of his life; who receives them on arrival at depot and lays them in order for the sawmill, and builds up the stacks of squares awaiting despatch to Europe, finally when the time arrives, placing them on the trollies for shipment; for he has the strength of a machine, and is not confined to the interminable repetition of a single series of actions.

The forests of the Ganges Division, which, as I have indicated, may be reached from Hardwar, may also be visited from the eastern side from the Kohdwára station of the Oudh and Rohilkhand Railway. There is good fishing to be had in the Ganges just before the snow-water comes down in April, for those who enjoy the use of heavy bait and tackle, and, where the stream splits up into various branches, fishing from the bank with a flying spoon is practicable. In the smaller streams the so-called "trout," a black-spotted carp, is numerous, and will rise either to fly or to spoon on light tackle. When he is on the feed, dozens may be taken in a short time. The best time appears to be when the sun is bright and hot, for discoloured water sickens the fish, and much harm is done by unusually high floods, which carry away the whole stock of fish to the big rivers, and thus for long after an abnormal rise the sport remains inferior. It is advisable to have weapons at hand when fishing these rivers, for one never knows what may happen, and it is trying to feel helpless in the presence of wild animals even if they have no evil intentions.

I had not much success with tigers in these forests. They seemed shy of returning to their kills, and caused much annoyance by slaughtering my baits and leaving them uneaten. There was a tigress at Chila who was proficient at this form of teasing, and in evading my efforts for her destruction. I was then building the house at that place, and removing for material the great stones from the ruins of a Buddhist temple discovered in the jungle, and this tigress was continually around the camp, frequenting the stream which lies to the east of the plain. She killed five buffaloes in succession without feeding on any, not even breaking the tethering ropes or dragging them away; in fact, she would neither leave the neighbourhood nor take any risks. One evening, hearing the alarm cry of the spotted-deer telling of panther or tiger, I took my rifle, and, followed by my orderly, went out to investigate; but on reaching the herd I for some time could detect no reason for alarm, till, following the direction of their startled gaze, I discovered my tigress crouching in the grass. She rose and strolled away through the forest, but I had learnt the lesson not to fire at the hind-quarters of dangerous game, and followed, hoping for a favourable opportunity. After a time she stopped, and, turning, drew up her lips with a snarl, to intimate, perhaps, that further pursuit would be resented. Immediately I had fired we lay still in the undergrowth listening to struggles, roars, and groans, close at hand, and not till these had subsided, and silence once more reigned, did we cautiously creep towards where the tigress lay in the trampled grass. I was glad of every tiger slain in this neighbourhood, lest some should have the taint of the man-eater in their blood, which death only can eradicate.

The charm of these forests lies in their mountains, where one is free of the high grass of the lowlands, so that stalking the sámbhar and spotted-deer is a constant pleasure. They were not in those days so frequent as to cause the sport to become monotonous, but yet sufficiently numerous to give a zest to the forester's work, and lead him to explore many places he might not otherwise have inspected; while the fear of surprise visits at inauspicious moments had a good effect in hindering the dishonesty of subordinates and contractors, and in preventing negligence, for the preservation of these forests from fire was then being first attempted, though at the present time it is a matter of course that they should not be burnt. The country, too, is very beautiful as one marches upstream on the banks of the Ganges River, and the islands, covered with "shisham" trees, are a joy in the springtime. At Gorighat there was a camping-ground with an evil reputation for spirits, the natives refusing to sleep there alone, and I had one night a curious experience there. My guest woke me in the small-hours with loud cries for help, and, rushing over to his small sleeping-tent, I found him much agitated and somewhat unwilling to explain. Ultimately his story was that through the flap of the tent he had seen a human hand stealthily descending on his face; that, unable to move his head from the pillow, he had been forced to watch its approach till a clammy touch had given him the strength of terror to shriek for aid. There was no doubt of his firm conviction of the fact of the occurrence, and I felt that he must know more about it than I possibly could; but the subject was not discussed with that detail I could have desired, especially as the natives took the absolute truth of the story as a matter of course.

During my stay in the Ganges Division I investigated the reason of the peculiar cry uttered by jackals, which is never taken up nor in any way acknowledged by the pack. The vernacular term for this call is "pheau," in imitation of the sound; but it is necessary to hear it echoing in the still night, and responded to by the started deer, in order to appreciate its mournful weirdness. There can be no doubt that the "pheau" is merely an alarm cry, and that in the forest it most frequently signifies that the jackal either sees or hears a tiger or panther, or has crossed the fresh track of one or the other. On one occasion I watched a jackal sitting some 20 yards from a tiger who was drinking on the river-bank. The jackal uttered this cry frequently, and ultimately followed the tiger as he wandered slowly into cover. Another time when riding I heard the cry, and saw a jackal sitting in the forest path ahead, and in a few minutes a tiger walked slowly across the road. This beast killed a woman the same evening not far from the spot. My method of investigation was to stalk the jackal, and watch him till I discovered the cause of his alarm; and it did not at first strike me that this might be located in the trees above as well as on the earth beneath, till I observed a jackal gazing at a large python coiled in the thick branches of a tree. It then, of course, was self-evident that any semi-arboreal animal, such as the panther, might well be sought for at a height from the ground, and that jackals particularly had good cause to remember this fact. Finally, on hearing a jackal, when run to earth by dogs, utter this cry in the extremity of fear, the conclusion was arrived at that, like the tales of the "wer" wolf, those of the "pheau" have originated in the nursery, to be adopted gradually into the folklore of the country.

The submontane forests of the Himalaya are of peculiar interest to the ornithologist; for they are not only rich in resident types, but are visited by many migratory birds during the winter months. In them is a variety of thrushes, of woodpeckers, and of birds of prey, three kinds of hornbill, while many other families are represented. Mr. Osmaston, whose name I have already mentioned, is a notable authority on the birds of this region, having made the study of their nests and eggs a speciality, and possessing a unique collection of the latter.

From the Ganges forests I went to Europe on furlough, and on my return found myself posted to the forests in Kumaon. These are now accessible from Haldwáni, a station on the Rohilkhand and Kumaon Railway on the route to the hill-station of Naini Tal. The charge extends about thirty miles both to the east and west of that town, and comprises mountain forests up to an elevation of nearly 6,000 feet; those of the Bhabar, or waterless tract lower down; and, lastly, those of the Tarai, where the soil is more or less water-logged.

The forests of the Kumaon district towards the east had in those days an evil name for malaria and for cholera, and not without cause. Such inhabitants as there were were chiefly migratory from the hills, where they returned in spring; they consisted of graziers from Kali Kumaon and shepherds from Thibet, men who were prepared to resist any forest regulations that were deemed to restrict their trade, and who were on the whole uninteresting and unfriendly. There was but one house, that at Chorgalia, or Thieves' Gully, where the Nandhaur River debouched into the plains; there were no roads save a particularly inferior track leading from Haldwáni to Barmdeo, from the one mart of Thibetans and hillmen to another on the banks of the Sarda River. Footpaths there were on which a good hill-pony might climb, but there were no cleared camping-grounds in a country of dense forest, and no wells in a land of impure water. Matters have been much improved since then; there are roads and houses, wells and bridges, for the lesson has been learnt that all these are necessary either to exploit the forest or to maintain in health those on whom this duty is imposed. The loss of life in the early days of forest conservancy in India must have been great, and the lists of wounded, men with constitutions ruined by repeated attacks of malaria, must have been lengthy; and thus the large sums that have been, and are being, spent in the protection of the staff have been easily recouped by its greater efficiency.

In the Kumaon forests game was plentiful. Below the hills, whence numerous watercourses proceeded, were the forests of Horai and Jaunla Sal, and between these spread vast plains of high grass wherein sheltered in the winter both swamp-deer and hog-deer; but this part of the country was much shot over by parties from the neighbouring districts and from the native State of Ránpur, though these did not enter the tree-forest to any great extent. Through the centre of the Jaunla Sal forest runs a broad grassy plain, ending to the south in a swamp, and here in the summer months up to four hundred swamp-deer have been counted as they grazed on the new grass; they are then bright chestnut in colour, their hides flecked with lighter spots, and the stags carry no heads. Jaunla Sal is almost the most westerly limit of this species. In the swamp above referred to there always were, and still are, tigers in the hot weather; in fact, Jaunla Sal is a good centre for a couple of weeks' shooting, whether on foot or from an elephant. The wild-elephants later in the season retreat across the Sarda River to Nepal, and their departure is welcomed, for in this flat country it is difficult to evade them when they are disposed to be unpleasant. It was in this forest that I saw the dead body of a tuskless male elephant, and the Forest Guard informed me that for three days before my arrival a fight had raged in the forest; and he added that, though he had been too fearful to go and see it, there could be no doubt that the victorious tusker must be of enormous size. The natives believe that in these duels the tuskless elephant has the advantage, as he does not hesitate to strike a foul blow by seizing his adversary's tusks and breaking them off, and it is true that the tuskless males always seem to have a more massive head than those with tusks; but on this occasion the tusker had evidently thrown his opponent, and then gored him to death, and I could only regret the loss of a unique opportunity of being an eyewitness of this battle of giants.

From the high bank of the Sarda River, below Barmdeo, one looks on a lovely landscape; the river is broken up into many narrow channels separated by shisham-clad islands, and a background is provided by the hills of Nepal in the distance. The fishing here is good at the right season, and the water quite manageable with 150 yards of line; while the islands used to afford cover to deer, and even tigers, visitors from the forests on either side.

I recall when in camp with Mr. Greig and his wife, our tents pitched on the bluff above the river, we proposed in a joking mood to take our tea on the island below, and catch a fish and shoot a tiger before nightfall, and actually carried out the programme. Mr. Greig was soon into a fifteen-pound mahseer, which he landed before tea, and later we mounted our elephants and wandered through the dense groves of trees. Shortly after I fired at a hog-deer that rushed behind my elephant, and the report woke a tiger, over whom the bullet must have passed. In the confusion that followed, the brute had covered 150 yards before the elephant was steadied and gave a chance to fire. He then laid up farther on, and it was a pretty sight to see him charge across the open and fall dead before he reached the elephant; for Mr. Greig was one of those certain shots who was never expected to miss, and who seldom disappointed this expectation.

To the west of Haldwáni the Kumaon forests in those days extended to Ramnagar on the Mohán River, and from here to the south-west lies the forest of Garibulchand, where good winter shooting was to be obtained, though later on in the year the big game retreated to the hills. To the north-east of Haldwáni lies the forest of Sitabani, a very favourite resort for tigers; but there was so much work to do in these forests, and so much to contend against in the way of sickness, that there was little time for the study of natural history or for sport. But I recall more than one hot season spent at Chorgalia, and at this distance of time my memories are chiefly of the icy winter wind that blew for twelve hours each night, with fell effect on the man or beast exposed to it, and of the furnace blast of summer that lasts for twelve hours of the day; of the attempts to introduce fire conservancy; and of the daily longing for the monsoon to arrive, when the forester might with a clear conscience leave his charge, knowing that none other would have the courage to brave its dangers and discomforts during his absence.

After about three years of hard work in the Kumaon forests, I was fortunate enough to get the charge of those of Garhwal, and the period spent there was as pleasant as the former had been miserable. The country lies between the Kumaon and Ganges forests, and comprises various "doons," or high-level valleys, such as the Kotah Doon, the Pátli Doon, and the Kothri Doon. Through these flow perennial streams of various sizes, the largest being the Ramganga River in the Pátli Doon; all of these rivers hold fish of a size proportionate to the volume of water, and afford good sport, while the configuration of the country, with its mountains and passes, supplies constant change of scene, and obviates the drawback of monotony. There are now roads and houses all over this area of about 500 square miles; but at that date the house at Dhikála, standing on a bluff above the Ramganga, was, besides the building at Ramnagar, the only adequate shelter in these forests.

Dhikála is a charming spot in an open plain, with low hills all around, and in the spring, when the hill forest is white with the "sâl" blossoms, and the lowlands shaded with the young foliage of the "shisham," while the river flows in wide sweeps between, it is one of the most delightful headquarters that either a forester or a sportsman could desire. Often from the upper veranda of the house hundreds of animals might be seen grazing on the new grass, and at one and the same time elephants, deer of several kinds, and pigs, might have been observed. During the winter, when the grass is high, most of the animals keep on the high ground, but in the spring they descend to the "doons"; at that season it was but natural that the tigers should take up their quarters close to their food-supply, and, as they were then not much molested save by occasional shooting-parties, the Forest Officer had to slay many, if only to protect the cattle working in the forest. But I here again suffered a rather serious reverse.

The mahouts came in one May morning and reported that there was a tiger obstructing them in cutting fodder for the elephants, and it became a duty to proceed to investigate the complaint; so, taking with me one stanch female elephant and one much younger and still untried, I proceeded to the spot, and soon found the tiger. He was very morose and gave me every chance, and, when struck by a ·500-bore hollow-fronted bullet, went some distance and lay in the grass. It was extremely hot, the gun-barrels were burning to the touch, and both men and elephants felt the sun greatly, so that I wished to go home, and return later in the evening or next morning to recover a beast that was evidently in no way disabled; but I foolishly listened to the clamour of my men, who insisted, as usual, that the tiger was dead, and consented to follow him up almost at once.

As might have been expected, he instantly charged, selecting the small elephant, who as promptly fled, and might indeed have made her escape, as the tiger was merely striking in an undecided manner; but, unfortunately, he inflicted a slight scratch on her hind-leg, and the foolish animal turned on him. She was at once seized as in a vice, the claws of both fore-paws being embedded in her head, and the fangs in the base of her trunk. From this grip there was no escape, and, the tiger continuing to pull in heavy jerks, the elephant came down on her knees. At this stage the driver described a parabola through the air, and lay motionless in the grass; while the tiger, still pulling, turned the elephant on her side. I in the meantime stood watching at a few yards off, unable to fire on account of the deep agitation of my own mount, who could hardly be restrained from either fighting or fleeing, and could not be made to stand steady. The tiger ultimately disappeared with one bound into the grass, the prostrate elephant slowly arose, blood pouring from her wounds, while the man lay still, and some minutes elapsed before he staggered bewildered to his feet, picked up his turban, and sought safety on my elephant. It was a melancholy procession that returned to Dhikála, and there was an anxious time to follow in tending the elephant day and night till her wounds healed and she was herself once more. The remains of the tiger were found not far from the spot later on, but I had little interest in the matter, because I felt that, in yielding to the foolish persuasion of my men, I had brought about a disaster that might have been much more serious than it actually was.

It is a curious circumstance that even in moments of greatest stress natives will insist on recovering their turbans and shoes—even, sometimes, at the risk of their lives. I have given an instance of this in the preceding narrative, and I recall two or three other occasions of a similar nature. In one case a mahout who had dropped his turban wished to descend to recover it, thus leaving his elephant unattended in the face of a wounded tiger, and deeply resented my refusal to allow him to do so; later on we found his head-dress torn to scraps by the furious beast, which merely seemed to the man to supply a proof of my tyranny in not permitting him to pick

ELEPHANT WITH "KATOLA."

up his property before it had been destroyed. There is with Mohammedans probably something of a feeling of disgrace attached to returning bareheaded from the hunt, and, ridicule being most keenly felt, they will take any risk to prevent it.

The "howdah" appears to me to be a most unsuitable arrangement for the solitary sportsman, its sole advantage being that a wider field of vision is afforded, and this is convenient in long grass; on the other hand, the angle of fire at a near object is difficult, and only verbal directions can be given to the driver. The latter objection is of more importance than the former, for the human voice carries far in the forest, and he who talks will seldom see much game, and, moreover, in moments of tumult verbal directions may easily be misunderstood. Again, if the sportsman is seated on the "pad," he is at all times insecure, and may easily be thrown by any sudden side movement of the elephant; while on steep ascents and descents he must occupy both hands in clinging to the breastplate ropes, and becomes thus helpless even for self-defence. The most convenient saddle for the elephant probably consists in what is known as a "katola," which resembles an inverted bedstead, with the four stout wooden legs cut short; seated on this, with head just above that of the driver, and a foot on either side of him, it is easy to direct his movements in silence, while at the same time the elephant can be efficiently protected from frontal attacks. Nearly all the contretemps I experienced in tiger-hunting occurred when shooting from a "howdah," and were directly referable to the fact that the elephant was not controlled by my wishes, but either by his own or by those of the driver; the latter, from a lower elevation, necessarily seeing things in a different aspect from what I did. Of course, when many sportsmen are occupied in shooting one tiger, it is immaterial how they ride their elephants, as but one can be attacked at a time, and the relieving forces are near at hand.

West of Dhikála is situated Boxar, where there is a house built on the ruins of a sawmill, which I believe was erected just before the Mutiny, and was never worked. A canal had been dug across a bend in the Ramganga River, and power was to be obtained from a turbine. It may some day be found profitable to attempt again to utilize the water-power of this river—not, indeed, solely for sawing timber, but to produce hydro-electric power for industries to the south. Meanwhile there was at Boxar good fishing, and in Shishamkhata, a forest above the house, there are always tigers and deer, which afford good sport until the arrival of some shooting-party, when they are driven up to the fire-trace to the north of the forest, to guns posted at intervals along it. About twenty or thirty elephants are required to carry out this scheme successfully.

South of Boxar the road runs to Kalagarh, where the Ramganga debouches on the plains, but a more interesting route may be taken through the low hills some thirty miles to Ramnagar; at each camp tracks of tigers are certain to be seen, and at Jamnagwar there is a famous ravine where they congregate later on in the season, when water is becoming scarce, as many as four or five, and even more, having been driven out and bagged in one day. Of course such slaughter cannot be indefinitely repeated, but the tiger is supposed to be vermin even when he lives twenty miles from the abode of man, and is quite incapable of harming him, so that his extinction appears to be a matter of time; for no Government would face the rare opportunity which would be afforded for misrepresentations by taking steps to protect so interesting a beast from extermination. Pity it is that he must disappear, and with him one of the greatest charms of forest life, and also a form of sport that has been not only enjoyable, but beneficial, to hundreds of exiles.

It was at this place that I was able to observe the grim defence of an old boar against a tiger, and to admire the pluck of perhaps the most courageous of all the beasts of the forest; for here the camp was kept awake all night long by the sound of a duel to the death which was proceeding a few score yards from the tents. There was no mistaking the roars of the tiger and the furious grunting of the boar, and I think our sympathies were all with the latter; but when dawn broke we found him lying dead in the grass, scored all over with wounds; evidently it was not till the tiger had succeeded in leaping on his back that the boar had succumbed. No doubt the tiger had not come off scatheless; we found him on the summit of one of those water-worn gravel hillocks so frequent in this part of the country, and unapproachable save by climbing up the loose surface; and having to hurry away, we left him to enjoy his hard-earned victory. At the next camp a pathetic tragedy had once occurred, involving the death of two men who were sleeping for the night in a grass shanty by the side of the path. A tiger seized one of the men as they were sitting at their camp-fire, but the brute was driven off, and the wounded man was carried by his companion into the hut. But here the tiger returned later on, and dragged away the brave man who had already risked his life for his dying friend. One hardly likes to think of the anguish of terror and of despair that must have been suffered during that night in the lonely forest.

Proceeding to the east of Dhikála, the valley narrows considerably, and at Sarapduli there is a grassy swamp below the road which has an evil reputation among the travellers who pass along this path on their way to the hill-villages higher up. Farther on, where a road strikes off to Mohán, there is a forest bungalow whence good fishing can be obtained, for, continuing up the river, the hills close in rapidly on either side, there are frequent rapids, and the water is less disturbed by the passage of bamboo rafts.

Here one day while I was fishing a native ran to inform me that two large snakes were fighting in the road, and, hurrying up, I found what I thought to be two pythons in deadly combat. After watching them for a while I proceeded to interfere, when one rapidly glided away, and the other threateningly erected his head, displaying the well-known hood of the cobra. I then knew that this was the dreaded hamadryad, and regretted that I had not left the combatants alone, as I might then have seen for myself how this great snake kills and disposes of his prey when of size equal to his own. He certainly had time to strike the python before my arrival disturbed him, but either he had not done so, or the effect was not instantaneous. Now he retreated, always stopping when followed, but never attacking, until my rifle arrived and the hunt was finished. This snake was about 11 feet long, and had huge fangs, so that the poison would be deeply injected, and a man would probably succumb in a few minutes from its effect and from the shock of the stroke.

Few snakes are seen in the forest save those species which are arboreal in their habits, probably because the others are concealed during the winter in holes underground, or in trees, and in summer are nocturnal in their habits. Pythons, however, are found all over the forests of Northern India, but the specimens I have measured never attained a length of 20 feet; they are fond of lying in marshy ground, but are frequently found in trees in the dry season, probably because their appetites are then more insistent. It seems improbable that a python should rely on obtaining food by crawling on the earth, whence he has a limited horizon, when from the convenient branch of a tree he can command a wider view and drop suddenly on his unsuspecting prey; for that this is the method adopted seems more than likely. The snake's teeth are not adapted to hold a large struggling animal, and on the occasions that I have seen the python with a spotted-deer enwrapped in his folds there were no signs of laceration; moreover, it is hard to believe that a python, generally one of the most sluggish of reptiles, should climb trees except for a better reason than, for instance, to take the air or to enjoy the landscape: he may be credited with a more practical outlook on life. The python can strike a severe blow with his head and also inflict a sharp bite, but it is not correct that the grip of his jaws once fixed is not released. Kipling no doubt uses poetic licence when Kaa breaks marble with his snout, but I have seen quite a small python strike a fowl with such force that it staggered to die bleeding some paces away, and several minutes elapsed before the snake proceeded to investigate the effect of its blow; it may therefore well be the case that the blow of a heavy python would be sufficient to stun a passing deer until it could be enfolded in the grip of the snake, and that this method of hunting may supplement the sudden and more deadly attack from overhead—the more so as a python, when threatened, sometimes raises its head to a considerable height, and widely distends its jaws, as if prepared to strike as soon as opportunity offers.

Cobras are frequent in the forest, but are mostly inoffensive unless inadvertently intruded upon. There were two in my hut at Chila for many days, and they could be heard rustling in the thatch morning and evening as they returned from the hunt or left for water and food; yet I should not have seen either had I not one morning met the male snake in the doorway, he being somewhat later, and I earlier, than usual. Fortunately, he it was who paid the penalty of his want of punctuality, and his partner, following on the trail of the dead snake in the evening, gave an easy shot in the open. It was interesting to recognize that there might be some truth in the native belief in attachment between the sexes in snakes, and in their ability to run a trail by scent.

CHAPTER IV

ON THE HABITS OF TIGERS

THUS far nothing has been written of the habits, the propensities, and temperament, of the Indian tiger; and this may perhaps best be recorded by a consideration of how he may be hunted by the sportsman who has at his disposal merely the usual equipment of Englishmen in India, who, in the majority of cases, are not in a position to spend large sums on sport.

The female has as a rule three or four cubs; I have never seen more with the mother, and probably their number is often reduced by untoward accidents during infancy. The permanent canine teeth are present at three years of age, when the young tigers measure from 7 feet to 8 feet in length, and until then they are not well able to support themselves—that is, they cannot kill the larger animals of the forest; and if for any reason deserted by the mother, they must content themselves with smaller game, such as peafowl, porcupines, and young deer or pig, which their extraordinary agility enables them to capture; in times of stress they will even feed on frogs, which may be found in large numbers in the drying pools during the winter and spring. The mother does not always remain close by the cubs, even when they are only half grown; but she knows where they are, and either returns to them or attracts them from a distance by her cries. That she continues watchful over them is shown by the fact that, during a beat in the Sohelwa forests, a tigress, who was safely behind the guns, walked through them and towards the beaters as soon as the drive began, and I had to shoot her to prevent any possibility of injury to the men; her three cubs were driven out in front of the line of beaters, and one of them savagely struck a coolie on the hand—a fact I recall, as it was the only occasion in which I had a man injured when hunting in India.

So soon as the canine teeth are grown, the young tigers either wander away from the mother, or are driven off by the tiger who has appropriated her. The male tiger does not seem to be addicted to infanticide, though, when they are in confinement, this crime is reported as not uncommon; in fact, I have seen him in company with cubs of all ages, and it is probably the difficulty of finding food for many voracious mouths that ultimately enforces a separation. The cubs after becoming independent doubtless have a poor time until the impetus of hunger teaches them to become careful hunters; perhaps it is for this reason that the young tiger frequently does wanton mischief in the forest and to the village cattle, and is most easily roused to fury. They continue to increase in length, and more so in bulk, for many years if they escape injury to teeth and claws; but with regard to the size they attain I am unable to make any definite assertion, beyond stating that I personally have seen at least two hundred dead tigers, and have never measured one over 10 feet $3\frac{1}{2}$ inches in length as he lay, though others may have been more fortunate.

However, the length of a tiger is no sure criterion of his weight and strength, and probably skull measurements give more accurate results; for the larger the head, the larger also are the muscles of the jaws and neck, and, given a powerful neck, it is probable that the muscles of the shoulders would be in proportion thereto, the fore-quarters of a tiger being much more massive than his hind-quarters. I give below some skull measurements of tigers as compared with their length:

TIGERS.

Where Shot.	Length.		Skull.		
	Ft.	In.	In.		In.
1. Marhá	9	9	$13\frac{1}{4}$	by	$9\frac{7}{8}$
2. Sohelwa	9	9	$13\frac{1}{4}$	by	$9\frac{3}{8}$
3. Changanála	9	0	$13\frac{1}{2}$	by	$10\frac{3}{8}$
4. Bankati	9	9	15	by	$10\frac{1}{8}$
5. Sathiána	10	0	$14\frac{1}{4}$	by	$9\frac{1}{2}$
6. Domoháni	10	0	15	by	$9\frac{15}{16}$
7. Dudua	10	2	$14\frac{3}{8}$	by	$9\frac{1}{4}$
8. Central Provinces	10	3	$15\frac{1}{8}$	by	$10\frac{1}{2}$
9. Garhwál	10	$3\frac{1}{4}$	$14\frac{1}{4}$	by	$10\frac{3}{8}$

TIGRESSES.

Where Shot.	Ft.	In.	In.		In.
10. Oudh	8	9	$12\frac{1}{4}$	by	$8\frac{1}{4}$
11. Oudh	8	6	$12\frac{7}{8}$	by	$10\frac{3}{8}$

It will be seen that No. 8—which, I believe, is the largest shot by that excellent sportsman Mr. P. H. Clutterbuck—heads the list as regards both length and size of skull, and was probably the heaviest tiger of all here listed, but that No. 4 runs him close in skull measurements, though 6 inches less in length. This latter was a most formidable animal, and I was much disappointed when the tape was put over him. No. 3 was also a massive tiger, as the width of his skull will prove; his measurements were larger than those of a twelve-foot tiger reported from Bengal, and he would probably have given that animal, not only the three feet, but a beating, if he had met him in the flesh. On the whole, it is probable that skull measurements combined with weight will give the best index to the comparative size of these animals, and the weight will probably be found to vary in a full-grown male in good condition between 400 and 600 pounds, increasing with the breadth of the skull.

There is, I think, no question as to the permanent deterioration either of the tiger or of any other species in India, but they have not now opportunity to attain to the large size of former years. It was easier for them to live to old age before the bow and arrow and the firelock were replaced by the high-velocity rifle, and before the village shikari was ousted by crowds of well-equipped and eager sportsmen. The sanctuaries now created in the Government forests may have a great effect in increasing the size of trophies, but only if their sanctity is strictly preserved, and if the locality remains undisturbed for a long term of years. The three years proposed as the term for which one forest shall remain closed to hunting may increase the number of animals, but cannot be expected to have an appreciable effect on the size of the trophies they yield.

Putting aside the method of shooting tigers by driving them by coolies or by elephants to the sportsman who is seated in a tree or in a "howdah"—a method very expensive, and, even at any outlay of money, often impossible by reason of the configuration of the ground or the height of the grass—the question remains, What means must be employed to come to close quarters with the quarry? First, it is evident that, if you cannot go to the tiger, the only alternative is that he should be persuaded to come to you; and if the habits of the animal are familiar, there is some chance of arranging a meeting.

The tiger is apparently quite content if he can secure a sizeable animal about once a week; but to do this he has to range a considerable area of country, unless, indeed, he is one of those uninteresting pensioners on the cattle of his neighbours who has lost all the characteristics of his species save that of gluttony. Writing of the tiger who feeds on wild animals, we will imagine that the pangs of hunger have induced him to travel. He has the period between afternoon and early morning to wander—say sixteen or seventeen hours—and in this time can cover many miles even at the slowest pace. He will proceed with the greatest caution, for, once his presence is known in the forest, all its inhabitants are on the alert and his difficulties are enormously increased. We will suppose that he has killed a deer or a pig, surprised out of the sense of security induced by the absence of any of the carnivora for the last few days; that he has dragged it away to deep cover; and that he is lying near it, feeling at peace with all around. The dawn breaks, and the crows pass over the forest in flocks to some savoury food-supply they had abandoned at nightfall; from their elevation their sharp eyesight detects something amiss, and one or two will perch in the neighbouring trees for further investigation. From that moment every animal in the forest is on the *qui vive.* The tiger remains to protect his larder from the vultures, and every movement is watched. He goes to drink water, and his progress through the forest is heralded by bird and beast; he returns to his evening meal, and the same publicity is his portion. Even during the night the grazing deer, nervous with their knowledge of his presence, are startled by harmless sounds, and false alarms are passed from herd to herd. Even if the hunt of the night before has been unsuccessful, the tiger is bound to be detected; for as his hunger increases his caution grows less, and he recklessly exposes himself, to his further disadvantage, so that soon but one course is left to him—namely, to move on to where he is unexpected; and he sooner or later must do this, probably with deep roars that signify both his impatience and his departure.

The successful tiger returns to his kill until the supply of flesh is exhausted. A cow or buffalo will generally last him three days, and there may be some unsavoury pickings on the fourth, but these he generally abandons to others. He eats voraciously in huge mouthfuls, skin, hair, and bones, being all acceptable, and yet in an incredibly short time his stomach is empty. I once shot a tiger in the act of feeding on a buffalo. The bullet struck the liver, and, as is invariably the case, produced violent sickness in a few minutes. The tiger, when followed up, was found dead beside a heap of buffalo flesh, which my orderly estimated to weigh a "maund," or 80 pounds; it was certainly at least half that amount. On another occasion I fed a tiger with a two-year-old buffalo. He ate the whole of it in two days, and I offered a second. On the evening of the fourth day I watched him come to the second kill, of which then only the head and neck remained, and I shot him on the spot. His stomach contained nothing but a small quantity of fluid. When the three days of plenty are over, the tiger generally strolls unconcernedly away, ignoring the presence of game or of any tempting bait that may be offered. His hunger will not be pressing, though his stomach may be empty; nor will pressure sufficient to drive him forth once more occur till three or four days later, when the same proceedings will again be followed.

Bearing in mind the enforced restlessness of the tiger, and the fact that he is suspicious to a degree, and only bold by force of hunger, or in places where he has not learnt to fear man, the best way to proceed is first to discover whether there is a tiger within reasonable distance of the sportsman's camp, and next whether it is of suitable size and sex; and this can, of course, be accomplished by careful tracking, which will afford information, not only as to how long a time has elapsed since a tiger has passed, and the direction it has taken, but also of its sex and weight. And then, given a good knowledge of the forest, an early riser finding fresh marks will be

Visiting the "Baits."

able to judge where the beast is harbouring for the day. He will also give a good guess as to the trails the animal will be likely to follow when starting on the evening's hunting. If there is time, it is best to make sure by tracking in a wide circle, on the chance of finding that the tiger has left; and if not, then on each of the exits a young buffalo should be tied in a manner that does not arouse suspicion. Then there is a chance that during the night one may be killed, unless, indeed, the tiger has secured a meal within the area that has been examined. It arouses suspicion when an animal is tethered by a rope round its neck, when it is placed on a road or path, when it is provided with a pile of wheaten straw and a drinking-trough—in fact, when there is anything unusual in its attitude or surroundings; therefore the buffalo should be secured by the fore-foot, so that it can stand or lie down at pleasure; and it should be supplied with leaf-fodder, and be placed to one side of the road, and under the shelter of trees, so as to present the appearance of having strayed for the purpose of grazing. Moreover, there must be in the close vicinity both cover and water, so that the tiger may drag his kill away, and remain to protect it during the day from jackals and birds of prey.

It is a mistake to visit the buffaloes too early in the morning, for often a tiger will hunt all night, and, being unsuccessful, will return to kill a buffalo he has before despised; and unless you have a perfectly trustworthy and truthful man, the latter being rather rare, it will be best to visit the buffaloes yourself, and so judge of the size of the tiger, and, from the direction of the "drag," surmise where it has been taken. Later on, some two or three hours before sunset, it will be time to follow up the trail, and while doing this, though it is useless to endeavour to be silent, any unusual commotion should be avoided. The party should proceed as if they were workmen or villagers passing through the forest. No intrusion on the "drag" should be allowed, for the tiger frequently returns along this to his kill.

Should the tiger growl at your approach, it is probable that he intends to hold his ground, and in that case immediate action can perhaps be taken. If an elephant is available, the tiger may be driven off, or perhaps shot at sight. If not, it will be well to ascend a tree to obtain further information; but in the ordinary course of events the tiger will move silently away, and then a suitable tree must be selected from which the kill can be commanded. The height at which the seat is tied depends on the hunter's taste. At 18 feet there is safety from a tiger's spring, but at that height the angle of fire is often unpropitious, and, moreover, the sportsman will be more visible against the sky, and will find difficulty in descending in the dark. About 12 feet is a suitable elevation, though if thrills are desired, or there is no better choice, 8 feet will serve. Lower than this the height of the grass may entirely obstruct the view. The platform, or "machán," is usually a portable framework of wood supporting a tightly laced canvas or other suitable material. A size of about 3 feet by 2 feet is ample for one person, but to seat two this should be increased to about 4 feet by 2½ feet. To secure the "machán" does not take long, and as soon as possible the men retire by the way they came, conversing in even tones till out of hearing.

The first half-hour of the vigil is of the greatest importance, for the tiger may be close at hand, and rush out on the kill as soon as he thinks the coast is clear. I have seen tigers do this before the men had time to go more than 50 yards, and in such cases there must not be delay in shooting, or the kill may be quickly dragged away into cover. If there are no signs of the tiger being near at hand, the first alertness may be somewhat relaxed, and then comes a period of the greatest interest, when Nature can be best studied: for attention need not be concentrated on one animal; there may be others—there will certainly be birds and insects—all around, and the moment will pass in pleasurable excitement till darkness falls. It is especially amusing to watch the effect on the birds; not one but will express surprise or horror at the sight of the dead buffalo. The ground-thrushes will chatter loudly, and even the small birds that frequent the tall grasses will warn their fellows; the magpies will sit around, and sometimes venture to alight and feed; but the behaviour of the crows will give the most useful information. If the tiger is anywhere near, a sentinel will be posted over him while the other crows snatch a hurried meal; but the vultures will not dare to drop until the crows feed at ease, for they are slow in rising, and need a run of a few yards before they can leave the earth. The warning note of the crow, once heard, will not be forgotten. It is uttered only for the benefit of his friends, but all the wild animals know it, and respond by hasty flight. It is curious, too, and sometimes humorous, to watch the approach of jackal or hyena full of hope that he may snatch an unearned meal. If these animals fall to without ceremony, it generally means that the tiger is not returning; but if their hair stands erect along their backs, and they shuffle off with hurried apologies, it may be inferred that the owner has left his own mark on his prey, and that there is grave risk in interference. What is learnt in one evening spent in hiding in the forest will be more than could be picked up in a month of wandering through it: for in the one case you are watched by a hundred hidden eyes, whose owners are all intent on self-preservation, in the other the jungle-folk are seen in real life, and many new facts are stored up in memory which will serve to good purpose in future, even if the tiger should not appear.

If, however, the tiger is returning to the kill, his mode of approach cannot be foretold; for it is one of the greatest charms, in hunting these animals, that no two act exactly alike, and therefore that inferences from former observations are not always infallible. One tiger may come to his evening meal loudly roaring, with the object of scaring away intruders; another may approach more quietly, but snarling with ill temper; and yet another may arrive so cautiously that, unless the trained eye can detect any unusual movement of stalk of grass or of green leaf, he may come, and, perhaps scared by an incautious movement, disappear unnoticed. Such a one will perhaps stretch a paw from the cover around, and draw the kill towards him while himself invisible. But whatever the method of approach, there is pleasure in expectancy, and more in its fulfilment, and at the same time there is no necessity to shoot, if for any reason there is no desire to slay. You have no duties toward the bag, as is the case when a party is in the field, and, if you so wish, the camera or the notebook can take the place of the rifle. My wife and I once watched for nearly half an hour a tiger who lay directly beneath our feet, and I have rejoiced in the gambols of mother and cubs a few feet away; while there are many opportunities in such circumstances of learning characteristics of wild life which are soon lost when the same animal is in confinement. But if the sportsman is out to kill, he should before firing remember that the game has to be retrieved single-handed, and that the shot, if badly placed, may change the calm strength of the tiger into fury that only death will appease.

When fired at, a tiger will almost invariably charge in the direction he is standing, and hence a facing shot is generally the worst that can be offered. To fire at the head from the same level may result in the bullet glancing from the skull, and the mark selected should be the base of the neck. Here the opening into the chest cavity is small, and if the bullet passes outside the shoulder-blades into the great masses of muscle little damage will be done; but otherwise a conical solid bullet of ·577 bore will traverse the length of the body and be found mushroomed in the hind-quarters, while the same bullet fired at a broadside target within 30 yards will pierce both shoulder-blades, and may be felt under the skin on the other side. When a tiger is mortally wounded, he will often rush away with tremendous bounds, and then return in his tracks, suddenly falling dead. The tiger whose skull measurements have been given under No. 4, when shot, dashed into dense grass, appearing at each bound well above it; then turned, and came in the same manner directly towards where I was concealed, and at the last leap lost his balance in mid-air and fell headlong almost at my feet. It was a magnificent spectacle, but it was hardly realized till later that the grass was 10 feet high, and almost concealed the approaching elephant. Another, a full-grown tigress, literally shot through the heart, ran about 60 yards, and sprang at a cliff full 18 feet in perpendicular height, hung with her fore-paws clinging to its edge for the fraction of a second, and then fell in a limp mass on the ground below. It very rarely happens that a tiger is killed outright save by a fortunate shot in the head. However severe the wound, even if the main arteries of the heart are severed, he will go for some distance, generally at full speed, before subsiding. On the other hand, if the injury is slighter he will soon break from a gallop into a trot, and then into a walk, and you may hear him growling savagely as he retires.

If the tiger has not been killed outright, it will be best to follow up the trail in the early morning while it is still comparatively fresh. The method I employed with success was to put two armed trackers to follow the trail, and place myself, mounted on an elephant, between them and the tiger, searching all cover and likely places before the men reached them; that is to say, the men always tracked towards the elephant, they always remained in open ground, and never were permitted to enter high grass—in fact, they were there to ascertain the direction in which the animal had retreated, and nothing more was expected or allowed. Even for this work a stanch elephant is required, and the tracking if prolonged becomes tiring, as an incessant lookout has to be kept for any signs of the proximity of the wounded animal; but if care is taken, and the work is done cautiously and quietly, there should be little danger when the sportsman is sufficiently experienced to note and take advantage of the signs of the jungle; they are frequent and unmistakable enough, when a wounded tiger is on foot, to convey a timely warning. If no elephant is available, the only way is to track with several men—the more the better—and to have the ground carefully surveyed by an intelligent man from a tree before moving forward. If the wounded animal has taken refuge in heavy cover, buffaloes may be driven in, but there is little chance that he will abandon his retreat save in the stillness of the night. The tiger seldom charges silently; his growls increase in volume until they merge into a roar, and sometimes he will swerve at the last moment and gallop away as if his courage failed; but when a tiger trots towards his adversary with head lowered, it is seldom that he changes his mind.

The method of capturing prey differs from that adopted in attacking an enemy. In the latter case the tiger seldom springs, but rushes close up to the adversary, and then, rising on his hind-feet, clasps with claws and teeth. He can reach at least as high as the length of his body, so that the rider on an ordinary-sized female elephant is well within his grasp. But when endeavouring to escape from his foes he springs with great certainty to considerable heights. For instance, I have seen a tiger jump on to the back of an elephant and down the other side without intending or doing any harm, and the manner in which precipitous ground will be negotiated is astonishing in so heavy an animal. His methods of hunting are various. With large animals, such as buffaloes, of twice or three times his weight or more, the tiger will almost invariably attack from behind, leaping on the victim's back, and endeavouring to break the neck by pulling back the head; hence the scratches on the haunches, on the shoulders, and under the chin, and the marks of teeth on the back of the neck. Smaller animals the tiger will seize by the throat from alongside, or will strike at them with the fore-paws when running, in the hope of throwing or hamstringing them.

I once in the Pátli Doon watched a tiger who was interested in some hog-deer grazing in the open plain at about 150 yards distance from the banks of a small stream. He seemed at once to recognize the spot where he would be nearest to his intended prey, and proceeded under the cover of the bank towards it. At a bend in the stream a small crocodile about 7 feet long was lying, evidently fast asleep, and to this the tiger paid no attention, perhaps in his eagerness mistaking it for a piece of driftwood; but when he suddenly became aware of the reptile his discomfiture was amusing : he bounded into the air and ran a few yards, then turned, snarling with ill temper. When this tiger at last found himself in the most favourable position for attack, he spent some time in adjusting himself for the start, arranging and rearranging his feet to obtain perfect balance, and finally shot across the open at full gallop. He had covered the first half of the distance before the deer realized their danger, and was within a few yards before they had got up their speed and fled with startled cries. Their escape was narrow enough to prove that luck might be sometimes against them, and that, though the tiger on this occasion returned grumbling with vexation, he might on another be successful in securing a toothsome meal.

Tigers will sometimes roar when approaching a kill, and often do so on leaving it ; the differences of intonation are easily recognized after hearing them a few times. They are also particularly noisy when seeking a mate, and their courtships are often accompanied with bloodshed ; for not only do the males fight amongst themselves, but apparently the females do not always escape punishment. An instance of this occurred at Kateniaghát, where I heard two tigers fighting off and on during the night, and next morning found the tigress close by with somewhat severe injuries to the chest and throat ; judging from the muddy state of her coat, she had apparently been pinned down and worried. The tiger was lying some 200 yards farther up the stream, and had not fled on hearing the shot fired at his mate; he seemed to be in an evil temper, growling threateningly as he walked away, and consequently presented the easiest of targets.

Besides the noises made by tigers in calling to each other or in expressing hunger, repletion, loneliness, and other sentiments, there is another sound which is used under the stress of sudden alarm, and consists of a squeaking noise repeated at intervals; it is very like the bleating of the swamp-deer, and may sometimes easily be mistaken for it. Such a sound may be heard in the night when a tiger comes suddenly in view of the camp-fires, or in the daylight when startled by the unexpected intrusion of man, and it is generally followed by a hasty retreat. Tigers sleep long and soundly, and when well fed they snore loudly, and are difficult to awake; at Murtihá I listened for over an hour to a sleeping tiger, who was concealed not 20 yards away under a dense clump of "bauhinia." I was momentarily expecting this animal to wake up and come forth, especially when a gallant jungle-cock arrived to investigate the noise, and stood swearing loudly, his eyes and comb suffused with blood till there seemed danger of apoplexy; but not even the intentional breaking of twigs or the rustling of branches could arouse the sleeper, and it was quite dark before he moved away towards water.

On the whole, the tiger is a pleasant-mannered and even-tempered beast provided he is not interfered with; if the reverse is found to be the case, it is probable that there is some reason for a soured or angry disposition, and it is therefore best for the sportsman to be on his guard until he is certain what may be the mood of the moment.

Vultures on a Carcase.

CHAPTER V

CONSERVATORS' WORK

In the spring of 1890 I had completed nearly sixteen and a half years' service, of which, barring periods of leave, three-fourths of each year had been spent in pioneer work in forests that had not yet become fashionable; and I had attained to the rank of a fourth-grade Deputy Conservator, whose pay was then Rs. 6,000 a year, a sum that at the present rate of exchange equals £400 sterling. It was then that I had the good fortune to be promoted to administrative rank, and was gazetted as Conservator of Forests to the Central Circle of the United Provinces. The change was important to me in more ways than one. In the first place, I was able to give orders instead of receiving them, and this permitted the exercise of professional initiative; secondly, my salary was doubled, thus enabling me to live in more comfort and acquire better horses and better weapons, both rather necessaries than luxuries in the life I was called upon to lead; and, further, I was freed from the harassing executive work which, especially in the protection of the forest from fire, entailed incessant strain throughout the dry season.

I confess that I was becoming weary of the

summers spent at Dhikála, at Chorgalia, and elsewhere, a solitary Englishman in the centre of an inflammable area of hundreds of square miles of forest, awaiting reports of any distant smoke during the day or of any glow of fire during the night. I was becoming tired of the incessant struggle against theft by the villagers or contractors, and against the corruption of subordinates, of the constant effort of vainly teaching in practice how work should be done, of the hours spent either in petty details of vernacular office-work, or in compiling the voluminous schedules with which "red tape" was gradually restricting the field-work of the executive officer; and maybe it was personal experience that aroused sympathy for my Indian subordinates, who led the hardest of lives on the smallest remuneration, so that to recruit the superior class of men that was required for the efficient working of the State forests was becoming yearly more difficult. It was a great step gained to be to some extent free from these insistent preoccupations, and to be able at least to suggest from experience some, perhaps not entirely unimportant, improvements.

I remained in the Central Circle but a few months, and then was transferred to Oudh, where the next eight years were passed; and here an attack was at once made on the system of departmental exploitation of the forest, a system whose pernicious effect both upon silviculture and upon the staff had become so apparent to one intimate with its working. A change in a system of management in any industry does not, of course, necessarily imply adverse criticism of previous authority, and especially is this the case in forest administration when in its infancy. It is well to recall that the methods of the past were at one time new, and doubtless involved difficulties in their introduction, and that they were probably the best available under former conditions; but there can be no progress without change, and the successful introduction of changes does but indicate that opportunity has been seized for making that progress.

In the case in point, the Kheri forests were being worked on the "selection" method, a system for which they were not ready, and which resulted in an inadequate outturn. The felling, the carting, the floating of the "sâl" logs to Bahrámghát, their sale or sawing to indent—all these operations were carried out by a multitude of petty contractors, and the accounts of these men remained open for many months, being complicated with frequent cash advances; while at the same time the control of large quantities of timber spread over many miles of a slow and risky waterway, and its disposal at a distant sawmill, was not under efficient supervision. In the forest, again, the system led to serious silvicultural disadvantages; the best trees were, naturally, selected for felling, and the inferior stock was left on the ground, so that in theory as well as in practice we were depleting the forest capital instead of building it up. It was not without some misgivings that the sawmill at Bahrámghát was closed after investigations that, to put it mildly, exposed many serious irregularities; and the question then arose, how to induce the extremely conservative members of the Indian timber trade to risk a new departure in a forest with which they were unacquainted.

Fortunately, my dealings with these men in past years had given them sufficient confidence to follow me in my transfer to Oudh, and from this side there was not much difficulty; that lay rather in closing accounts with contractors and subordinates, a task which occupied much time, and revealed some transactions almost humorous in their impertinence.

When this distasteful work was completed, it remained to make for the area a regular working plan, fixing for a term of years its treatment and its yield; and in this work I first made the acquaintance of an Indian Forest Officer, Mr. Keshavanand, a man who, though delicate in health, never spared himself in the service, and who, being of a studious nature, had built securely on the basis of a short scientific training received at the forest school at Dehra Dun. To enumerate all the trees of two species in three-age classes over nearly 150 square miles of forest is a lengthy undertaking, but when it was finished a good foundation was furnished for determining the amount of timber to be yearly removed, and it was satisfactory to find that it totalled in number of trees about four times those previously felled, and in volume even more than this would indicate; for now sawing was carried out in the fellings as well as logging, in order to utilize the inferior stuff that came under the axe.

The promise conveyed in the working plan of a yearly outturn for a fixed period of years was sufficient inducement to the Rohilkhand and Kumaon Railway to construct a branch of its line from Mailáni to Dudua, and this new departure finally insured the success of a change in system which liberated the Forest Officer from the duties of lumbering, of conveying the timber to market, or of milling it, and gave him some time to devote to the scientific working of the forest. I have been informed that this forest railway is the best-paying branch of the system to which it belongs, for it now serves the timber and grain trade from Nepal; and as similar railways have since been constructed to tap the forests and villages of Bahraich, Gonda, and Gorakhpur, touching the Nepal border at other points, and have been extended gradually to form a complete system in a tract of country hitherto neglected, there seems good reason to believe that my information was correct. So encouraging was the success that followed the issue of the working plan for the Kheri forests during the next few years that plans were compiled for the whole of the workable forest areas of Oudh. The period covered by these plans has long since expired, but they have been since followed by others that are similar, but even more exact and more effective, because at the time of their compilation more detailed records of the past were available as to the rate of growth of the timber, as to the reproduction of the species, as to varying effects of soil and locality—in short, with regard to all those items of local knowledge that are essential for the progress of Indian silviculture.

The next matter that claimed attention was demarcation. In consequence of the opening up of the area, cultivation was pressing on the forest boundary, which in many places was intricate or even disputed, and consequently far from being satisfactorily defined. It was therefore decided, where possible, to make exchanges with various landowners so as to simplify the forest boundary, which was afterwards permanently fixed by means of numbered sandstone pillars from the quarries of Mirzapur; and between each pair of pillars a bridle-track was constructed, so that, whether on horseback or foot, inspection could easily proceed. The system to be employed in demarcation presents a serious problem in the extensive forests of India; preliminary work has to be carried out quickly, so as to permit of early survey, and the manner in which this is done is often most ingenious. For instance, in some places a large cylinder of bamboo matting is filled with stones, a stake being erected in its centre; in others, a green stake of fig or "jingan" is driven into the soil, in the hope that it will take root and flourish; in others, again, the trees at angles in the boundary are blazed. But such makeshifts do not permanently demarcate the boundaries; they are easily removed, and are also liable to be destroyed by wild-elephants and by village cattle, which seem to take a curious pleasure in wilful mischief. Monoliths, on the other hand, though initially expensive, are subject to no damage even in the vicinity of villages, although the people may use them to sharpen their sickles and axes, for sandstone of a suitable hardness is generally rare.

The exchanges between the Government and the landowners proceeded with the exasperating delays of the East, where, though life is short, the people appear to have infinite leisure; but the eager acquisition of landed property and the struggle for its retention are traits with which we of the West can sympathize, for there must always be pressure from those who have not on those who have, possibly increasing until landownership brings neither honour nor profit. But ultimately even this matter was arranged, and thereby the cost of demarcation was lessened and inspection rendered easy, while trespass, when it occurred, could be regarded almost with certainty as intentional.

One of these exchanges, however, implicated the area of about 30,000 acres peopled by the Thárus of Kheri, whom it was desired to bring more under the influence of the Forest Department, a position they also wished for; for being in close touch with the Forest Officer, and dependent on the forest for their welfare, they did not appreciate the interference of both forest and revenue officials in their affairs.

Now the establishment of forest villages in India is one of the operations most conducive to success in forestry, for thereby a local population is created who are given scope for agriculture, and at the same time are provided at their doors with a special form of labour in which they rapidly become efficient. The system, too, obviates the introduction of labour from outside, which is expensive and often unsatisfactory; for malaria and dysentery take heavy toll of new-comers uninured to the hardships of the jungle. Moreover, the villagers thus settled in the forest soon take a special interest in its protection, and, even if they themselves sometimes pilfer, they will carefully prevent such attempts by others. Orders to hand over the Thárus to the charge of the Revenue Department were received, therefore, with much reluctance on either side, as those will understand who have experienced how strong becomes personal attachment to a locality or population in whose welfare interest has been taken. How strong this feeling may be can be gauged from the fact that ten years later, when opportunity occurred for the reconsideration of this question, every detail of the transaction was clearly impressed on my memory and available for the information of the Government of India; and when the villages reverted to the charge of the Forest Department, I experienced intense satisfaction that was, I am glad to say, shared by the villagers themselves.

A third matter that cost infinite trouble and labour was the preparation of the Record of Rights for the villages near the forest. All villages within three miles of the boundary (and there were many in a now more populous country) were enumerated, with particulars as to inhabitants and houses, cattle and farm buildings, acreage of arable land, demand for timber, fuel, grass, produce and grazing; and schedules were then prepared recording the annual grants of each for which the people were eligible, so that the demand on the forest could be estimated, and information afforded as to the proportion of its yield that remained available for sale in the open market. This work extended over some years, for it necessitated constant reference to the Revenue officers, and on completion it received approbationary notice by the local Government, though later the same Government, under other leadership, revised many of the details that had at first been accepted as desirable.

These three important considerations of working plans, demarcation, and settlement, gave full and interesting occupation when added to the routine work of a Conservator of Forests. To both special and routine work reference may be necessary later on, but it still remains to present some idea of the official attitude to the work of the forester, as this had more influence on the progress of State forestry than even the attitude of the population, whose views were naturally, to some extent, reflected in official policy. To the executive Forest Officer the position assumed by other officials was not of vital importance, for any irremediable differences of opinion could be referred to the Conservator, who had access to Government, and from whom orders were taken; but during the first half of my service I could not but note that the feelings towards the work of a new department were as a rule biassed either by indifference, by distrust, or by dislike, and this caused the more astonishment to one who was accustomed to the very different conditions prevailing in Germany, where the Forest Officer enjoys the highest consideration and status.

But Indian official sentiments of those days were founded on a perfectly natural and explicable ignorance. England has no need of forests. Her water supply is assured, and crop failure may entail distress, but not disaster; her hills are quiescent, and their feeble crumbling does not require that the soil should be upheld by the root systems of forest trees. Such silviculture as was required in the past in the interest of sport and scenic beauty was entrusted to land-agents and foresters, who did good work guided by rule-of-thumb and by the traditions of their ancestors. The Englishman abroad admired the forests of France and Germany, but failed to appreciate the significance of their absence in Italy or Greece. He believed in the term "inexhaustible" as applied to the woodlands of Scandinavia and America, and took no interest in timber save as regards its quality and price.

How matters have altered in this regard during the last fifteen or twenty years has been set forth in many writings, but now sufficient has been said to indicate that at the time of which I write it would have been impossible to undertake in England any study of forestry which could have been useful to those recruits of the Indian Civil Service who were to develop into India's future rulers; while the position of those who had already attained was, in the majority of cases, as regards such technical knowledge, even more hopeless. There was therefore no blame attached in this instance to want of perspicacity. For instance, what these officials thought they saw was a band of enthusiasts who were engaged in the pernicious occupation of land-grabbing at the people's expense. The band of enthusiasts existed, but it was engaged in saving the forests for the nation—indiscreetly sometimes, no doubt, as is the case with all enthusiasts. What they imagined they detected was an attempt to make revenue by restricting the rights of the people; what was happening was that the people were having their rights so liberally acknowledged that they could not fully utilize them, and that at the same time large sums were yearly being paid into the State Treasury. Such comparisons might be continued almost indefinitely, but they now serve no useful purpose. These gentlemen acted up to their lights when they exclaimed that protection from fire might result in such an increase in insect life that the adjacent crops would be destroyed, or asserted that natural regeneration could make way against excessive grazing, or that the actual presence of the forest proved that it was immune from the attacks of man, and no argument could convince them that their lights were darkness; for in those days Lord Curzon had not introduced the now all-powerful expert-specialist to the notice of the Indian Empire, and the protests of the forester, sometimes uselessly violent, passed unheeded.

In practice, therefore, if not in theory, forestry was arrayed on one side, and the people on the other. The outcry against restrictions imposed on the present generation, so that something might be left to their successors—the prohibition, in short, of spending the capital instead of only the interest—was to some extent misunderstood to voice the claims of the future as well as of the existing population, and Revenue officials who took this view were right in defending such claims, not knowing them to be imaginary. It was but very slowly that confidence was created, but each Revenue officer who became a convert to the importance of State forestry was capable of exerting, both on the people and on other officials, an influence more effective than the labours of a multitude of solitary foresters; and when, perchance, the knowledgeable interest of some high official was aroused, the progress made, even in a very short time, was incredibly rapid. Only when a a new arrival, imbued perhaps with preconceived notions based on his experience of forest policy in another Province, proposed to reverse the decision of his predecessors, did the Forest Officer awake from his dreams of the millennium to find himself again fighting for principles that he had thought secure.

Fortunately, however, high officials in India were then little concerned with forestry. The subject was not, in their view, of sufficient Imperial importance, and, moreover, it was vastly unpopular with the people in its interference with pleasant and lazy customs; so that even the most versatile of Viceroys found no relaxation in remoulding forest policy, nor did Lieutenant-Governors pay continued attention to it during the period of their rule. All of them, no doubt, enjoyed from time to time the free life and the escape from worries that the greenwood confers, but none of them have their names prominently associated with the forests of India; they have, happily, left that honour to the men who have spent their lives in the wilds, so that when Indian forestry is mentioned the names of foresters, and not of statesmen, are recalled.

And this is as it should be; for consider that during the arrival at early maturity of even a fast-growing tree some two dozen Viceroys and the same number of Consuls have passed on their transient careers, and think to what changes of policy, to what varied idiosyncrasies, such a one has been exposed. And if there still stand some rugged stems, now too stiff with age to bend even to the fiercest blast, which have calmly looked down for centuries on the works of man the destroyer, there is cause for thankfulness for that love of trees which is innate in the heart of every Englishman, even though he may not have knowledge as to the requirements of the forest. Perhaps it is partly due to this affection that there has been some sympathy in the attitude adopted towards forestry amongst those in high places, for failing their concurrence such progress as has been made would have been impossible. It would, indeed, have been more rapid had that sympathy been earlier expressed, for to make a new scientific department at once dependent upon its earnings for its success is not a mistake likely to be repeated in these days, when initial liberality is held to be essential to rapid development.

Enough has now, perhaps, been written to present the conditions of the struggle in the past according to the impression received at the time, so that from their consideration the success of forestry in the present may be the better understood and appreciated.

The charge of the Oudh Forest circle carried with it residence in the hills, for Naini Tal was the summer seat of the Local Government. The place is too well known to require any detailed description. Compared with other hill-stations, it possesses considerable advantages, for some temperaments in its lake, on whose borders sociable gatherings are continuous, and for others in the facility for leaving the populous basin formed by the hills of Liria Kánta, Chinar, and Skerkadánda, and at once entering the Government woodlands at the back of these mountains; so that one may spend the day in the forest with a chance of seeing "gural," "serow," or barking-deer, and be back in the settlement in the evening. The climate of Naini Tal, save in the late autumn, is somewhat relaxing. The rain falls from June to September, often with excessive violence, and the houses highest on the ridge are those most sought after. In the autumn, when the sky is clear, the air brisk, and the dahlias in flower, Naini Tal is a delightful and healthy resort. Ranikhet and Almora can be reached by good cart-roads or by shorter bridle-tracks. They lie at a distance of about thirty miles, but neither is bracing. At Chaubatia, above Ranikhet, there is a Government orchard and a small forest rest-house, where a fine view of the snows can be enjoyed, as well as a better climate. The lakes in the vicinity of Naini Tal are well known to fishermen, and there are guide-books to the locality, and to the sport obtainable, that fulfil all requirements.

From Naini Tal the Conservator descends to his field-work at the beginning of November, and the first tour is generally made in the district of Gorakhpur, which is divided from the Province of Bengal by the great Gundak River, and is served by the Bengal and North-Western Railway. Gorakhpur is a district of planters and swamps, and in former days a yacht club existed, and good sailing was to be had during the monsoon. At the present time other forms of sport take precedence. There is a troop of Light Horse who arrange joyous meetings, and there are the usual station games, as well as shooting-parties, which fill the hospitable bungalows in the district. But there is not much big game in the forests of Gorakhpur, though spotted-deer and pig are not uncommon; while to the north, towards the Nepal frontier, tigers are often found in the grasslands on the banks of the Gundak River, and these sometimes stray some distance to the south.

Gorakhpur had a special interest at that time, as being the last stronghold in the United Provinces of the wild-buffalo, though these are still frequent in the adjoining territories of Bengal and Nepal. There were then reported to be a few cows and calves and one sizeable bull in the forests, and it was common knowledge that many sportsmen were eager in their pursuit. The animals roamed in the Government forests in the north of the district, and when we were camping in this direction fresh tracks were soon found, whereupon the local "shikari" was called in, with the offer of a reward of Rs. 100 if he was instrumental in affording the chance of a clear shot at the bull. Now began a dance that might have been recognized at the commencement as futile. At 3 a.m., in the blackest and mistiest of mornings, we passed in silence through the dark forest to lie in wait close to a ford by which the animals had certainly crossed some time before, but did not again do so. We spent the daylight in crawling up to mud-holes where they had once wallowed, but did not revisit. Often we heard the snort of alarm as the herd crashed through the forest, till at last the conviction could not be withstood that the buffaloes were my tracker's stock in trade, that to see one killed was the last thing he desired, and that his inopportune cough was not entirely due to bronchial affection. We parted without effusion of rupees or of thanks on either side, and immediately after this Jonah had been swallowed up in the distance, the hunter's luck appeared.

My wife, who during all my future wanderings shared my sport, one evening accompanied me on an elephant to ride through the tree-forest near the camp, and shortly after we had started the cry of the spotted-deer and the gruff grunting of a panther attracted our notice. Noiselessly we passed down a shady glade, when from a patch of high grass uprose a huge form, that stood with head uplifted and horns thrown back, eyeing us in defiance. The mahout was as deaf as it was possible for a man to be, but he muttered, "Wild-buffalo! what a chance!" and sat quiescent. Consultation with him was impossible, but having with me a ·500 Express rifle shooting hollow-fronted bullets, I manœuvred the elephant so as to get a broadside shot, hoping that the light bullet might perhaps penetrate the body. But the bull ever kept his face to the foe, leaving the question of fighting or of fleeing entirely to us. With a whispered word of warning to hold tight, the opening shot was fired, and, to the astonishment of all, the battle was over, the bull fell on his side and rolled on his back, the mighty fore-legs pointing uselessly to the sky. More shots in the neck did not disturb his attitude, and so we left him lying in the forest where he had ruled, a victim to over-confidence in his massive strength. He might at any time have driven the elephant off, or even overthrown her with little danger to himself, but he was content with threats instead of proceeding at once to action ; and so his funeral car was a cart with many bullocks, and round him sat all night a crowd of villagers, dividing his flesh and speaking of his prowess until, with the morning light, the vultures came from afar and fought for their share of the spoil, so that by noon only a grim skeleton remained on the plain.

The bullet had drilled an oval hole in the centre of the forehead and penetrated the brain, for it was always the unexpected that happened when bullets were weakened by the methods employed in olden days to increase their velocity by a reduction of their weight. The horns measured 8 feet 4 inches along the curve, which, outside Assam and Burma, would be considered to be a good trophy. The herd of buffaloes appeared to break up soon after. Some of the cows probably wandered away to Nepal, and Mr. P. H. Clutterbuck caught a young heifer, which grew up with the domesticated buffaloes, and became so tame that she allowed the herdsman to handle her. To see her, still immature, overtopping all her companions around her gave an excellent idea of the height and bulk of the wild animal. She was offered to and refused by the London Zoological Society, and went later to adorn a Raja's menagerie, where no doubt she proved a great attraction. The final scene of the extinction of the wild-buffalo in the United Provinces occurred shortly after, when the same sportsman met in the forest a bull that had perhaps returned to revisit the scenes of his youth, and promptly met his fate—perhaps a more kindly one than if he had lived long enough to attract many hunters, and to be fired at by a less experienced hand.

The Gorakhpur forests have been remarkable for other waifs and strays. A rhinoceros, perhaps carried down by the monsoon floods, once took up his quarters in the Government forest, and was soon observed, for in these small areas so large an animal could not be hid; and he, too, succumbed to a single shot from a Martini-Henry rifle, which easily pierced the tough skin on the shoulders. The history of one half of his hide, given to me by Mr. Clutterbuck, was curious. I brought to England a monstrous slab some inches in thickness, and it remained on my hands until I was due to return to India. Already I had in contemplation a midnight journey through London, to end by hurling it from the top of a four-wheeler into the murky waves of the river, when I fortunately met an enthusiastic golfer, who faced his drivers with rhinoceros hide, and attributed lightness and elasticity to the material. So to him joyfully I handed over the skin, and received in return a cheque for the cost of carriage to England, and a generous gift of two of the manufactured clubs; and later I often wondered, when congratulating myself on placing this skin so satisfactorily, how many pieces of the Gorakhpur rhinoceros were still wandering round the golf-links of the world.

It is curious how, as a rule, hunting trophies fail to fill any useful purpose in daily life, though amongst uncivilized men they are largely used both for articles of clothing and adornment, or even as weapons of offence and defence. The pleasure afforded by the sight of a fine pair of antlers or of a well-cured skin is a personal one, consisting chiefly in its power of recalling vividly the detail of the struggle that preceded their possession, and to none other—save, perhaps, the naturalist—can such trophies be of much interest. They are not like a picture, or a statue, or an Eastern carpet, which embody the conception as well as the skill of the artist, and receive their beauty from the soul as well as the hands that have created them. Yet even in civilized life buffalo hides make trunks that may last a lifetime, and spotted-deer skins can be changed into leather bags whose pliancy is a delight. For the wanderer in the Himalaya nothing is more convenient than to use the bamboo baskets of the country, covered with raw hides. The hair prevents the rain from penetrating, and the hillmen thoroughly enter into the mild joke of calling for the tiger, the panther, the bear, etc., when each package is designated by its distinctive covering. But as the annual list of visitors to India increases, even tiger skins have their value. America takes many to decorate the rooms of the wealthy, in spite of the enormous duty levied by the Custom officials, and the young and needy sportsman will have the less chagrin in parting with one or two of his trophies if their proceeds provide him with a trusty rifle with which others can be obtained.

The Gorakhpur district is famed for its wild-fowl shooting, which can be easily obtained on many tanks and lakes during the winter months; but numerous guns are sometimes required if a large bag is desired, as the birds soon become wary, and move readily from one sheet of water to another.

The district of Gonda is adjacent to that of Gorakhpur, and connected with it by rail, and here are the estates of the Máhárájá of Balrámpur, a relative of that potentate who earned his title by his loyalty in the days of the Mutiny. He it was who collected the magnificent stud of elephants numbering over one hundred, and all trained to some form of sport; for their owner was a mighty hunter, and it is from hence that arrangements were made every second or third year for elephant-hunting by "kheddahs," whereby the increase of the wild herds in the United Provinces is checked. It used to be a unique sight to inspect the stud at Balrámpur, and to visit the fighting elephants, some of enormous size, and so dieted as abnormally to increase their weight, on the same principle that the Indian wrestler is fattened. When both elephant and driver were under the influence of a drug that deadened all fear, some great duels have taken place with the object of occupying the attention of the lord of the wild herd while his harem was being ensnared; but on more than one occasion the trained elephant has been unable to stem the whole-hearted charge of the free animal, undertaken with fury and despair at the prospect of imminent capture. Some of the Balrámpur fighting tuskers were animals of unusual bulk, and their attendants sat as pigmies on their backs; but in the forest in those days were others who, judging from estimates carried out at a respectful distance, and from the measurements of the print of the fore-foot, were probably larger, and

A "Fire Line" in the Gonda Forests.

certainly more dexterous and agile. Not many such are now left, and it is rumoured that the order for the slaying of all solitary male elephants has already gone forth, so that the disappearance of the species from North-West India is probably only a matter of time.

From the house at Chandanpur, in the north-east corner of the district, tigers may generally be found, and are often beaten up to the guns, especially as elephants are easily available in this district, owing to the generosity of the Máhárájá; the configuration of the ground is broken, deep ravines being frequent, so that the line of retreat of the tigers can be readily guarded. As a rule it will be found that there is difficulty in these forests in persuading a tiger to return to his kill, perhaps because the area is not extensive enough to afford much choice of cover, or even freedom from intrusion by man.

Mr. B. A. Rebsch, who has shot as much big game as any man in India, developed here an interesting form of sport while in charge of these forests, that might still be practised with success. His aim was to circumvent the bears which nightly descend from the hills to feed on the wild fruits and roots in the plains below, and return before dawn to their mountain fastnesses; and with this object he reached the Nepal boundary, then marked by a cleared ride 30 yards wide, before daylight, and posted sentinels in trees at convenient distances on either side of him. These men could look down towards the forest below, and with coming daylight could detect the bears moving towards the hills, and thus were able to inform the sportsman of their approach by preconcerted signals. Accordingly the bear, who was intent on crossing into foreign territory, was met on his arrival by the sportsman, with varying results; at least on one occasion Mr. Rebsch was severely mauled by his opponent, but I suspect that he found satisfaction in giving the bear every opportunity to show fight, for his "shikari" complained in the vernacular idiom that he used to let the bear "climb on his neck" before firing.

The Gonda forests hold some good sámbhar stags during the autumn, that may also be stalked by the sportsman who will take the trouble; but the lengthy frontage of the area exposes all the wild beasts to constant intrusions, and many have apparently been killed off, though some have retired farther west. From the house at Nandmahra good small-game shooting can often be had in those places where high crops adjoin the forest boundary, for peafowl, jungle-fowl, and hares, frequent this cover in the early morning and evening, and can very satisfactorily be driven over guns posted along the edge of the forest; I believe that sixty or seventy brace of birds have been killed in one day's operations carefully carried out in this manner.

Proceeding on inspection duty, the district of Bahraich is entered, and the camp pitched at Sohelwa, a place already recommended to the sportsman; but in the winter months the sámbhar stags have already left for the hills, and other game must be looked for.

Once in the forest near the camp a tiger had been tracked to cover, and arrangements were hurriedly made to drive him out; his only exit was by a narrow path along the bank of a wide watercourse that was dry at that season, and here on the sloping trunk of a tree, some eight feet from the ground, a "machán" was quickly placed, and I and my wife took our seats, while the few men available in camp undertook to walk through the forest towards us. No tiger appeared, and perhaps it was fortunate he did not; for we were full in sight, barring the only path for escape, and we were already feeling thankful at our want of success, when a she-bear, accompanied by a full-grown cub, appeared on the scene. As she halted and raised her head, her muzzle twitching from side to side, she was dropped in her tracks; but she instantly recovered, and, seeing us, charged at once at the tree. The second barrel missed fire, but fortunately another rifle was handy, and, as she was stretching out her paw to claw us from our perch, she was shot through the chest and fell backwards. Meanwhile the cub was capering round, apparently anxious to join the fight, till he got a bullet through his ribs and retired, so giving us opportunity to despatch his mother and descend.

To risk defeat on account of inferiority of ammunition appears to be incredibly foolish, and we had hoped to get a reliable supply before more trouble followed; but it so happened that before this could be arranged we had an urgent call to a tiger's kill some seven miles to the west, and started at midday in heavy rain that continued with unbated violence for the next twelve hours. We sat, drenched to the skin and miserable, listening to the perpetual drip in the empty forest. We knew that the jungle animals would be snugly under shelter—the pigs in the little grass huts they cunningly construct when warned by approaching storms; the deer under the densest foliage, with faces to the wind and ears turned to the rear to detect any suspicious sound; the birds clustered side by side on the lee of the warmest trees —and that only such stolid and hardy creatures as the vultures, who one hour are in the sultry heat, and the next in the icy drifts two or more miles above, would make light of the drenching mist and heavy showers that passed over the forest. But we also knew that we had to keep heart in our hunters, who themselves, in spite of weather, had brought us news of the kill, that if we failed them on such occasions we should be branded as fine-weather sportsmen, and that our example would soon be followed by our men.

Then the tiger appeared to put life into our shivering frames; a big male of sullen aspect, his hide darkened by the universal moisture, his temper short with the showers that fell on him from every bush he touched, he came slowly but determinedly towards us till the click of the hammer as the first cartridge missed fire brought him to a halt, and as the left barrel followed suit he gazed around with an angry stare. The second rifle lay between us under rugs and hats and all the paraphernalia collected to protect from the elements the two human beings who crouched in a space of some four feet by two; it was dragged out with pressing haste, and still the tiger could not detect the whereabouts of danger, yet, growling uneasily, he turned to go. At that moment he was shot through the heart, and bounded high in the air, striking in his fall a stout sapling some six feet from the ground, and snapping it off as he fell with it. But when we reached camp, famished and dripping, our first care was to collect and destroy every cartridge that was not above suspicion, lest after two warnings further neglect should end in mishap.

From Sohelwa, too, and from the next camp at Bachkáhi, we made interesting Nature studies of the forest panther, and learnt much of the romance of his daily life. The panther, surely, is a beast endowed with most superior cunning and forethought, so that he seems sometimes to be capable of those reasoning qualities that we claim as exclusively our own. He is a clean feeder, and has no taste for hair; so in eating he folds back the skin by degrees till it lies like an empty glove. He circumvents the vulture who are watching for his departure by placing his kill high in the branches of a tree, where there is no space for their greedy tearing and rending; and if he finishes his meal before dawn appears, he will cover it up with dead leaves, so that it may not be observed by those who pass. His approach is always silent and stealthy; he displays infinite patience, and his attention is not fixed on the ground below, but passes to the trees above. He is a consummate master in still hunting; none can hide as he, and none are so quick to recognize a chance for flight or for onslaught. Finally, with him there is no indecision as to the course to adopt, which in the case of the tiger so often puts that animal at a disadvantage; so that when the hunter at last stands over the seven foot of spotted hide, and can quietly admire its beauty, he feels the satisfaction of having outwitted one of the most cunning of animals.

Yet even the panther is not infallible, and is sometimes bested by man or beast. We were once watching over the melancholy remains of a goat, facing in opposite directions so as to command a wider view, and in that absolute quietude so necessary for success, but so irksome when long continued, with every sense strained for some indication of the panther's whereabouts. Three crows also sat around, uttering cries indicating the depression of weary waiting; they dared not descend, nor would they at first leave the inviting repast, till, suddenly changing their minds, with one accord they flew to the north, and we were left alone. In the distance—perhaps 1,000 yards away—we soon heard again the clamour of the birds loudly scolding and vociferating; then the panther was seen approaching, led or driven by the noisy birds who would give no respite, till the drowsy beast arrived, and, with a glance at the kill, lay down under our seat. In the tension of the moment we could hear our hearts beating loudly; the slightest movement would have ended the episode, and it was not till the word "Asleep" reached me in the slightest of whispers that I dared cautiously to turn. The process seemed to occupy many minutes before I, too, was able fully to admire, at a distance of a few yards, the sleeping beauty; he had been aroused from doubtless just as comfortable a slumber, brought to his kill, probably, by barefaced untruths as to its safety, and then left to his fate without remorse, simply in order that his betrayers might gain a hearty meal. He passed to happier hunting-grounds without awaking, and we had scarcely left the spot before the crows were fully enjoying the result of their astounding treachery.

CHAPTER VI

CONSERVATORS' WORK (*Continued*)

IN the Bahraich District we attached to ourselves a Mohammedan of the name of Abdul, who remained with us till his death, the most courageous, eager, and faithful servant and friend that it was possible for any man to have. To him we owed most of the success attained at this period in the Oudh forests, for it was he who found out where the big game lay and concerted with us the arrangements for a meeting. Every day before dawn he was away into the heart of the forest; at every camp he arrived a day before us, and without his skilful help we should never have had time to spare from professional work for both tracking and hunting. Nor would his assistance have been so valuable had he not been able to distinguish in his reports between fact and imagination; supplied with the former, our intimate knowledge of the forest stood us in good stead, while his patience, courage, and sharp-sightedness when tracking, seldom gave any opening for escape to a wounded animal. Thirty-five tigers and an unrecorded number of panthers and bears we killed together; and to the last, when he fell a victim to dysentery, that scourge of the jungle, we had the fullest confidence in each other as brother-sportsmen.

ABDUL RAZÁK, SHIKARI.

"PICKLES."

The opinion of Anglo-Indians must naturally vary as to the characteristics of their fellow-subjects, according to the classes with whom they come in contact, and to the mutual respect they bear the one towards the other; for to that collection of nations comprised in the term of India no such general attributes can be assigned as would be possible with a homogeneous population. Speaking of the Mohammedans of Northern India, with whom I have been associated during the whole of my service, I can testify to the good qualities they possess, and of these, perhaps their exceeding loyalty is the most conspicuous; they have served me in all conditions both of ease and discomfort, from Kashmir to the wilds of Burma, and I have found them always the more cheerful as difficulties increased, willingly undergoing hardships similar to, but necessarily even more pronounced than, those suffered by their master. A Kashmiri or a Burman might desert at any moment when difficulties became distasteful, or even when self-interest called; but a Northern Indian never does before arrangements have been made to replace him, and his promise of return may be always relied upon. Perhaps we have been fortunate in the servants that have attached themselves to us, yet from other parts of India similar testimony will probably come from others who know better the peculiar conditions of west, east, and south. Thus, in Burma the Indian is in bad repute, for the reason, probably, that many had fled there on account of crimes committed at home. There are black sheep in every flock, but I can only write from personal experience.

The reasoning of a native of India starts from a basis not always understood by those who are unfamiliar with his mode of living and mode of thought; he will not reveal himself till he has trust in his master, and even then he is often childish in his temper and in its mode of expression, for he has behind him centuries of oppression, when, as an aged villager once said to me, to wear a clean muslin cap on a feast-day was enough to invite a visit from the authorities in search of hidden wealth; and in those circumstances the only defence lay in deceit and lies, which were justified as necessary to safeguard the home and family. The people are what their rulers and their priesthood have made them, and the introduction of new methods and new laws can but slowly affect the ideas of a vast population; and so it is that, when a truthful servant is found, one is apt to feel astonishment, though perhaps in the West this may be almost as great a rarity. Yet, curiously enough, the introduction of these Western methods and laws does not always bear good fruit; for the more uncivilized the people, and the wilder the life they lead—in short, the greater freedom from oppression—the greater often is their natural truthfulness displayed: for independence doubtless produces as nothing else can self-respect and fearlessness in the individual.

Here is a characteristic narrative of a Tháru from the north of the Bahraich District, who walked forty miles or more to give himself up to the magistrate at headquarters. His wife had been enticed away by one of the Nepalese guards who watch the boundary of that State, and the Tháru confessed his crime in a few words: "I took my bamboo and went up to the guard-house; my wife was there, and when I told her to come out the Nepalese attacked me with his knife. I struck him over the head with my bamboo, and he lay still; then I brought my wife to her father's house. The village headmen said that this would cause trouble in the village, so I came to say that I alone am responsible." His story on investigation proved to be correct, and it is satisfactory to think that the verdict was "justifiable homicide," for the community would otherwise have been much disheartened. "How," they would have said, "can we live here if we are not allowed to protect ourselves against these robbers?"

The forester is often safer from theft and other dangers when dwelling with the jungle tribes than when amongst a more settled population. There such happenings as robbery, and even murder, are not infrequent, and almost every Forest Officer will have some instances to relate. The following, which took place at Amángarh, in the Garhwál District, is a characteristic case of civilized but sordid murder. It was the custom at that time to send the forest revenue collected during the day to sub-treasuries at a distance, and on this occasion the Forest Guard was late in arriving, and doubts were freely expressed as to his honesty. Next morning inquiry showed that the man had left his quarters with a heavy bag of copper coins; he was traced as far as a broad drive running through dense forest, and thenceforward nothing more was known till the trackers supplied further information. The victim had been joined by two men, who walked on either side of him, and a few hundred yards farther on there had been a struggle, whence a trail led into the forest to the spot where his body lay. He had been bound with his own turban and decapitated with his own knife, and, so far as I remember, while the police were discussing whether the crime had been committed within the borders of one district or the other, the culprits got clean away.

The western extremity of the Bhinga Forest lies on the banks of the Rapti River, infamous for its treacherous quicksands, which engulfed with heavy loss a party of cavalry who were driving the mutineers from Oudh into the Nepal Tarai. Even to-day care has to be taken when crossing the ford at Kakadari, or the sight may be witnessed of a string of laden camels reclining in the stream, their long legs presumably held captive by the clinging sands. The camel is certainly a fearsome beast on any but dry and solid ground ; on clayey soil he will slip till his straddling legs are past recovery. He is perhaps the only animal that absolutely refuses to make an effort to save his own life when out of his depth in water ; while only strangulation will persuade him to cross the gangway on to a roomy boat, where, once shipped, he must be bound down in a sitting posture, lest he should wave his irresponsible limbs, to the destruction of the crew and cargo. He has his virtues, for he can walk in paths where wheeled traffic is impossible, and he is not liable to attacks from wild beasts ; his savour saves his life from tigers, and wild-elephants will flee from his approach, but his value in Tarai country is doubtful, and he kicks and bites with equal skill and ferocity.

The forests of Bhinga present a curious appearance to the forester. Thirty years ago the area was peopled with ancient trees that rose abruptly from a bare soil hardened by the hoofs of numberless cattle; there was no young growth, the parent trees were without progeny, and as they fell from natural decay their place was filled by a thorny growth, impenetrable to man or cattle. It was Nature's last despairing effort to protect the fertility of the soil. For a generation the forester fought against fires, cattle, and man, and yet there was no response in the appearance or in the continuance of seedling growth, till later, under the protection of the thorns, a few little trees began to show, and, encouraged by the admission of light, sprang up to give in their turn protection to hundreds of their own kind, to assure the tardy regeneration of the former forest, and so permit their ancestors to pass away in peace, their duty accomplished. To one acquainted with the past history of this forest, two questions naturally presented themselves—whether a whole generation was required to rest a tired soil, and whether the planting of any other than the existing species might have met with success.

The origin and sequence of tree-growth in Northern India is interesting, and may be well studied in the rivers flowing from the hills. It takes but a small obstruction in the current to form a sand-bank that shall just emerge from the lapping waters; a stranded tree-trunk from the mountains, a boulder displaced from the bank, may lay the foundation of a forest, for in a few days the sand and silt it arrests springs into life from the seeds that are thrown up by the stream, and that germinate so soon as they come to rest. In this way the "shisham" and the "khair" forests appear, and at once consolidate their vantage-ground with roots interlaced to stoutly resist the removal of the soil; while any additions to the solid earth are accepted with joy, and added to by the débris from the superabundant vegetable growth. The trees erect dams with their discarded branches, and hold up the silt of the encroaching waters while permitting the off-flow of the surplus floods. Then, in a surprisingly short time the island is above flood-level; it has become a forest of gregarious species that in due course bring forth fruit, not to rear their progeny at their feet, but to follow the practice of their forefathers, and engage busily in the formation of new colonies far below.

Next, as age advances and the serried ranks thin out, there arrive other species, sown by the tempestuous winds of the monsoon or carried by birds. Soft-wooded trees, such as the fig, the cotton, and others, all come to take the place of the passing generation; the new population in turn covers the soil with shady boughs, and enriches it with its falling leaves, till over the boulders and the sand there is a layer of porous and fertile vegetable mould suitable for the growth of the more exacting hardwoods. These, eager too for extension of their territory, send their seeds in whirling showers—sometimes, such is their vitality, with germination already commenced ere they reach the soil; or other ways more difficult are adopted that prove successful only after many assaults and many losses. But ultimately they take possession, to hold the conquered province, perhaps, for several lengthy generations, while they look down on the river, now many feet below, and watch new territory being built up for their successors, or maybe the crumbling away of the banks on which their ancestors have stood.

But the hills cannot dwindle and subside without leaving some mark in the plains below; their configuration may not, indeed, be altered perceptibly during the life of a man, yet even during his short term he cannot fail to observe how Nature disposes of the débris of their crumbling. Whether he stands at the foot of the Himalaya or in the deltas of the waterways 1,000 miles away, he cannot remain ignorant of either the levelling up that is daily progressing, or, once his eyes are opened, to the part that the forest plays in the stupendous work that is proceeding. Just as in the sub-Himalayan tracts of Northern India the rapid torrents deal with the boulders and sand on the steeper slopes, so in the thousands of square miles comprised in the delta of the Ganges there is a similar force at work to deal with the finer earth that has succeeded in completing the long journey from mountain to sea.

Imagine the south-west monsoon hurling the waters of the Bay of Bengal against the land relentlessly for many months of the year, and defeating its own fury by the sand it throws up just above high-water mark. At once the forest takes possession, and forms a dam of living fascines, a barrier to further progress. Yet in this embankment must be openings for the muddy waters of the Ganges to find an exit, and through these openings the tides flow strongly many miles up-country; they hold up the fresh water, cause it to flood the low islands, and to deposit at least a portion of its rich silt ere the ebbing tide carries it away to the sea. Upon these islands, again, the forest, ever watchful, seizes. The mangroves rapidly line the waterways and define them; their seeds fall on the mud-banks at low-water, to stand upright on spiky ends, or on to the moving tide, to float away in the hope of meeting some other congenial resting-place; and once found, there is scant delay in asserting vitality. They cannot, as do other trees in more secure positions, await for months or years such conditions as may be the most favourable for their growth; they have a part to perform that brooks no delay—the duty of arresting the débris of the hills, so that, after hundreds of miles of preparation, the soil, that has become ready for the propagation of the food-producing plants for the use of the food-consuming animals, may be fully utilized.

Nature has a serious task when arranging for the continuance of plant-life, in whose absence animal-life must soon cease, and the study of her methods will surely supply material for never-ending research. In Indian forestry we know but little of the rotation of species, and many silvicultural failures have not improbably been due to our ignorance. In the preceding lines the narrative has been on each occasion broken off: in the one case with the establishment of the hard-woods, and in the other with the victory of the mangroves, which themselves disappear so soon as out of reach of the tides. We may indeed suspect that an endless succession of crops of hard-wood is not entirely possible, for there is reason to fear that the toxic effect of the excreta of gregarious trees may be inimical to the continuance of seedlings of the same species; and it is certain that the mixture of species such as is found in a natural forest is provocative of healthy vitality, and that, in pure plantations, insects and fungi find a pleasant field for their enterprise. Such knowledge leads us to pause in the endeavour to unduly increase the proportion of the more valuable timber trees, though we are checked more by the practical results of our experiments than by having entirely fathomed the causes that compel these results.

Moreover, we suspect that such chemical constituents of the soil as are necessary to tree-growth are present in almost every soil in sufficient quantity to support tree-life, and that the physical qualities of the soil are those that have an even greater influence in the maintenance of a forest. There remains, then, to be discovered what other, if any, additions to a soil are responsible for hindering the indefinite continuance of any one species, and whether there may not be an interposition on the part of Nature prohibitory of interbreeding, whose ill effects are so marked in the animal kingdom. We may some day light upon the causes that are at work when studying, as we now do, to remedy their effects, and then will become open to us those silvicultural secrets with regard to teak, to "sâl," to other valuable Indian timbers which at present so often stand in the way of the forester in his efforts to aid in the regeneration of those trees on areas where magnificent forests once flourished, or stand in splendid maturity even in the present day.

From the Rapti one crossed a stretch of level wheat and rice lands extending for miles before reaching the small Government forest of Charda. This is an area covered with an almost pure growth of "sâl," and opinion is divided as to whether it will grow timber or only fuel and small poles. The tree behaves as if it were disgusted at its isolation; it shows unusual sensitiveness, and refuses to grow either in the low-lying glades or on the "dihs," or elevated hillocks. These latter, they say, were the village sites of olden times; now they overlook the fruitful plains around, deserted save by the "nilgai," which loves such open spots. A curious antelope this, and sometimes a terror to the peasantry, whose crops he destroys, while meeting the objections of their owners with counter-threats which are not all vain; for the male has been known to turn on and kill his pursuers, and we ourselves were once held up by a fine specimen, who would not yield way to our horses. We had on this occasion no weapons save hunting-crops, and these he despised, snorting, grunting, and pawing the ground, as we approached; nor would he be driven off by two Forest Guards, who thought to treat him as they would a refractory bullock, so that, unwilling to have him a danger to passers-by, we had to send for a rifle and so end the affair. On another occasion a wounded bull charged an elephant with great determination; he was allowed to advance until there could be no possible doubt of his intentions—so near, in fact, that he fell dead at her feet when struck by a bullet between the shoulders.

These animals fight each other with desperate ferocity; their passion obliterates every other instinct, and the hunter may approach within a few yards and watch the duel. The horns are seldom more than 9 inches long, but they are sharp enough to penetrate the thick hide of the chest and neck and to inflict serious wounds; and if one of the combatants is shot, the sound of the rifle does not deter the survivor from goring the fallen foe, in the belief that his prowess is alone responsible for the victory. In such cases it is best to slay the victor also, for "nilgai" are vermin, and will not tolerate any other deer in their vicinity. Their impertinence and other selfish qualities are due, doubtless, to their being classed by the natives as cows, and therefore safe from the village "shikari," though the villagers are glad to have them butchered so long as they themselves do not incur the penalties of mortal sin. I have seen in the dawn an endless procession of "nilgai" on the banks of the Koriala River, and could have slaughtered a score without trouble; but there is a limit to being a cat's-paw, even though, as the natives evidently thought, a few more sins made no appreciable difference to the "sahib's" hereafter.

There were panthers in the Charda Forest, a wily crowd who declined all allurements; one patriarch in particular was fond of goat, but would eat only in perfect solitude, and I believe that his age was held to entitle him to a full stomach before his companions or descendants would dare to approach. And thus many goats were unavailingly sacrificed. His custom was to watch the kill, and never approach till the last man had left; then, secure from immediate interruption, he at once proceeded to his repast, and I had no doubt in my mind that he could count with sufficient accuracy to insure that there was no interruption. For him, the spoil-sport of the locality, a trap of devilish ingenuity was laid. First, his kill was placed in a "zareeba" of thorns, and across the opening a gun loaded with buckshot was sighted; no confidence was placed in the long silken thread which is supposed to pull the trigger by the pressure of the chest of the victim, for this animal was too cunning to push against even so slight an obstacle, but a weight was arranged to fall at the least touch on a tight cord attached to the trigger. We strolled away, talking freely, and had not gone 200 yards, when a shot resounded through the forest, and, returning, we found that the panther lay dead close by. He had no tail or ears, and his neck and chest were seamed with scars—a vicious beast that might, as he became feebler, have turned into a man-eater, and have been even more difficult to destroy.

It was at Charda that I saw the effect of the great frost of 1905, when in one night the foliage wilted over hundreds of square miles of forest, and myriads of trees were killed throughout the country. The cold air seemed to lie in strata varying with the locality. In some places the upper half of the tree was frost-bitten, and in others only the lower portion was affected by the intense cold; but in result the young growth was either partially or totally ruined, while the effect on the field crops was most disastrous: it was as if a fierce fire had passed over the land and burnt up the vegetation in its course.

In the Chakhia Forest, which lies one march west of Charda, is one of those old forts which the chieftains of olden time held against their brother-robbers as a stronghold for the loot gained in ravaging the country around. The general design of these forts varied but slightly with their size, and consisted of outer defences of ditch and bank enclosing a citadel similarly guarded, the whole commanding a perennial stream that was sometimes approached by a covered way. During the Mutiny such forts had often caused much delay and loss to the British forces, though with modern artillery they would soon become untenable under shell-fire from a distance. At present the earthworks have crumbled away; they lie mysterious and suggestive in the silent forest, their overgrown ditches and mounds affording shelter and the security of a distant outlook to the wild animals which frequent them. The wild-dogs and hyenas have their burrows in the deserted slopes, and panthers love to bask on the ruins of the walls; even tigers are grateful for the solitude that now reigns where once rapine and bloodshed were frequent.

At the ruined entrance to the Chakhia Fort I sat one evening in a small tree that scarcely topped the remains of the outer wall at my back. From thence to the "machán" was but a short spring for any agile animal, but no other vantage-ground had presented itself. On either side the fortifications stretched away till lost in the evening gloom; the bushes near at hand took on ghostly shapes against the dark background of trees; from the distance came the sound of voices and of cattle returning to the shelter of the villages; in front, a winding pathway led to the ruins of the ancient citadel, and imagination peopled it with throngs of men in chain-armour, with round shields slung over the shoulder and sharp "tulwars" ready on the thigh. The jungle-cocks had uttered their last shrill challenge, and the rustling of the roosting peafowl had died away in the branches of the high trees. A fishing-owl was anticipating good hunting with deep booming notes, when a movement was observed on the shadowy path. It took no shape or form in the dim light, nor was there any sound to guide the eye, already strained with watching. The apparition must be left to declare itself either jungle animal or jungle spirit, for no human being would silently roam this spot at night. Gradually a grey outline was defined against the blacker background, so close as to call for instant action, and a flashlight picture was immediately impressed on the brain, of a tiger rearing high in the air, and then smiting the earth with his fore-paws as if to annihilate an enemy. In the black darkness that followed the flash of the rifle the thudding of feet was heard, as the beast sprang up the bank and disappeared behind me.

The morrow was occupied in tracking around the fort and in the steep ravines in the neighbourhood, but no glimpse of the animal was obtained. The following day we resumed the search, and found and pressed him towards the open country, where at last, after furious roaring, he stood at bay. From the elephant only an indistinct mass of yellow fur could be seen in the bushes, and the driver remained unmoved by entreaties to approach. He was unnerved by the angry threats of the tiger, and fearful lest his elephant should be attacked; and then it was that, weary of further argument, the valiant Pickles sprang from the "howdah" and disappeared in the bushes, his departure rousing the courage of the mahout, who felt he could not refuse to follow and rescue a favourite dog. We moved a few paces forward, and met for the first time face to face. The tiger took no notice of the dog, who hung silently from his ear, but he fixed his yellow eyes unblinkingly on the hunter, then slowly sank to earth with a bullet in his neck. Of the crowd who returned to camp, Pickles was perhaps alone without regrets. He had done his duty according to his lights, and often, surely, lived the fight over again when, with twitching feet and muffled yelping, he lay asleep before the camp-fire.

The Chakhia Forest holds a fine stock of panthers, and our black goat, Satan, called up several to their death. She became an adept at the sport, and lived to an honourable old age without an accident. But some wily beasts there were who would not reply to her winning cries; to those we had to sacrifice strange goats on the altar of sport, in hopes that an aroused appetite might lead to their destruction. In the Mandnála there lived such a one, reputed to be of great size and cunning, so that our endeavours were scoffed at by the villagers as foreordained to failure. Abdul, however, took a delight in attempting the impossible, and one morning announced that this panther's hour had come. It did not so seem to us when we saw the "machán" tied amongst a group of saplings, and visible enough even when empty; but it was explained that the undergrowth was thick, and that there was a better chance than was apparent. The panther put in an early appearance, but though we were able to remark his size and the paleness of his colouring, indicating age, he showed no hurry to approach within shot, and kept us in a state of tense excitement for some time. It is well on such occasions to decide beforehand at what point the shot will be fired, and to have the rifle in readiness pointed in that direction; for it is impossible to raise the weapon suddenly without being instantly detected, while, on the other hand, to keep a heavy rifle to the shoulder for any length of time is trying. This panther at last approached the line of fire, stood for some time on the alert, then proceeded to cross it, and lay dead in his tracks. The villagers came afar to see him lying in state, and each had some tale to tell of goats, of calves, even of cows, killed during the years gone past.

Here also we made experiments in the climbing powers of panthers, fixing the kill in a branchless sapling some 15 feet from the ground, and thence the panther recovered it with ease. We secured it still higher, and watched in the hope that we might see how the panther severed the rope to reach his prey; and while waiting, lo! an unexpected tigress appeared on the scene, gazing with an indifferent eye on the jungle signs around her. She was miserably thin, and looked as if just recovered from a deadly disease or injury, so that the bullet that struck her behind the ear probably afforded a painless exit from a painful life; but though we could detect no external injury, we felt that such animals were dangerous to man, and should, when possible, be made away with.

Across the river to Motipur is a short march, and here I met a friend of my youth in old Premgir, the "shikári," now white-haired and bent, but still so keen that his eye brightened as he spoke of the old hunting days that we had had together. He told me that his chum, Moti, had been killed many years before, when beating out a tiger from a boggy stream that the elephants could not enter. The animal refused to go forward, probably because too much noise had been made in placing the guns, and lay skulking under some bushes in sight of the beaters, who wisely halted. Moti, with foolhardy recklessness, the result of many years' successful hunting, approached him with many injurious epithets, and, loosening the brass water-vessel that Hindus carry, attached to a long cord, for drawing water from wells, struck the tiger with it. In return he was viciously clawed over the head. He made light of his wounds, but they proved fatal a few days after.

But what most amused the old man was the recollection of a stalk after a noble spotted-stag in an early May morning before the sun had dried up the moisture in the jungle, and when each leaf and blade of grass was still bespangled with dew, when the increasing heat was drawing up the water from the surface of the soil, so that a soft mist enveloped the silent forest-trees, now heavy with their spring foliage. From a distance of a few score yards, unknown to the hunter, I watched his proceedings: saw him strip off the brown cotton cloth and throw his turban aside; then noted how, almost naked, he crept cautiously along to intercept the stag in his leisurely retreat to the jungle. It was good to see the old man stop and fire, and the smoke eddying gently, as if in rhythm with the echoes that rolled back from the high wall of vegetation in the background; to see the stag, startled but unhurt, standing an instant as if to locate the danger, and then falling to a second shot before he could spring into his gallop; but best of all was Premgir's almost terrified astonishment at my intervention, which I firmly believe he attributed to a "bhut," or jungle spirit, before he recognized me coming slowly towards him. As we strolled together into camp, I had to soothe his feelings by pointing out that it was only to his inferior weapons that he owed his defeat, and that the distance was too far for the old gun he carried. We could afford to laugh now at the many occasions when we had been bested by the jungle animals, and to realize that it is not always victory that is the most interesting, and that being hunted often affords even more memorable sensations than does hunting. Poor old Premgir never reached his home from his last visit to me. He died on the way from cholera, which is perhaps sometimes a synonym for poison administered in the heat of a domestic feud. He had himself wives young and old, and children of all ages, and sufficient property to cause jealousy in his household.

But I have already described these forests, and can now cross both the Girwa and Koriala Rivers to the Kheri District, where the house at Bilraien stands on the edge of the forest looking over the rice-fields to the hills of Nepal. This was a notable place for panthers, and sometimes the sportsman might save himself the trouble of looking for them: they came to him, and could be seen from the veranda stealing through the dusk. One killed two of our herd of sheep, dragging them out from a grass hut, and during the following day was seen repeatedly in the adjoining scrub, and as often disappeared when followed up. Evening had come, when, weary of the constant alarms, I went out for the last time, and found the beast, also possibly fatigued, crouching on the cross-roads. The bullet struck the earth in front of his chin, and, passing between him and the soil, ripped open his stomach as if cut with a knife; but such was his vitality that he got clear away, and was found dead two days later by indications afforded by the useful crows.

Here, too, a curious episode occurred. As I was roaming through the sâl forest admiring the natural regeneration which had followed on closure from cattle, so that the young growth was now man-high, and so dense that the grass had been completely killed down—musing, in fact, on matters silvicultural, and not thinking of sport—the elephant stopped dead, nearly jerking me on to the mahout, and there in front of her lay a tiger crouching. Abdul at my back seemed to spend hours in extracting the rifle from its case and handing it to me with a couple of cartridges, and I surely took days to load the weapon. The tiger never turned his gaze from mine during this anxious period, nor did he move when I fired, nor even when I proceeded to reload, so as to have more than one shot available in case of trouble. Then I said to the mahout, "Is he hit?" He replied, "I don't know, but there is blood trickling from his nose;" and as he spoke the muscles relaxed and the beast rolled over on his side. He was not 5 yards from us the whole time, and none but the stanchest elephant would have stood so unconcernedly for so long, or, indeed, would have resisted the impulse to back away, if not to flee, at the first surprise.

Between the next house at Bhádi Tál and Bilraien are two famous "nálas," where many tigers have lived and died. The first is narrow and deep, flowing through high "ratwa" grass, and is unpropitious ground to fight a wounded tiger with a single elephant. We found it best to wait in such cases till the beast moved towards one of the large lakes to the north, and then track him through the tree-forest if he was still able to travel, and therefore powerful to hurt. One such Abdul reported to have left cover, growling savagely, as soon as evening fell, and we were on the trail by daylight. It was easy following for about a mile in fairly open ground, so that at a distance we could see a great clump of elephant-climber, almost the only shady retreat that we had come across. It was also enough that on a high tree above a dejected crow sat silent, and the trackers were at once taken off,

Footprints in the Sand.

and ascended to safety amongst the branches, while we very slowly advanced towards the suspicious spot. At 40 yards there was no sign, and step by step we reduced the distance, till the tiger sprang out with a roar, and was stopped before he could reach the elephant. Such moments and such sights are the best tonic the forester can take. They are worth many ounces of quinine in warding off malaria, for they make the exile's blood glow so that depression and lassitude are as if they never existed.

At Bhádi Tál is one of the best spots to become intimate with the forest fauna, for all are there in plenty. It is the stronghold of the swamp-deer, and of their remorseless follower, the tiger. A few forest panthers also make it their headquarters, and there is also, alas! good hunting-ground for the wild-dogs. In the "nála" to the south-east of the house, close to the road to Khairigarh, Abdul had one evening tied a "machán" for us in a small tree with scanty foliage. We sat for some time watching the antics of a most beautiful jungle-cat who was feeding on the tiger's kill. He was nervous in the extreme, and would dash away at the slightest sound, returning very cautiously, the while growling and swearing under his breath as if to scold himself into better courage. Then the startled cackle of a jungle-cock was a warning not to be disregarded, and the cat left hurriedly, not to return; and with good reason, for there, walking proudly along the bank of the "nála," the owner of the kill was coming to investigate.

It is seldom that a tiger is seen at his ease on open level ground, and so, also, it is seldom that his height and size can be fully admired. In grass and foliage only glimpses of his tawny hide are visible, and it does not seem as if he stood a foot higher than an ordinary table, though as long as one that would seat many persons in comfort. We had leisure to admire this tiger as he boldly approached —indeed, we let him come too near, with the result that we had to take a facing shot as he stood and stared suspiciously. He left, showing certain signs that he was not badly hurt, and in his hurry stumbled over a sloth-bear in his path. What actually happened to this unfortunate animal is unknown, but his roars of rage re-echoed through the forest long after the tiger's footfalls had died away, until Abdul's reproachful voice was heard asking why we had fired at a common bear. He was delighted when assured this was not the fact.

The next morning showed a perfect piece of tracking that lasted for nearly two hours, till we arrived at a muddy pool in the forest encircled with a ring of light green but heavy grass. As we approached ahead of the trackers, the mahout pointed to the black tuft of a tiger's tail protruding from the grass, and no time was lost in getting Abdul to mount the elephant at my back. We proceeded to visit the water, so as to find from the tracks whether or not the tiger were disabled, but had no time to carry out our intentions; for the beast appeared on the high bank above us about 20 yards away, and looked decidedly threatening as he turned toward us. The principle of the efficacy of first blow is nowhere better exemplified than in tiger-shooting, and this one answered to the shot by rushing at the elephant with a roar. It was but the veriest fraction of a second before he had passed through the grass and emerged on our side, only a few yards away; a still shorter time elapsed before three shots were fired almost simultaneously, and he lay dead under the elephant's tightly curled trunk, so close that she receded half a pace to avoid his fall.

Similar incidents of sporting life in Oudh might be multiplied. It might be told how we opened a campaign against the big tigers of Duduaghát, which for so many years had roamed that part of the Kheri forests, not unmolested but unscathed; how in the space of one month we bagged four tigers, measuring in the aggregate over 40 feet in length, and how their quarters were almost immediately occupied by other but younger animals. But enough has been written to prove that the solitary sportsman may find pleasure in camping in the Government forests, and, with good trackers and a knowledge of wild beasts and their ways, may yet make a fair bag without incurring any great expense.

In these histories of successful sport it is, however, due that a narrative of a third defeat should find place, lest the impression should be given that there was no ill success, no failure to bring the great carnivora to the gun, and no clumsy handling of the rifle when the supreme moment presented itself. Such occasions were, indeed, more frequent than was desirable, and memory still returns with a pang of regret to opportunities lost by wrong interpretation of the signs of the jungle, by want of attention or foresight, and, worst of all, by hurried, ill-aimed shooting, for which there was not even the excuse of inexperience. Each such failure should bring with it, and surely does to the ardent lover of Nature, a wider knowledge and a keener zest in applying it; while as the sportsman grows older the desire to kill diminishes, and the love of the hunt is increased; he devotes his attention to the most experienced of the jungle animals, not so much because the trophy he may wrest from them may be superior, but rather because the greater skill and care is needed in its attainment. And even when at last you stand over some defeated king of the forest, and recall how he has survived through long years of danger to reach the magnificent proportions of his prime, a feeling of remorse is born that you, who are yourself imbued with the spirit of the forest, with a love of its silence and of its freedom, should have been guilty of depriving another of what you have learnt to value.

One march to the west of the Bhira railway-station lies the forest-house of Kishanpur, and here were, when we arrived, the tracks of a tiger and tigress, evidently young beasts, and probably not long separated from their mother; with the appetite of youth they had killed a buffalo on the side of the road, and carelessly dragged it to a forest of saplings. There was no suitable tree to tie the "machán," but eventually it was supported between three slender poles about 10 feet from the ground, where it rocked with each movement and swayed with each passing breeze. The tigers made no attempt to conceal their approach; they could be heard growling from a distance, and the nearer they came to their evening meal the more threatening was the attitude of the tiger to his mate: he was evidently insisting on his prior right to the meal. At 25 yards away he looked an evil beast that would be ready to attack on the slightest provocation, over 8 feet in length, but slim, with the unformed muscle of youth. The bullet struck him as he faced the "machán," and, missing the cavity of the chest, ploughed through the shoulder muscles, and he retreated, growling angrily.

Darkness had fallen before we returned to camp, and the carts were being loaded for the night march. The spare elephant had already gone on to the next camp when we started at daybreak to look up the wounded tiger. There was no blood after the first hundred yards, and tracking was slow as we travelled towards the swamp that lay to the north. So the morning was already well advanced when we arrived on its brink, and the grass and foliage was beginning to stir with the first wafts of the hot wind that would shortly blow with violence. We could see or hear nothing, but at a little distance in the grass was a small pool surrounded with unhealthy-looking trees, and on these sat some silent crows. We proceeded to investigate the reason of their interest; but before we reached the spot a heavy body came hurtling through the grass, passing within 6 feet, and coming to a standstill some 20 yards away. The tiger had charged an unseen foe, and, himself unseen, was now standing at bay. Merely to precipitate matters, a shot was fired in his direction, and it had that effect, for again there was a rush through the heavy grass, then a shock and silence. The agitated mahout now explained that the tiger was clasping the elephant's fore-legs, and we implored him to move onwards. With difficulty the elephant took a step forward; the tiger now lay on his back, biting her belly; another step, and she was preparing to yield to pain and fear and subside, when Abdul remarked that he could see the tiger. Lying on my face on the "pad," I lowered the rifle with one hand over the crupper ropes, and fired into a writhing mass below, and the elephant was free and staggering away. We took her to the open country outside the swamp; she had thirteen bites and innumerable scratches, and we led her away, fearful lest she should die of loss of blood on the journey to camp. It was many months before she was recovered, but she was then as stanch to tiger as before.

Meanwhile Abdul remained to watch the ground and warn the villagers of the danger in their neighbourhood. The next morning he drove a herd of buffaloes into the grass, which were driven out by the tiger, who still lay on the same spot; then, unwilling to own defeat, Abdul went himself into the swamp to reconnoitre. Advancing through grass that rose many feet over his head, he suddenly entered an area of trampled herbage, and saw the blue sky above him, while almost at his feet lay the tiger, who greeted him with a loud roar. He fled, leaving his shoes in the sticky mud; and now his position was the worse, in that he feared to return to camp without them. Better death than ridicule, so again he faced the danger, this time pushing his rifle before him as he slowly crawled along, and so finally was able to respond to the menace of the wounded tiger by a bullet through his brain. And thus he triumphantly rejoined the camp with both skin and shoes, and was happy in spite of severe reprimands for his foolhardiness.

CHAPTER VII

FORESTERS' LIFE IN BURMA AND THE ANDAMAN ISLANDS

In 1899, after eight busy years in Oudh, I proceeded to England on furlough, with the knowledge that I should not return to those forests. The prospect of a change was not unwelcome, because the most interesting work—that of the organization of the area—was practically complete; moreover, the head-quarters of the Conservator had been transferred to Lucknow, with the option of spending two and a half months at Naini Tál, involving the prohibitory expense of renting a house at each of these stations. Yet the last place I desired to visit was Burma, for there a total ignorance of the language cut me off from intercourse with the people, and both the climate and the mode of life were different to those to which I had become inured after twenty-six years' service in Northern India; but there was no escape, and I arrived in the Northern Forest Circle in that Province in the beginning of January, 1900.

Of the sport in Burma I can record nothing, owing to the fact that I never enjoyed any, for it afforded me no pleasure to be led up to a beast whose local name even was unknown to me, and whose habits could only be learnt at second-hand through an interpreter; so that only weapons of self-defence were retained when marching in those vast forests, and occupation depended almost exclusively on professional duties and on efforts to pick up some knowledge of the ways, not only of the people themselves, but of the various nationalities who are engaged in commerce and other work in the country.

I soon found that all of the comforts and many of the decencies of camp-life had to be abandoned in this new country, where there were no roads, and often even no paths, to those places that the forester had to visit. The duplicated outfit of tents and camp-furniture laden on many carts, the horses and traps, the troupes of servants, and the patriarchal herds of cows, sheep, and goats, that followed the forester through the jungles of Northern India were now all absent; three elephants (one generally incapacitated by a sore back or a lame foot) provided all the available carriage, and a bed, a chair, and a table, all the possible furniture. The country supplied fowls, eggs, rice, and coarse vegetables, such as pumpkins and spinach, and thus the most precious part of the equipment consisted of canned milk and butter, of bacon and wheat-flour, and of candles that gave a dubious light after dark. A change of clothing and a bottle of whisky were not forgotten, and so, with two servants instead of twenty, we plunged into the wilds in January, to emerge three months later after walking some four or five hundred miles through the primeval forest.

An elephant carries from six to eight hundred pounds, and can cover daily some ten to fifteen miles if carefully laden and looked after; and though each animal is accompanied by two men, these can exercise but slight control, for the Burman does not sit on the elephant's neck, but professes to direct him from a precarious perch on the piled-up baggage by means of a short bamboo spear. In these circumstances there are likely to be many mishaps, but when most of the conveniences of camp-life have been abandoned at the start, these have little effect on the traveller.

We took ponies with us, but they were little used, as a foot pace was rarely exceeded on account of the absence of all paths save those leading from one village to the next; and when these did not serve, a way through the forest had to be hacked with "dahs," the useful knives of the country. We generally started from our tiny tent at dawn, and were led by a guide who was changed at each village we reached; but often he had no luck, and was forced to accompany us during the entire journey. At about 10 a.m. we ate the breakfast we had brought with us, and then continued the march; and it was often evening before the new camp was ready, sometimes on a spot hastily cleared in the dense forest, at others in a monastery courtyard or near a village site. In the early morning the forest was wet with mist, and at midday the sun beat fiercely down, so that it was not surprising that even Europeans adopted native clothing; for this is certainly most suitable in climatic conditions where the wearer is continually drenched either with dew and rain or with perspiration.

The forests seemed magnificent in their vastness, in the size of the trees and in the dense undergrowth of bamboo; but at present it is impossible to utilize more than a few of the most valuable species, and attention is chiefly directed to teak for export, and to pyinkado for railway sleepers. It is rare to find pure teak forests of any great extent; as a rule the tree is scattered amongst other species which have little marketable value, and in evergreen forests some magnificent specimens are observable. During native rule the teak was a royal tree, and the monopoly has been maintained by the British Government, and, as the timber is never felled green, there is the less difficulty in enforcing State ownership. It is customary to "girdle" the standing tree, so that seasoning proceeds during the two or more years that elapse before felling, and in this condition the logs will float about two-thirds submerged in fresh water, which would not otherwise be the case. As the timber has to traverse some hundreds of miles on a journey that frequently takes a couple of years before reaching the distant market, the importance of this method of seasoning is apparent.

The procedure in the matter of the exploitation of teak is as follows: The forester "girdles" such trees as he considers are silviculturally fit for removal, and this involves him in an arduous task, as he may only find one suitable stem on every three or more acres traversed. After "girdling" he impresses each tree with the Government mark and with the year of "girdling," and so important is this work considered that it was, ten years ago, entrusted only to European officers, and that not only for the reason that the future welfare of the forest depended on proper removal of the mature timber, but also so that the registers whereby the future fellings were checked might be correctly and honestly maintained. At the present time this work has been proved to be beyond the strength of the European staff, and is entrusted to provincial officers and subordinates under the supervision of the superior officers, and these, no doubt, carry it out with equal efficiency.

The area that has been treated by "girdling" is two years later leased out to timber trading firms, who fell and remove the dead trees in the manner they deem most suitable. It will be seen that there is here opportunity for fraud in arranging for "girdlings" outside those registered by the Forest Officer, and advantage has sometimes been taken of this opening, and of the difficulty of checking the removal of the girdled trees, especially when the subordinate staff was poorly paid, and when a distasteful mode of livelihood debarred any but the most needy from entering the service. But in the present day more reliance on the contracting firms is justified, for these replenish their staff by well-educated youths of good social status selected in England, and the forester finds that he is assisted rather than hindered in his work by the presence of contractors' employees in his forest. Of the Burma timber firms, the Bombay-Burma Trading Corporation takes the first place, in virtue of the magnitude of the interests involved, and in the extent of the country worked over in Burma, India, and Siam; and a young man joining this corporation, and bringing with him health and energy, should have a prosperous career before him. I was much helped during my Burma service by my acquaintance with the leaders of the B.B.T.C., who knew all that there was to know about the exploitation of the forest, and were at all times ready to give every information, as well as to settle any disputed matters, with courtesy and liberality.

The general method of removing the felled timber is to drag it by elephants to a neighbouring water-course which it is expected will be heavily flooded during the monsoon; should this hope be realized, the jumble of logs is accompanied by elephants, who refloat such as may be stranded, and, when a jam occurs, relieve it, often at the risk of life. In this way the teak logs at last enter the great river Irrawadi, or one of its affluents, such as the Chindwin, and are then tied into rafts with cane ropes before the journey to Rangoon is undertaken. On the way adventures are not uncommon; the rafts may be stranded or may break up, and in these circumstances it becomes difficult to protect or recover the drifting logs from the practised river thieves, who are always on the alert, either to quickly bury their find in the sand, or even more rapidly to saw it up, so that the marks of ownership may be obliterated. The laws governing forest produce in transit by water are necessarily strict in Burma, but whether they were quite effective in the absence of organized river police is doubtful; it is probable that were such a body supplied with swift launches its cost would have been soon recouped, and the morality of the river population considerably improved. The teak logs on arrival at Rangoon are brought into depot, where again the elephant proves his usefulness, and are ultimately sawn up, the better quality going to Europe or America, and the remainder supplying building material to the East.

Of late years there has been a very serious falling off in the quantity of teak available for export, and the reason is not far to seek. In former days the forest was full of "girdled" timber of all sizes, awaiting the pleasure of the ruling Government, while there was also a surplus stock of over-mature trees of so large a size as to be difficult to utilize without special appliances. The yearly outturn therefore was at first larger than the increment of the forest at that time, and when this excess supply was exhausted the outturn naturally fell considerably. It is doubtful if in the future such large-sized trees will be available in as great a quantity as in the past; when new areas are opened out, the over-mature trees found therein will probably yield a certain number of magnificent logs, but after their removal the future working of the forest will seldon be based on a much higher girth than seven and a half feet, and such a size, though commercially useful and financially remunerative, will not supply those immense squares so often seen in former years, when the giants of the forest were eagerly handled by European firms who had the men, the elephants, and the machinery, to cope with them.

It is probable, then, that the teak harvest of the future in Burma will consist principally of medium-sized but well-grown and sound timber, in quantities gradually increasing as the forests respond to organization and protection; but whether the demand for teak at a price that will afford a fair remuneration for the cost of handling it will continue must remain a matter of opinion. The timber market brooks but little interference: a constant supply of the same wood of similar quality and at about a similar price seems necessary to its satisfaction; and if these factors are not present in the case of any given timber, the market seeks them in another. If it cannot get the best timber in the quantity and quality desired, the next best that fulfils these requirements is sought out, and such a timber might be difficult to oust when the time arrives that teak can be offered in greater quantity and better quality than during the last few years.

Of other timbers, those required for railway sleepers are at present the most valuable, but the cost of conversion and carriage leaves but little to book as the value of the wood. Burma has not at this time a population large enough to fully utilize locally her forest crop, as is the case in India, where the people themselves consume by far the greater portion of the outturn, and it is because there is no pressure on the forest that a State forest property can be built up at leisure that shall in the future efficiently serve the welfare of a much larger population. There can be no doubt that the resources of this rich Province will at some future day be utilized to the full, and, as the Burmese as a nation can hardly be expected to multiply so as to fill the land, it seems likely that an outlet for emigration from the populous West will be afforded to a hardier and more laborious people. Already the occupancy of rich, hitherto ownerless, soil follows in the track of the few lines of railway that tap the wealth of the more populous portions of the Province, and it is not unlikely that if the establishment of foreign settlements were encouraged, and a through railway journey from India provided at no great expense, the Indians of the east and centre of the Peninsula would flock to a land where Nature is kind and taxation light.

As for the Burman, if it is agreed that he is a person who as a rule finds happiness in ease, his charm is undeniable. The peasant who devotes three months to agriculture, and for the rest of the year can reside in a well-built, comfortable house supplied with every requirement of his simple life; whose womenfolk will wear either gold ornaments or none; whose dress on the gala-days that occur so frequently in this beautiful land is always of silk, may be pardoned for refusing to work in order that he may possess more than he can use, especially when the accumulation of wealth does not, in Burma, appear to bring more luxury or more refinement in life. The people are already refined; they have charming manners and a charming hospitality; but if work is waiting to be done, it is better to employ the Chinaman or the native of India, although these may be actuated only by the interested motive of improving a hard lot, and not by the truly Western incentive of pleasure in work for work's sake.

Already in Lower Burma there are signs that the Burman may be supplanted by his more energetic fellow-subjects from the West, and, when to a natural indolence of temperament is added the love of gambling and the general recklessness characteristic of his race, there can be little doubt that even laws designed to protect him against himself will merely delay, but not prevent, his final disappearance. It is doubtless the good manners of the Burman, his cleanliness, his dainty attire, the cheerfulness of his disposition, the buoyancy of his demeanour, which make him a favourite wherever he goes; the reverse of the picture is too seldom seen to have much effect on the general appreciation of these attributes, and yet many a Forest Officer, entrusted with the management of an area extending over thousands of square miles, must have felt it almost hopeless to cope with the attitude of those around him; and thus the good work that has been accomplished is all the more a splendid record of devotion to duty and a proof of the effects of personal influence.

In the winter of 1900 I marched through the forests on the west bank of the Chindwin River, and thence, crossing above Kindat, traversed the watershed between the Chindwin and Irrawadi Rivers, reaching Kathá about the end of March. The chief impressions conveyed by the forests of Upper Burma were those of vastness and solitude; villages, often only a collection of huts in a forest clearing, were eight or ten miles apart, and in the whole of the Chindwin District, with an area approaching, I believe, some 20,000 square miles, there were only about 2,000 square miles under cultivation, and this was situated principally in the south. Camp was most frequently pitched in a hastily-made clearing in the forest, but wherever a monastery was found, its courtyard was occupied after permission had been asked; and there was unfailing interest in watching the monks—often apparently earnest, holy men—in the discharge of their duties, teaching the young folk from the neighbouring villages, reading from their sacred books, or strolling around in the cool of the evening. On these occasions there was always regret that want of knowledge of the vernacular prevented our closer acquaintance.

The daily march through these giant trees, whose tops were often invisible in the morning mists, through the swaying bamboos that arched 50 feet above the traveller's head, through grasslands wet with the clinging dew, had the charm of novelty, but the isolation of the lonely European when no brother-officer was within reach became after a time trying in the extreme. Of animal life little was seen; the tracks of tiger, bison, elephant, and "sámbhar," were there, the cries of birds and of the melancholy hooluk monkey were often heard, but the eye seldom lit on any living creature, a depressing change from the forests of India, where game still existed plenteously. This objection did not apply to insect life, which swarmed around, many species being predatory on the human body, and so compelling an interest in their proceedings. Communication with the outer world was restricted to the weekly steamer plying as far as Kindat, and beyond that river-port was dependent on the good-will of the messengers, who leisurely followed my quicker movements; and so it happened that after two days' marching up the bed of a watercourse, always ankle and sometimes thigh deep, I arrived on the slopes draining towards the Irrawadi River, having had no letters for eighteen days, and no news of the world for twenty-five. Here I met an Indian geologist, who imparted to me the news of the first victories won by the British in South Africa, and looked on curiously at my belated expressions of patriotic satisfaction.

From Kathá I went to Mandalay, and found a climate that seemed familiar in its arid heat, but amid surroundings that were totally inadequate to withstand it. The wooden houses with latticed windows failed to exclude the hot winds, therm-antidotes were unknown, and when the Burmese "punkha"-puller started off for the nightly theatre or music-hall, and took with him all chances of restful slumber, there arose a great longing for the decrepit old Indian, male or female, who pulled spasmodically, yet conscientiously, through the weary nights. During the last ten years, many customs, first based on stern necessity, have disappeared from European life in Upper Burma; houses of brick and stone have replaced those of wood and bamboo, electric light and power have lessened the heat and improved the ventilation; in fact, there is less dependence on the inhabitants of the country, and more on the scientific amenities of the West. And these amenities were badly wanted where in winter the difference between day and night temperature might amount to 30° F. and more, and where the evening at the club might be passed in a furnace of 108° F.

From Mandalay to Maymyo is but forty miles, but they bring with them a reduction in the summer temperature of some 19° F. We were fortunate enough in being able to rent a house from the Recorder of Rangoon, a double-storied wooden erection, through whose walls the monsoon rains literally spurted, and through whose floors notes might be dropped to the occupants of the rooms below. In those days Maymyo was in its infancy, but under the fostering care of various Lieutenant-Governors it has sprung into one of the best hill-stations in the Empire; its polo-ground is perhaps unsurpassed, the golf-course is interesting, there is some hunting, and good roads invite pleasant excursions in many directions. There is a club, a hospital, and a travellers' rest-house, and the officials and visitors have fine houses and gardens. But in the beginning it was not so, and the place was in itself unhealthy, while there were many other inconveniences incidental to a new settlement. It will hardly be realized what an important part hill-stations have played in the social life and morals of exiles in the East. By making it possible that white women and children should make their homes there, these mountain settlements have altered the whole tone of society, and have raised it to a level which the pleadings of the Government or even its stern, and sometimes inappropriate, edicts could not compel. To Sir Frederick Fryer is due the credit for having established Maymyo as a summer resort, as well as for the changes that have followed on the creation of not one but several mountain resorts, where the isolation and other drawbacks of a tropical summer may be obviated or ameliorated.

After a few months spent in Maymyo we started on a summer trip on the Irrawadi River. The Government launch was a fine stern-wheeler, capable of a speed of about twelve miles an hour, and possessing a spacious upper deck with a tiny cabin; but this was seldom used, as the weather was so warm that an open-air life was no hardship; in fact, it is one of the greatest charms of the country, outside the limited dry zone, that even the walls and windows are designed to admit all the cooling breezes of the monsoons. The launch had a draught of about 30 inches, so that the danger of stranding on the numerous sand-banks was reduced to a minimum; but, on the other hand, she was extremely top-heavy, and, when the side-awnings were closed to keep out the rain, she sometimes heeled over considerably to the wind, and more than once the captain ran her alongside the banks for safety. The crew consisted of Chittagong Mohammedans, seafaring by caste and custom, men reliable in emergency and adepts at manœuvring a boat in narrow channels, where often swift currents were encountered. The river is buoyed out by the Indian Marine Department by means of long bamboos anchored to sand-bags, but the system has the disadvantage that at low-water these bamboos lie on the surface, and in high floods their painted tops are submerged, so that a local knowledge of the water is a most valuable asset at all times.

The Irrawadi is a noble stream during the monsoon. Its length of more than a thousand miles no doubt satisfies the craving of those who take delight in statistics; but what appeals to the imagination is its breadth, the volume of its waters, the beauties of the tropical forest, at this season dipping its foliage into the murky waves, and the relentless strength of its current. The winter tourist in Burma sees the

Irrawadi at its cold-weather level. He passes between sandy or rocky banks that obscure the distant view, at a season when the forests have already lost their full vitality; he cannot realize the greater charm of being borne on the summer floods high above islands, of struggling against the foam-capped waves on the open reaches, or of fighting against cross-currents and whirlpools that are concealing the fair-weather waterway. He will not see the great wooden boats with high sterns and bellying sails blown against the stream by the more powerful monsoon, nor the timber and bamboo rafts like floating villages sullenly swinging with the current. He travels in ease under brilliant skies in an Irrawadi Flotilla mail-steamer, and recks little of the adventures of those who in smaller, sometimes tiny, craft brave the dangers of this noble river.

The Burmans are excellent sailormen, and at home on the water. They manage their own boats with consummate skill, and it is surely only owing to their general untrustworthiness that the less volatile Mohammedan is chosen to man all European craft. From the villages the whole population turn out daily to bathe, and much fun and chaff goes on at this social hour. It is a lesson in skilful modesty to watch the manner in which the women undress as they gradually enter the muddy water, and don their clothes as they slowly emerge, to stand on the bank radiant in their dry costumes.

The small boys at the same time will be disporting themselves by towing a log laboriously to the head of a neighbouring rapid, and whirling down astride it, often falling off and swimming like frogs to land, to repeat the amusement. Then from the nearest monastery arrive the acolytes with bamboo water-pots, 6 feet long and 7 or 8 inches in diameter. They swim out into the stream, and fill them with unpolluted water for the use of the monks. The evening falls with the tinkling of pagoda bells and the booming of gongs, commencing at first with single slow notes, and rising in rapid crescendo till the air is converted into waves of sound, the one following the other with the hurried regularity of a breezy sea.

One cannot proceed at this season beyond Bhámo, for the two upper defiles bar the way, and even the third defile is often difficult in heavy water. The river, compressed within narrow space, flows under the left bank with smooth and silent power; under the right bank is a return current flowing in the reverse direction, whose waters are perceptibly higher than those in the main stream, so that it seems quite simple to float up-current on its waters, until at their meeting the boat is swept round with irresistible force, and may not escape from the whirlpool without hard labour and anxiety.

On each pinnacle of rock a pagoda marks where one of the faithful has paid a vow or publicly professed his gratitude for temporal blessings enjoyed. The country is full of these offerings, and pity it is that their maintenance should not be considered so marked an expression of piety as their construction, for then there would be fewer ruins, both of works of art and of public utility, than is now the case. In every well-known religion man has to work out his own salvation by faith and the works that result therefrom, and in each he has an appeal to higher authority than man, which is of infinite value to the suffering and distressed; but the Buddhist would seem to be self-centred in his preparations for the next step on his long journey to absorption in the infinite. He gives the impression of standing alone in his struggle for the future happiness of rest; yet surely he often must feel the need for assistance, and surely, too, the women who prostrate themselves in the shrines of the founder of their faith present many a petition to an unknown god, although they have the assurance that it is useless.

Anchoring at Bhámo, we left the launch with strict injunctions to the crew to watch the river, which in falling water may run off six or more feet in a night, and leave you stranded till an opportune rise that may be deferred for months. Then we enjoyed the varied interesting sights of this most cosmopolitan city. British troops no longer occupied the fort, Indian police battalions holding this frontier of the Empire. In the streets, Chinamen, Sikhs, Pathans, Burmans, Jews, Parsis, Kachins, and many other nationalities, good-temperedly jostled each other, and many were the quaint trifles that could be picked up by the curiosity-hunter, or bought in actual wear on the wild visitors from a distance. At a distance of some twenty miles from Bhámo the Chinese frontier begins, and at Sinlum Kabar is a British outpost, some 6,000 feet above the sea-level, in a bleak, disforested country. Here the caravans of mules pass in from China with their rough drivers, professing the Mohammedan religion, but paying slight attention to its precepts; and here one may sit over the evening fire far above the sweltering river, though it is perhaps more sentiment and home-longing than chilliness which leads you to enjoy it. It is, in fact, a rite rather than a necessity.

In the cold weather of 1901 we started on a long tramp, commencing in the Mu district, and ending on the Irrawadi. The first march was eventful, for we walked for sixteen weary miles through a jungle where the "dahs" were frequently in requisition to cut a path, our object being to pitch camp by the side of a stream of running water that was known to the guides. It seems strange in a tropical country, where evergreen vegetation is not infrequent, that scarcity of water should be such a common hindrance to roving through the forest, yet in all the Provinces of the Empire that I have visited Burma is easily the most prominent as regards the difficulty of the water-supply to the wandering forester. No sooner does he leave the main watercourses than he is confronted with the inconvenience of filthy water, often so pronounced that the filter worked by a force-pump would require to be cleaned after it had yielded a pint of clear fluid. On this occasion, parched with thirst, though bathed in perspiration after a trying walk, we hurried over the last mile, to find our stream a sandy watercourse destitute of moisture. Ten miles was the distance to the next water-supply, and instantly everyone was digging frantically, in the hope that the spring-level was still within reach; and soon from many little basins in the sand clear water was trickling in welcome streams. It reminded one forcibly of childhood's days on the sea-shore, where water-level is sought under no penalties, and the wooden spade of the seaside would have been most useful in the present emergency.

The elephants alone showed no sign of trepidation; they knew by scent, by the movement of the soil beneath their heavy tread, that water was not far below the dry sand, and that they could reach it with a few kicks of their fore-feet; yet, like all domesticated animals, they wisely waited till man performed the service which in wild life they would have finished, perhaps more speedily, themselves.

At this camp a curious incident occurred, giving matter for thought as to the instinct or reasoning power of the elephant. At midnight the camp was aroused by wild trumpeting and squealing of elephants, and immediately everyone was on the alert, the Burmans throwing green bamboos on to the fires, which exploded with loud reports as the moisture between the nodes was vaporized with the heat. Then two of the trained elephants were seen each fondling, with extravagant gestures of joy, a newly-arrived calf, evidently their own property. These young animals, some 5 feet in height, had been left weeks before about thirty miles away, to be handled and made fit for light work; but how they had ascertained where the camp was, and how found their way through the pathless forest, is a matter that still requires explanation. Early next morning the men in whose charge these calves had been left arrived, without kuowing that the animals were before them. They related how the calves had run loose in the forest, how they had tracked them for two days, and, finding that the tracks had joined those of a wild herd, had given up the pursuit; then,

THE MORNING BATH.

learning of our camp in the vicinity, they had come to report. Their astonishment at the events of the night before was great, but they could not explain the occurrence, and we were content to believe that the birds of the air had conveyed the matter to two wandering orphans in distress.

At Manlé we reached the depository of one of Buddha's numerous teeth, which we were told had been presented by a German scientist, who had acquired it in Ceylon. The relic, which appeared to be of solid ivory, and similar in shape to the tusk of a walrus, did not afford so much interest as its custodian, a venerable Abbot with a charming presence, and manners calculated to command reverence, and even affection. We went to call on this gentleman, who, though debarred by the customs of his religion from approaching any woman, thought he had sufficiently deferred to the prejudices of his subordinates by placing me between himself and the lady visitor, and thus seated he related to us the history of his life and work. Later on he took us to the small pagoda in which the sacred tooth was kept behind the barred iron gratings. The monks lined the sides of the narrow staircase, and the beaten-gold shrine containing the relic was handed down from hand to hand, received by the Abbot, and placed on an altar under the trees. Then all bent in silent, almost tearful, adoration. There could be no doubt of the intensity of the feelings evoked, and when I forced myself to ask whether the Abbot believed that this was a human tooth—an impossibility save by the force of simple faith—the reply came firmly that the relic was entrusted to him as sacred, and that he had received it and retained it in all good faith. We left this Abbot, a gentleman in the truest sense of the word, with regret.

It is curious to note the tendency to express merit or divinity by figures of colossal proportions, as is so often the case, not only in Burma, but with the Jains, and sometimes even with Hindus. This practical aggrandizement of deities and others probably leads the uneducated, who are too prone to accept the symbol for the actual representation of unseen powers, to picture to themselves, not the human body with Divine attributes, but a figure possessing in reality grotesque additions which depict these attributes. It would follow that a simple Buddhist would base his conception of the "Light of Asia" on the huge models in brass and alabaster which he sees in the temples, and demand that his tooth should be in proportion. The educated men, of whatever religion, fervently deny the imputation of idolatry, asserting that the images they revere have in themselves no intrinsic power or merit, but are useful merely in calling to remembrance the attributes of those they adore; so that, while admitting paganism, they demur to being classified as idolaters by the breezy confidence of the West. And thus, seeing that it is the educated who lead religious thought, there might perhaps be more success in proselytism if further consideration were given to this subject by those who take a practical interest in it.

Leaving the Mu district, we proceeded northwards and met the officer commanding an escort of Gurkhas, with whom we hoped to travel to the jade-mines that were situated in a somewhat unsettled locality. The system then in force was that the official entrusted with the receipt of Customs valued the jade that was brought down, and presented his demand for the payment of a royalty according to a fixed percentage on this value; if the owner found this estimate too high, he was at liberty to claim in cash the amount of the estimate, when the jade became the property of Government. In this way a tolerably fair result to either side was arrived at; but the estimate at the best was merely a speculation, for until the huge lumps were cut open no exact idea of the colour and translucency was possible. The greater part of this product goes to China, where it has a quite fictitious value, based on the properties believed to be inherent in the stone. We did not reach the jade-mines, however, for, owing to the indisposition of the Commandant, the escort set out to return to headquarters, and, disappointed, we determined at least to see the Indawgyi Lake before the return to civilization.

The first sight of this large sheet of water was more mysterious than impressive. Tiny wavelets of clear water lapped a sandy beach that was crowded with myriads of minute shells; at a short distance the ripples were lost in a haze of mist blocking out the farther shore; to the left a cluster of houses topped a small promontory; to the right was a forest of huge trees, some of which lay felled and logged on the water's edge; and even when the sun asserted its sway and the landscape cleared, there was but little beauty in the scenery, and nothing of interest save the solitude of the waters between profanation of historical antiquity by its adaptation to the needs of modern life.

During the cold season of 1902 various tours were made in the districts of Lower Burma, where climate and surroundings were different from those in the north; the country is, of course, more populous, and in consequence there is greater pressure on the forests, and the forester has other duties besides exploration and protection. Exploitation is in some districts here carried out departmentally, involving an enormous amount of labour both in the field and in the office, while the plantations of teak and "khair" absorb more time than the staff can afford. The timber depot at Rangoon was supplied from the Government forests, and monthly auctions were then held with the object of controlling the price of teak. Whether this object was attained is questionable; no doubt the auctions tended to force up prices, but these, for various reasons best known to those acquainted with the working of the timber trade, do not always represent the actual market value of the wood.

The depot is served by the tide which at high-water fills the creeks that intersect it, and in consequence the elephants, when arranging the logs, worked laboriously in deep mud, and casualties were numerous. For some years past various schemes for mechanical haulage of the timber have seen the light, and may be one has been ere this adopted; but personally I was in favour of the abolition of a Government depot, being an opponent of Government-managed industries, and holding, with Professor Marshall, that Governmental intrusion into businesses which require ceaseless invention and fertility of resource is a danger to social progress, except, indeed, in those cases where both private capital and expert knowledge are lacking to inaugurate some new commercial departure that seems essential to industrial development. The demand for land in Rangoon and its neighbourhood has already justified large expenditure on reclamation, and the site of the Government timber depot is one that would probably prove to be a remunerative example of the extension of such work.

The chief silvicultural questions of that day were the advisability of extensions of plantations, and the effect of protection from fire on the natural reproduction of the teak-tree. With regard to the former, the plantations of Burma extended over an area of about 100 square miles, and had mostly been created with the object of growing timber—in this case teak and "khair"—by sowing these species together with field crops. That is to say, forest land was broken up for cultivation on condition that forest seed was sown with the field crops; and the cultivator thus had the advantage of free land, besides payment for surviving seedlings when he quitted his temporary holding. There is no doubt of the ingenuity and efficiency of the system, but it involves certain drawbacks that were perhaps not fully recognized in the past.

In the first place, the best soil was naturally selected for raising the field crops, and on such land natural regeneration of forest trees was in itself probable. If the selection had been always made in areas where tree-growth was inferior or wanting, a evening anchorage we listened with pleasure to the sounds of the village life near by, and watched the lights of the belated boats as they, too, hurried past to safe anchorages.

In April, 1901, I proceeded to England on leave for six months, and on my return found myself transferred to Lower Burma, with headquarters at Rangoon. Any description of this city as it was eight years ago would fail to be familiar to the traveller of to-day, so vast are the improvements that have been made in this short space of time; it will suffice to say that then there were neither electric lighting nor fans save in a few public buildings: for those who have lived in tropical cities before these two necessities of the West were introduced will appreciate the difference that they can make to the dweller in the East, and will agree that light without heat and cool slumber during oppressive nights are factors in maintaining physical and mental health that cannot be too highly prized.

The climate of Rangoon is equable both as regards air temperature and moisture, and the roads and public gardens display all the beauties of tropical vegetation; while above all soars the golden pinnacle of the great pagoda, visible from many miles, whether approaching by water or land. Pity it is that the Burmans, who, judging by their pleasing dress, by their beautiful work in silver and wood, have a truly artistic temperament, should have so little feeling with regard to a national monument as to permit its grand terrace to be crowded with shrines designed in such detail that the tired eye becomes confused; or that the authorities should permit the use of corrugated iron sheeting in the repairs of this or indeed in any of the ancient and inimitable monuments of Burma Under the influences of a utilitarian policy, stucco and sheet-iron shrines are springing up to replace the beautifully designed and decorated works of former years, and the Buddhist of to-day expresses his devotion in a cheque given to a contractor from Hindustan, where his ancestors, collecting the most expert of workmen, spent years in directing their labours to his liking. If the money spent on new buildings were devoted to the restoration of the old, many vanishing works of art would yet be saved to the country; or if even more of the beautiful carvings, now rotting in deserted monasteries in silent jungles, were collected where they could be seen of the people, and so serve to recall more frequently the art of the past to their memory, it would perhaps help to show that their conquerors appreciate skill and talent, and that, although at present fully occupied with public works designed to serve only material purposes, they have not lost sight of the spiritual needs of those they rule.

The interest enforced by Lord Curzon in the protection of the archæological monuments of India was surely one of the most important features of his viceroyalty. Though in practice the work is always hampered by the insurmountable difficulty of obtaining workmen possessing the spirit and the leisure of the past, and though the restorations must therefore be but makeshifts evident to all who inspect them, yet they connote an attitude infinitely preferable to the desecration of neglect or to the profanation of historical antiquity by its adaptation to the needs of modern life.

During the cold season of 1902 various tours were made in the districts of Lower Burma, where climate and surroundings were different from those in the north; the country is, of course, more populous, and in consequence there is greater pressure on the forests, and the forester has other duties besides exploration and protection. Exploitation is in some districts here carried out departmentally, involving an enormous amount of labour both in the field and in the office, while the plantations of teak and "khair" absorb more time than the staff can afford. The timber depot at Rangoon was supplied from the Government forests, and monthly auctions were then held with the object of controlling the price of teak. Whether this object was attained is questionable; no doubt the auctions tended to force up prices, but these, for various reasons best known to those acquainted with the working of the timber trade, do not always represent the actual market value of the wood.

The depot is served by the tide which at high-water fills the creeks that intersect it, and in consequence the elephants, when arranging the logs, worked laboriously in deep mud, and casualties were numerous. For some years past various schemes for mechanical haulage of the timber have seen the light, and may be one has been ere this adopted; but personally I was in favour of the abolition of a Government depot, being an opponent of Government-managed industries, and holding, with Professor Marshall, that Governmental intrusion into businesses which require ceaseless invention and fertility of resource is a danger to social progress, except, indeed, in those cases where both private capital and expert knowledge are lacking to inaugurate some new commercial departure that seems essential to industrial development. The demand for land in Rangoon and its neighbourhood has already justified large expenditure on reclamation, and the site of the Government timber depot is one that would probably prove to be a remunerative example of the extension of such work.

The chief silvicultural questions of that day were the advisability of extensions of plantations, and the effect of protection from fire on the natural reproduction of the teak-tree. With regard to the former, the plantations of Burma extended over an area of about 100 square miles, and had mostly been created with the object of growing timber—in this case teak and "khair"—by sowing these species together with field crops. That is to say, forest land was broken up for cultivation on condition that forest seed was sown with the field crops; and the cultivator thus had the advantage of free land, besides payment for surviving seedlings when he quitted his temporary holding. There is no doubt of the ingenuity and efficiency of the system, but it involves certain drawbacks that were perhaps not fully recognized in the past.

In the first place, the best soil was naturally selected for raising the field crops, and on such land natural regeneration of forest trees was in itself probable. If the selection had been always made in areas where tree-growth was inferior or wanting, a stronger argument in favour of the practice would have been forthcoming. Secondly, the plantations required continual and expensive supervision. During the first few years frequent weedings and cleanings were necessary, and later on judicious thinning alone could result in healthy maturity. The expense of such operations was calculated to affect the value of the final crop to a very serious degree, even if they could have been carried out; but neither the supervision nor the labour was available, and without these reversion to the original type of forest in the neighbourhood was but a question of time, while the dangers incidental to the creation of pure forests were also liable to assertion in insect and fungus damage, which could not be combated in a multitude of comparatively small areas scattered over a vast extent of country. There existed, therefore, very serious reasons for a careful reconsideration of the subject. It was finally resolved, after detailed inquiry, that the forester in Burma had sufficient work in tending the natural forests without undertaking the somewhat doubtful task of creating new ones on a system that Nature had in her experience not found to be suitable to the conditions she imposed.

With regard to protection from fire, it had for long been noticed that its effects were more marked in their benefit on the inferior species, on shrubs and on grasses, than on the more valuable trees which it was intended chiefly to affect. The effects of fire upon established teak-trees, young or old, was not disputed; even leaf fires of small intensity produced injuries in the base of the stems that soon caused dry-rot and other unsoundness in the heart of the timber. But not only had the question of the quality of the existing crop to be considered, but also the effect on the production of a new crop. The teak had to be aided, not hampered, in the reproduction of the species.

Speaking generally, the teak-forests of Burma may be divided into evergreen and deciduous. In the former class the most magnificent specimens of teak are to be found. They have been forced by the struggle towards the light to keep pace with and to overtop the gigantic trees common to this type of forests; but they are prevented from the reproduction of their kind, for their seed will not germinate, or at all events the seedling will not continue to exist, under the dense cover of the evergreen undergrowth. Now, by the practice of universal protection from fire, there was danger of introducing a similar condition of affairs into the other and more important type—that of deciduous forests.

The evergreen species are the most sensitive to damage from fire; they have not the power of resistance that the deciduous trees often possess, while at the same time, given suitable conditions, they tend to extend, and to so consolidate themselves that accidental conflagrations or intentional firing become alike impossible, because there is no inflammable material to feed it. As may be imagined, in the controversy that followed extreme opinions and propositions were not infrequent; but it was recognized by thoughtful foresters that there could be no general verdict for or against the practice of fire protection, but that the local circumstances of each forest must decide the case on its individual merits. On the one hand, the extension of the evergreen forest must not be unduly encouraged, nor must the drawbacks of excessive undergrowth in deciduous forests be permitted; on the other hand, the damage caused by fire to the standing stock in deciduous forests must be minimized as far as possible, and only condoned when it became absolutely necessary in the interests of the maintenance of the principal species.

The rank growth of bamboos in Burma, and its effect in checking the tree regrowth, is also a matter of very great importance to the future of these forests. It is idle to anticipate that the labours of the forester will either check or seriously diminish this evil. Here, as elsewhere, only the continuous attacks of a large population over many generations will be able to overcome the overwhelming vitality of these giant grasses. Considerable but undue stress has been laid on the well-known fact that the bamboo seeds gregariously after periods varying in the case of different varieties from thirty to sixty years, and that thereafter the clumps die down, often over very large areas. It was suggested that advantage should be taken of the temporary absence of these shade-giving plants, and of the fertilizing ashes that would be yielded by burning the dry clumps, to sow teak and other forest trees. In practice, however, though we know that the burning of a seeding area, and the dibbling in of teak seeds, might result in the creation of a valuable forest, yet such knowledge is merely academic; for it is impossible, owing to the scarcity of labour, to deal, with that promptitude which alone would command success, with the immense areas affected by seed years, more especially as Nature gives only a few months', or even weeks', warning of what is about to happen. The small patches of tree-growth resulting from experiments made in this direction show what might be done, but they also prove the very narrow limits of our powers in this direction. And yet the forests of Burma might, according to the report of an expert especially deputed for the inquiry, yield the best quality paper-pulp manufactured from bamboo at a remunerative cost. The amount of raw material available is, of course, enormous; and were this industry started, it would perhaps be the only instance on record when the demand for pulp insured the improvement of the forest, and not its destruction.

In May, 1902, we had the interesting experience of a great cyclone that blew for three days, wrecked several good ships, and caused considerable damage in the city by injury to buildings and by uprooting hundreds of avenue trees. The details that were impressed on the memory are trivial, in view of the widespread disaster. They are of the windows of the house being blown in with a loud report, and of the rooms being simultaneously flooded with water; of sheet-iron roofing skidding down the gale, threatening death to all it encountered; of attempting to reach office in a carriage that was ignominiously pinned against a wall by the wind; and, lastly, of the breaking of the boom confining several thousand logs in the Bombay-Burma Corporation's timber depot, and of their sudden appearance in the Rangoon River, driven by a flowing tide and the force of a cyclonic storm. These heavy logs, probably averaging 2 tons each, appeared to be enjoying their release and the return journey towards their mountain homes. They came in solid phalanxes, bounding like porpoises, crushing all the wooden craft they encountered, and bumping joyously against the iron steamers that lay straining at their anchors, and so passed out of sight in the gloomy night. Then with the ebb they returned; such as had not been stranded in the intricacies of tidal creeks sullenly heading downwards to the sea, unable to avert recapture, save in the case of a happy few that, buoyant in the sea-water, ended their journey, perhaps, on some remote island where axes and saw-mills were unknown.

The hot weather of 1902 saw us again at Maymyo, this time in a house made of matting, with elastic walls and flooring. It was owing to the kindness of Sir Frederic Fryer that we were able to pass some months in a better climate so far from our head-quarters. There was, however, much sickness in the station, and a change to Rangoon, with its damp warmth, from the chilly mists of Maymyo was often effective in staying the prevalent disease. I spent some pleasant days on the Strand there, in the magnificent house occupied by my friend the late Mr. Roberts, then one of the principals in the Bombay-Burma Corporation, visiting from thence various district headquarters by boat or rail to inspect offices and arrange for the next season's work; then in the commencement of the winter, while still retaining charge of my duties as Conservator in

Burma, I was deputed to Calcutta, to write the article on "Forests" for the "Imperial Gazetteer." I remained in Calcutta for about a month, and on my return started on a trip to the Andamans.

I had now completed twenty-nine years' service, and had not yet qualified for the highest pension; and I still found myself in a country where the enormous disadvantage of lack of intimate knowledge of local customs and language could only be partially made good by continuous arduous effort, and where the process of acclimatization entailed somewhat severe physical disabilities; and the question now arose, that sooner or later inevitably presents itself to every officer who has chosen foreign service as a career, whether a longer stay was worth the risks that accompanied it. In an undeveloped Province, life must necessarily be trying. Pioneer work involves the renunciation of many of the amenities of life, while sickness or accidents, in themselves trivial, may easily become serious when far from the reach of assistance. Men in the prime of their youth, and incited by the novelty of their surroundings, enjoy such a mode of life for a limited period; but when it is indefinitely protracted it becomes intolerable even to the hardiest, and a longing arises for a fixed place of abode, and a change from an existence whose sole landmarks are afforded by hurried visits to the Homeland. The question is usually decided either by financial considerations or by the prospects of obtaining more congenial work under improved conditions; but for my part I had concluded that I must leave either the Province of Burma or the Indian Forest Service. Meanwhile the Asiatic Steamship Company's boat waited at the wharf to take us to a new country, to a land of truly primeval forests inhabited by the remnant of a savage race, but ruined by the presence of thousands of India's worst criminals.

A day and a half on a slow-going steamer brings the traveller from Rangoon to the harbour of Port Blair, and perhaps it is not only to the passengers that there comes a feeling of relief at having escaped a meeting with the cyclones which apparently have their birthplace to the south, and their playground in the Bay of Bengal. Some of these passengers there were who would have been indifferent to barometric disturbances even if they had been acquainted with their theory: there were men who sat silently behind iron bars with manacled limbs, on the way to expiate crimes of jealousy or of passion by long sentences of exiles, from whence they had little hope of returning; there were others, professional criminals, who had little to lose, for they had no home—a word as sacred in India as in England—who looked upon transportation as an unpleasant episode in their career, and made light of it, while their companions were perhaps fretting against the treachery of intimates or at the failure of their revenge.

Port Blair, with its quiet, transparent water into which one may gaze fathoms deep, with its cocoanut palms and undulating hills, is always beautiful; while the coast line as it trends away in the distance, outlined by the breakers on the coral reefs or by the mountains covered thick with forest trees that rear their grey stems a hundred and more feet into the sky, produces a characteristic scenery that remains in the memory. But as soon as foot is set on this promising shore illusion vanishes, for the trail of the convict is over all; 13,000 in number, there are perhaps two free men to every hundred criminals, and the minority is guarded by armed police wherever it moves. As you walk along the roads lined with luxuriant tropical vegetation, you meet a gang of numbered slaves clad in coarse canvas, with light shackles tied to the waist; they halt, and deposit the implements of labour—axes, spades, and crowbars—at their feet, and wait with crossed hands till you pass. You enter a boat: the convict crew must be overawed by an armed officer, lest they murder the passengers and escape to freedom or death across the open sea. You sit at meals: your food has been cooked by one convict, and another stands to serve you. In short, you are never free from detected crime, and, in spite of the arrangements made to protect the lives of officials of the State in public, you know that in private you are at the mercy of any individual whose mental balance is upset by loss of liberty, or who finds his life intolerable, and desires to lose it by those quick legal methods commencing with a summary inquiry and ending even more abruptly with six feet of rope.

And if these are the sensations that the free man, still sensitive to his novel surroundings, may feel, what are those that the prisoner himself experiences? He has the advantage that his term of confinement in gaol is but short, and that the distraction of work, severe though it be, is soon afforded. But he remains even then at the mercy of the gang overseers, themselves convicts, who are in a position to make his daily life a daily torture; and if he escapes such a fate, he has still to run the gauntlet of malaria, dysentery, tuberculosis, and other minor disorders, which, if they fail to kill, will still leave lasting scars from their attacks.

In the star-shaped gaol now constructed the prisoners pass a period of probation, and, if their tempers endure the strain of silence and mechanical exercise, they are rightly considered to be trustworthy in better conditions. They are then drafted to public works — to the dockyard, to the saw-mills, to lumbering in the forest; the worst to hard-labour in the chain gangs on Viper Island, the most amenable to domestic service amongst the residents.

Another term completed, they become "self-supporters," and are given land for cultivation; or they may earn money by their labour, they may even marry a convict wife and bring up a brood with no past history, but perhaps with inherited tendencies from brains dulled by long loss of liberty, and with consciences unable to distinguish between right and wrong. Yet the best keep before them ever the prospect of return to the little hut in the native village, and dream, maybe, of the warm evenings when the sun is ripening the wheat, and when the mango groves are alive with birds; or of the flat-topped roofs in the distant hills, where the water murmurs between the fields glowing with Indian corn or crimson with the ripening millets. These are they who in emergency stand by their masters, who will risk their lives to save the shipwrecked, or will interpose their own defenceless bodies between the would-be murderer and the yet more defenceless woman and children, and who from time to time receive their reward in freedom, and return to their homes perhaps better citizens than when they left them in despair.

The climate of the Andamans is hot and damp, but the winds blow throughout the year from the north-east or the south-west, and if a house can be secured which stands open to both these breezes, there is comfort on returning from work carried on under the searching rays of the sun. Twice a fortnight the mail-steamer brings letters from the mainland, and, now that important news is signalled by aerial telegraphy, such a story as that of the coronation of His Majesty King Edward VII. being celebrated in these islands with joyous ceremony some time before it actually occurred will not again have opportunity to become current.

Except in the immediate neighbourhood of the Settlement, primeval forest covers the thousand odd square miles that comprise the Andamans and its archipelago. Where clearances of the overhead cover have been made by Nature or by man, a dense and impenetrable undergrowth springs up to prevent the recurrence of the domination of the forest-trees, whose seed falls only to be choked by thorns and dank foliage; but where that domination is still supreme there are aisles of lofty stems that block out the sunshine so completely that grass or shrubs refuse to grow on the shady ground. There are birds and pigs to keep man company in these forests.

The natives are like negroes in miniature, well-made and athletic, and they are either tame or wild. The former are employed in various works about the Settlement; they catch turtle and collect tortoise-shell and sea-slugs, they gather the crop of cocoa-nuts and edible nests, they track the escaped convict and bring him back safely to durance, unless he prefers to end a struggle with a three-foot arrow through his body. They are cheerful and pleasant people with a passion for tobacco, but they seem to be dying out as a race, perhaps contaminated by the convicts with whom they come in contact. The wild Andamanese, on the other hand, keep to the shade of their forests, and are happiest when ignored; they visit their permanent camps from time to time, and in their middens have been found relics of ancient wrecks thrown aside as of no value, for they are entering the Iron Age, and will do murder gladly for the sake of a convict's shackle or of an elephant's tethering chain. And when their camp is rushed with the object of bringing prisoners to Port Blair, in the hope that these may learn the pleasures of civilization, and thus voluntarily give up their freedom, they reply with arrows, irrespective of the rank or nationality of their seducers, to show that the proposed exchange is not to their liking. They will probably continue to exist as a tiny nation till the North Island is opened out to Western progress, and their final record will, maybe, consist of a few skulls and bones, of fish-spears and wooden drums, exhibited in museums to show to the curious and to the scientific what manner of men were those who could live happily where a European would die from starvation in the midst of that plenty which Nature has provided.

The inhabitants of Rutland Island are a finer race; they come over the sea in open canoes to declare allegiance to the British Government, and return gladly to that seclusion which wild races find so necessary to their health and existence.

The forester finds much to interest him in the Andamans, for here is a large area of forest untouched by man, and yet easily accessible from the sea, whose tidal creeks, fringed with mangrove, run far into the island. It would be difficult to find such favourable conditions elsewhere, and the fact that Andaman padauk, a timber of a beautiful red colour, is available only in these islands confers on their owners a monopoly that must enhance the value of the wood. The exploration of the North Andamans was undertaken only a few years ago by the Forest Department, whose work had till then been confined to the southern districts in the neighbourhood of the penal settlement; for it was evident that sufficient convict labour was not available to extend timber operations to the north, and it was at first considered that it would be impossible to have free labour in the islands, as this might afford too frequent opportunity for escape. It soon came to be realized, however, that there was little ground for this objection, for he would be a fortunate man who, unprovided with food or the means of obtaining it, should cross the pathless forest from south to north, and find at the end of his journey caste brethren or compatriots who would risk their own liberty to afford him a chance of deliverance.

The exploration of the North Islands and the compilation of a plan for their working disclosed the fact that about 10,000 tons of padauk and 20,000 tons of other timber would be annually available for export. The beauty of the former wood is undoubted, but experts report it to be difficult in working, so that for furniture it could not replace mahogany; they admit that for internal decoration such as panelling, staircases, flooring, etc., it is almost unsurpassed, and the large size of the timber makes it peculiarly suitable for this work. A trial contract involving the delivery of 12,000 tons had already been completed, the timber in the log at Port Blair fetching about half the price of good mahogany in London, and the greater part of this went to America, where it was much admired. That country has, however, now its own tropical island forests managed by expert and zealous foresters, and doubtless will not go abroad for what can be obtained from its home possessions. Of other timbers, some are ornamental, and others might serve well for railway sleepers after impregnation, or would be bought up in the Indian market for building native houses; and where Government possess, as in the Andamans, an excess forest capital whose reduction is advisable, so that a full rate of interest (that is, of increment growth) can be forthcoming on the remainder, it appears probable that it would pay well to accept a very moderate royalty on the surplus stock that has been accumulating during centuries, and that similarly lenient terms would provide a reasonable perpetual dividend when the forest was in good working order.

The trees now constituting the forest are large, and some of even enormous dimensions; it is reported that all are within two miles of tidal creeks, which, once reached by the aid of buffaloes or elephants, would conduct the timber without risk to one of the numerous harbours where vessels could lie in safety, but so far capital has not been attracted to this enterprise; it has perhaps been deterred by the trouble of arranging for the importation of labour from Madras, and of erecting huts and machinery for the accommodation of the workman and the conversion of the timber—in short, by all the details of starting a new industry in a new country. But it is hardly probable that this source of a good timber-supply will, now that it is known, remain for ever undeveloped, and it seems likely that, if the enterprise is undertaken with knowledge, it will prove remunerative to an unexpected degree. Meanwhile State ownership of forests can afford to wait both for the reduction of the excess capital and for the interest on the normal capital, offering meanwhile, to all who wish to read it, the excellent working plan drawn up by Mr. Todd, the Forest Officer who spent many arduous months in these wilds collecting exhaustive information about the primeval forests.

In the South Island the Forest Officer exploits the forest, and shows what may and should be done in the northern area. He has at his disposal some eight hundred convicts and twenty to thirty elephants, and has constructed tramways working by steam or bullock power to bring his timber to Port Blair; he has a timber boat that transfers elephants to the islands of the archipelago, and brings back the logs they have dragged to the creeks, and he has a sawmill on Chatham Island where timber is prepared for the use of the Settlement and for export beyond the islands. This work is on a comparatively small scale, undertaken chiefly for the requirements of the Settlement, and serving to show what might be done by an organized commercial undertaking; it is in addition to the forester's silvicultural duties of experimental plantations, of improvement fellings, and of protection, and the financial results are not by any means final. For instance, no serious timber-merchant would employ a mail-steamer of a few hundred tons to carry heavy logs, a trade for which it is entirely unsuited, and no person trading for profit would incur the useless cost resulting from the construction of tramways without skilled labour; these are examples of the makeshifts that are bound to occur in pioneer work which is undertaken primarily with a view to utilize the forest wealth, and to advertise to the world that it is available to those who will undertake its removal.

On Christmas Day of 1902 we invited a convict to tea, in defiance of all regulations to the contrary. He was a sturdy North Countryman, one of the two Europeans detained on the island, who lived in a hut of his own and filled the post of chief engineer to the sawmills then managed by the Forest Officer. His crime was that he has asserted to the death his supremacy in affairs marital; his attitude, that if again involved in such an emergency he would deem it justifiable to repeat his action. I think he enjoyed meeting his compatriots in friendly intercourse for a few minutes on one of the greatest Christian festivals, though there were doubtless reminiscences that created longings for freedom to visit once more the land of his fathers. We parted friends, and he testified his gratitude by a present of fowls and eggs the following morning. My wife took upon herself to plead the convict's cause with the Chief Commissioner when bidding adieu on the deck of the steamer that was to take us to Burma, for there was good opportunity in the clemency about to be accorded to thousands of prisoners throughout India at the approaching Coronation. But her efforts were in vain; there were, doubtless, official reasons why the prayer should not be granted, and so it was that she left the Andamans in tears. Our guest, we heard, died shortly after, and we could imagine that hope deferred had sickened his heart to death, and that he was glad of the release.

CHAPTER VIII

THE WORK OF THE INSPECTOR-GENERAL OF FORESTS

When I arrived at Rangoon, on return from the Andamans, in the New Year of 1903, a voluminous mail awaited me. From the Government Gazette confirming the appointment of a new Inspector-General of Forests, I passed through private correspondence till I reached a pile of oblong envelopes that denoted official communications; and here I found a letter from the late Sir Denzil Ibbetson, expressing a kindly welcome to the headquarters of the Government of India to officiate as Inspector-General until the retirement of the holder of that post.

It would be idle to say that I had not weighed my claims to such preferment against those of my immediate predecessor, for in any service where promotion depends on vacancies, so long as human nature remains what it is, such considerations must find place; but I had already put aside the question as settled, and my attention was at the time attracted to the vacant Directorship of the Forest School at Dehra Dun, an institution that had been engaged for nearly a quarter of a century in affording a technical education to Rangers and other subordinates of the Forest Service, a subject on which I, in common with many other foresters, possessed some definite opinions. Now the whole outlook was altered. I should be in position to direct that Director ; I should return to India, and be afforded an opportunity to travel throughout its vast forests ; I should be able to look back on the time spent in Burma as affording a pleasurable addition to knowledge that would aid in future work. And so I handed over charge of the Pegu Circle with joy, and on February 3, 1903, arrived at Calcutta, took over charge of my new office the next day, and proceeded to my initiation into its workings.

To comprehend the administration of the State Forests of India, it will be necessary to give a short sketch of the machinery of the Indian Government. The Empire is ruled by a permanent Executive Council, aided by a more numerous body of nominated Councillors, the whole under the presidency of the Viceroy and Governor-General, who holds the portfolio of Foreign Affairs. The other Executive Councillors are the Commander-in-Chief and the Ministers for the Home, Finance, Legislative, Industry and Commerce, and Revenue and Agriculture Departments. Finance and Legislation are administered by officers appointed alternately from England and from amongst the members of the Indian Civil Service ; while the heads of the other departments are as a rule recruited from that Service. In each department are Secretaries, Deputy-Secretaries, and Under-Secretaries, who also, with a very few exceptions, derive their origin from the Indian Civil Service. Each department is divided into branches, and these, in cases where special expert knowledge is deemed to be requisite, are presided over by officials who have the requisite training, either in England or through Indian experience. The heads of these branches, who as a rule are not members of the Indian Civil Service, communicate their advice to the Secretary of the department, who takes final orders from the Minister concerned, or, in case of disagreement between departments, from the Governor-General in Council. State Forestry in India is controlled by the Department of Revenue and Agriculture, and the Inspector-General of Forests is the expert in charge of its Forest Branch.

But he has also other duties outside the scope of that department. On him rests the initiative and control in the matter of forest education, and he is responsible for the correctness of the silvicultural proposals that are prepared under the orders of the Conservators for transmission to the Local Governments. Thus, not only is his advice demanded on all forest questions that are brought before the Government of India, but his orders are required in all matters affecting the professional treatment of the forests. In either case he is open to a salutary criticism which absence of local knowledge on his part would render peculiarly effective, and it is therefore of the utmost importance that he should acquire as intimate an acquaintance as possible with the varying conditions that obtain throughout the Peninsula. In respect of the two Provinces of Bombay and Madras, ruled by Governors appointed in England, and subject to only a general control of policy by the Government of India, such acquaintance was difficult to obtain; for the Inspector-

A Forest Stream, Central Provinces.

General could only visit these Provinces by special invitation of their Governments, and he received their silvicultural and other reports for information, and not for orders.

Provincial Governments showed marked jealousy of any restriction, real or imaginary, of their authority by the Supreme Government, and the visits of Inspectors were, therefore, not always welcome. There was the fear that the local staff might be tempted to look past its own Government to the Government of India; that it might perhaps accept from the representatives of that Government suggestions and opinions that would be repugnant to the provincial policy. Especially with regard to State Forestry, it was evidently considered that forest policy should be interpreted solely by provincial officials. Again, the relations of the inspecting officer with the members of his own Service were capable of presenting serious difficulties. The individual opinions of scientific experts are a most valuable asset in the decision of any new policy, and the presentment of the arguments in favour of or against such policy affords scope for much enthusiasm; but, on the other hand, acquiescence in, or opposition to, new proposals may not be entirely dependent on opinions on technical matters, and formidable obstructions may be raised by those who are impatient of outside initiative or of criticism that may be interpreted as interference with local authority. The foregoing remarks are introduced to exhibit the duties and difficulties incidental to the life of an inspecting officer. His pleasures consist in gaining experience in his profession by visiting new countries, and in having some share in introducing improvements either in management or in the conditions of service of those with whom he has been long associated; for amongst his other duties he should be the representative of a constituency with which he is intimately acquainted, and should be ready to promote its welfare whenever this coincides with those public interests that it is his first duty to forward.

Six weeks in Calcutta and a fortnight at Dehra Dun, in order to be present at the yearly examination of forest students, brought us to the beginning of April, when the transfer of the public offices from Calcutta, and the recommencement of work in the mountain headquarters of Government, necessitated a sojourn at Simla. It is not proposed to describe a Simla season, or to compile a record either of its official or social occupations; but it may be of interest to show how these impressed one official who spent six seasons in Elysium after nearly five times that number of years in the waste places of the earth.

Simla is undoubtedly the queen of mountain settlements so far as climate is concerned. Standing 7,000 feet above sea-level, near the thirty-first degree of north latitude, and far towards the west of the Peninsula, she enjoys a dry climate, and the monsoon rains are seldom excessive or prolonged. In the spring the greatest drawback is the dust, which is driven from the south and west, and sometimes obscures the landscape with a yellow haze; but the autumn weather is superb, and those who remain during the winter do not complain of the inclemency of that season. Snow falls after Christmas, but does not at that elevation remain long on the ground. The worst months are probably those of February and March, when cold winds blow with some persistency. Simla is, of course, not comparable with other hill-stations as regards beauty of scenery. Mussoorie affords grander views of the Himalaya, and so does Darjeeling; Naini Tál, in its narrow cleft among the hills, charms the eye, if it enervates the body; and Ootacamund, with its wide stretches of downs and the clustering forests in their hollows, bestows more freedom and expanse; but probably none of these possess a climate so suited to Europeans, though they may afford more facilities for enjoyment. For Simla is cramped on a narrow curving ridge with steep slopes on either side, and its "Chaura Maidan," or wide plain, is but 20 yards broad and some three or four times as long; and this will afford a basis for an estimate of other places whose breadth is not their crowning attribute. The ridge, which may be seen from miles away, attracting the eye by the extreme ugliness of its buildings, is crowded with church, assembly-rooms, and various outhouses, whose erection denotes the humane attempt to provide man and beast with shelter, but which are as out of place as they are inadequate; and, below it, swarming tenement houses cling to the hillside, where reside the majority of the 40,000 inhabitants who live on the spendings of the European community. At one end of Simla is Viceregal Lodge, at the other the residence of the Lieutenant-Governor of the Panjab; and, ensconced behind Jakko, the War-Lord, in the intervals of his martial zeal, beautifies his house with the display of those art treasures from many lands in which his soul delights. From Viceregal Lodge to the Post-Office nearly two miles of houses belong to the Government, and afford shelter, at preposterous rents, to high officials, who are believed to enjoy these dignified disbursements; the others hide where they may on the slopes of Jakko, and on other minor hills, in buildings which are, for the most part, dark and unsuitable; and they pay for this accommodation for the season any sum between £125 and £250 that their landlords can extract. Taxes are high and penetrating. Your dog, your servants, your rickshaw, your importations, are all watched by the Customs officials, and these notify in advance, even to the innocent, the fate that will follow any lapse from honesty.

Only three great personages, those before indicated, may drive on the roads of Elysium, and only this trinity enjoys the "light from the lightning," as the natives style that due to electricity; though to this there are exceptions when youth and beauty gather at the assembly-rooms, or bachelors, all young in gaiety if not in years, celebrate their mystic rites at the Club or at the Grand Hotel. The remainder of the population ride in rickshaws and burn paraffin. The rickshaw is not the five-guinea contrivance of the Far East, drawn by one palpitating wretch; it will cost you £30 or £40 to be equipped with a vehicle both smart and comfortable; and as your purse or your pride is, so will your team be; from three hillmen draped in simple cotton to five stalwart knaves bristling with buttons, silver lace, and monograms, even with crests instead of the armorial badges that should rightly be worn by these vassals.

In Simla the same things happen on approximate dates every season. The Sports Club at Annandale first revives under the genial hospitality of the Viceroy's Household, and Society lunches under the deodars on their invitation. Then follow gymkhánas, polo, and races, in due course, until the monsoon rain converts the playgrounds into shallow swamps. Meanwhile Viceregal Lodge has not been quiescent; it has satisfied itself of the allegiance of its subjects by inviting them to a Levée, and it tests their agility at a State Ball, and their appetites at a State Dinner, where one may behold the gambols of the gods or observe them relaxed by good cheer. Nor does it stay its magnificent hospitality at these official functions; it asks all to enter its doors to eat, drink, and dance, to their hearts' content, warmed the while by the genial approbation of the host and the charming courtesy of the hostess, and inspired by the gentle encouragement of graceful Aides-de-Camp.

Following this opening of the season, a thrill of hospitality runs through the Settlement. Members of Council and Generals, Secretaries and Colonels, even Deputy-Secretaries and Majors, entertain and are entertained at the evening meal, so that at eight of the clock the roads are full of rushing rickshaws, and the air resounds with yells of "Bahin háth," or "Keep to the left." Three hours later the return journey is undertaken by a still more joyous crowd: young men and maidens, light-hearted in the sparkling night; the middle-aged, happy in the recollection of good cheer and good fellowship ; and the aged, contented that they are on their way to bed without having prematurely fallen asleep during the feast. Meanwhile the Amateur Dramatics are amusing their audiences and themselves with performances grave and gay, both well staged and well acted by talented performers ; and maybe a zest is imparted to the proceedings by the fact that you are acquainted, not only with the cast, but with the audience—at least, to the extent of knowing their income and age, and also, so far as gossip can be trusted, their personal and family history to the third and fourth generations

With the monsoon arrives the season of dances and balls that continue till its close, and with it also cease the picnics to Mashobra and the neighbourhood, and the garden-parties that fill up any spare moments that may have been saved from work and play—for there is work at Simla. It has been called the "playground" of the Empire, but a reforming Viceroy directed that the word should be changed to "workshop," and took care that the term should be applicable, so much so that in the reaction that followed his departure it has been hinted that less efficiency would bring the rulers and the ruled in closer relationship—in plain language, that we should try levelling down instead of levelling up. But whatever the inspiration of the moment, it makes little difference to the toilers of the pen who stream to the various hideous public offices at ten of the morning, nor dare leave them till late in the evening, for the reason either that work is unfinished or that more is expected. Then may be seen the return of the labourers, remarkable for ostentation in reverse proportion to their importance; thus, the Member of Council strolls unassumingly to his home, the Secretary may be followed by a gold-laced orderly with a discreet despatch-box, but if you see a weary youth perched on a seventeen-hand charger, followed by a procession of coolies laden with tin coffers and typewriters, you will know that this is an Under-Secretary, who will take no rest during the night, lest India should perish, and will drive his reluctant neighbours to cards or drink by murdering their sleep with the help of the incessant ticking of his writing machine.

In India speech-making is at a discount, and only the great are given opportunity to practise this art; the majority must commit their sentiments to writing, so that they remain a record against them. And it is in writing that the slaves that fill the monumental offices of Simla and Calcutta are engaged. The vast majority still use the antiquated pen, and American systems of saving time with shorthand, typewriting, or phonograph, are not in favour. Each officer sits entrenched in a zareeba of files, for the most part in manuscript of the poorest quality, for this is not an art that is made perfect by practice. He is directed in the sequence of his labours by slips: blue, immediate by day or night; red, urgent, but not sufficiently so to interfere with food or sleep; green, early, but only as early as you can; and yellow, confidential, being what every clerk has read, but what you may not whisper to your colleagues. The wag who proposed a fifth label of purple hue, denoting to-morrow, attracted but little attention, though his suggestion met with the approval of all whose souls were not utterly deadened to a sense of humour by an unnecessarily overwhelming sense of responsibility.

The Indian official has not the time both to write and to talk, and it is a question whether the extreme verbosity and iteration of public speakers form such a pleasant or useful method of conducting public business as that of committing opinions to silent and unobtrusive foolscap; but it seems probable that an opportunity will soon be afforded in India to express an opinion on this subject from practical experience, when 352 men will take the place of the 146 previously licensed to talk in public on Imperial and local administration. These changes are certain to have a widespread effect on the Indian official; he will accept all with his usual silent loyalty, and will, without any verbal spur thereto, give his best endeavours to make them successful. But he is not debarred from retaining his own opinions as to the effects they may have on the welfare of the Indian people, though it might not be politic to express them. It would be interesting to compile a schedule of the opinions of men who know the peasantry and have lived amongst them; for this purpose only a few headings would be required, such as the following:

With regard to the population of 300 million, is it in a state of discontent with the Government, or interested in the success of unrest and sedition?

Does it understand even the principles of representative Council reform, or attach any importance to them?

Will the uneducated—that is, the vast majority—have any voice in the election of representatives on the Council?

Would they rather be ruled over by their own people or by the officers of the British Government, and have they even the slightest sympathy with, or do they expect any from, the comparatively tiny band of Indian educated progressives who have succeeded in obtaining a legal outlet for the expression of their own opinions?

The answers to these questions might go some way to furnish a reply as to whether the interests of the toiling millions of India have been fully safeguarded by this new scheme. It has been truly said that they will be if the Indian Councillors honestly interpret even to the depressed classes the aims and objects of British administration; they will not be if these Councillors discredit and harass it; and in the latter case the masses, who have had little voice in the change of system, will be much worse off than before: for the British administrator formerly stood between them and the privileged classes, from whom the Councillors will now chiefly be drawn, and if his authority is diminished, so also will be his power to protect their interests effectively. We must hope for the best from an honest attempt towards progress; if it tends to withdraw from the British administrator the most important and almost the only power left to him of initiating improvements and carrying them out in detail, the people cannot be held responsible for the consequences of transferring authority from that class which has in the past ruled with success to another class which desires to rule in the future. But Council Reform had not then been introduced, and Simla was still engaged in writing, and in this occupation I found my work. I came to it not only with experience of the requirements of Indian State Forests, but with the conviction that emoluments in the Forest Department were, as regarded Europeans, disproportionate to the value of work demanded and accomplished, and, as regarded Indians, frequently insufficient to meet the expenses of official life in the East.

The efficiency of any Service is based on various conditions, and perhaps the most important of these is the maintenance of a high moral standard; but it becomes difficult to insist on this standard unless adequate protection is afforded at least against lapses that are directly referable to unavoidable financial distress; and if such protection is withheld, relaxations of principle may occur that constitute a danger to official prestige, and easily lead to felonies punishable by the law. The grant of a salary calculated to meet the expenses of a public officer who is forced to live up to a certain social status should be therefore a primary consideration with his employers, but when taking steps to insure the payment of such salaries other points of interest are speedily brought to notice.

We are, for instance, often too ready with accusations of corruption and expressions of abhorrence with regard to the acceptance of illegal gratifications by Indians, without considering the difference between the standard of probity created by the British Government and that customary in the country before its arrival. With us, so-called illegal gratifications are penal, because such are rightly held to affect the impersonal service required by the State and the justice of its decisions; we expect an official to refrain from commerce, from speculation, from anything that may divert his attention from public to private interests; we make this a condition of his service, and punish, not only any breach of his contract, but also those who are accessory thereto. Under native rule the case was widely different; then salaries were often held to be the least part of the emoluments, and, indeed, appointments to onerous and responsible posts were often purchased, and it is but fifty years since the H.E.I.C. both ruled the country and exploited it to its own advantage. The time-honoured system of the past has to give way to the sterner morality of the present day, yet an Indian (not a Government official, who by accepting office has contracted not to increase his income by forbidden methods) sees no degradation, no dishonour, in adhering to an ancient custom, even though he may recognize the theoretical superiority of the new régime; and where this régime is not in force he continues the customs of his forefathers.

Thus, stepping across the boundaries of a native State, I once found a venerable officer who lived in a style suitable to his position, and moved amongst the people with the usual outward signs of authority. I was informed that his salary was 15s. a month, and he had recently been fined £125, or, say, fourteen years' pay, perhaps because his master considered that he could afford to contribute something to the privy purse. There is no doubt that this man was honest according to the moral code of his country and employer; but codes are various, and we cannot expect any general and instantaneous adherence to the details of any new one we may introduce. We have also a duty quite as stern as that of inflicting penalties for a breach of our laws, and that is to insure that no undue temptation has been allowed to assault the criminal; the higher the standard of probity, the greater protection should we afford against a fall. The question was whether this had been done in the Forest Department, which equally with the Police was constantly being held up to public opprobrium for the crimes of oppression and bribery; had the salaries of its officers been fixed after taking into consideration that emoluments formerly customary were now prohibited, and had they been increased in proportion with the increase of the cost of living and with the decreased value of the mediums of payment? The reply seemed to be undoubtedly in the negative.

Thirty years ago the basis of wages may have been fairly adjusted; they probably were so, judging by the ease of recruitment to the department; but since then matters had altered, as a few specimen instances would show. Then the price of wheat-flour, a staple food in Northern India, stood at about 40 pounds or more for the rupee, and other food grains at proportionate rates; the hire of a four-bullock cart was 1 rupee a day, and a coolie could be maintained for 4 rupees a month or less; while the value of the rupee was about 2s. It was now a token representing 1s. 4d.; wheat-flour oftener sold at 16 pounds than at 24 pounds, and cart-hire had been raised a hundred per cent. or more. The rise in emoluments due to so-called "reorganizations" had not kept pace with these changes, and in result the efficiency of the department was being lowered, while recruitment presented continual difficulties. In Europe competition to enter the service had practically ceased; in India desirable applicants were scarce.

An eminent Viceroy once expressed horrified surprise that every public Service in India was pressing for better conditions of service; the mental shock might have been softened had he recalled Becky Sharp's remark that it is easy to be honest on £5,000 a year, and then noted that the members of the Indian Civil Service, a body of men who make the laws of the country and apply them, and who fill most of the lucrative civil posts even outside their own service, were not averse from accepting compassionate allowances when promotion was slow, or from proposing and receiving better pensionary terms, meaning larger deferred pay; and had he also considered that those Services which did not enjoy equal advantages might be in even worse circumstances: for the smaller the income, the less is the margin for adjustment of expenditure to meet any adverse change in the conditions of daily life.

The cash requirements of the Indian peasantry are small. They live on their autumn crops, and pay the rent from the winter harvest; the homestead supplies nearly every necessary of daily life, save perhaps the cotton cloth or woollen blanket that forms the wardrobe; but when Government Service prohibits the enjoyment of home life, expenses rise to a very considerable extent, and, unfortunately, the opportunities of illicitly meeting them increase in proportion. If, then, it is pleaded that the public treasury cannot afford to pay the reasonable cost of an establishment originally maintained under more favourable financial conditions, the alternatives are obvious—to reduce the establishment either in numbers or in morality ; and if neither of these is accepted as suitable, then a third course remains, of maintaining fewer European and a larger number of Indian executive officers, leaving administration in the hands of a preponderance of the former.

The native of India, working in his own country, would, considering his expenses, be well paid at one-half of the sum required by a European to maintain his position. The house rent of the former is a trifle compared with that of the latter ; he is not pressed by custom, or even by preference, to live in the more artificial manner of the West ; he is amongst his own people, and pays market rates for his necessaries, and has no need of European luxuries ; he is not obliged to send wife and children to England for health and education, and thus to keep up two establishments on the earnings of one. It is highly probable that quite suitable Indians of education and honour could be found by degrees to fill a great many of the posts now held by Englishmen at one-half their salaries, and that such men would have more influence in defeating unrest than penal enactments and Council reforms; for they would come into closer contact with the uneducated classes—"the ignorant and emotional"—on whose prosperity British administration must be based rather than on the placidity of a small educated class, whose numbers are in comparison infinitesimal.

In a country held by an alien race, without entering into the question whether the hold is maintained by the sword or by the affection of the people, the subject race must first prove that it is competent to carry out honestly and efficiently the needful executive work under proper supervision. The grant of administrative authority should not be conferred on them as of right, but in response to approved merit, and posts conferring such authority should not be "reserved" for their occupation; they should be merely open to their attainment after practical proof of their loyalty both to the Government and to their country. And especially should their loyalty to their own country be above suspicion, for even if we pleaded guilty to the atrocities and brutalities of which we may be accused by any political visitor who in a three months' trip has unravelled all the mysteries of Hindustan, we might still pride ourselves that these are but caresses compared to the ill-treatment that their religion tolerated, and their history records, as the everyday habit of both Mohammedan and Hindu monarchs.

Such were the views which impelled me to endeavour to improve the conditions of service in the Forest Department, and I was glad when the late Sir Denzil Ibbetson gave me permission to place my arguments and proposals before him, so that they might, if approved of, be subjected to the fiery ordeal of criticism by the Finance Department of the Government of India.

CHAPTER IX

JAUNSÁR; THE SUNDARBANS; DARJEELING AND THE BENGAL TARAI

In the autumn, when the air is crisp with frost, when the Virginia creeper is hanging in crimson streamers on the deodars, and when the everlasting snows lie calm and white above the well-defined line of 16,000 feet elevation, an irresistible longing seizes the inhabitants of Simla to enjoy the beauties of Nature, together with freedom from social exigences, and they steal away in parties of two or three and more for ten days' respite from work, and from the still more exhausting pursuit of pleasure. All go to Fágu, the rest-house thirteen miles from Simla, overlooking the deep valley of Saing, and there their roads diverge: some reluctantly descend that valley, hoping for better things beyond; others pass along the Thibet road, branching at Narkanda to Kulu or to the Sutlej Valley, and the woods are full of officials and their families, relaxing even under this short glimpse of the primitive life; they would probably rather meet a bear or a pheasant than even a Viceroy, for this short holiday is all too precious to be curtailed by those amenities, whose insistent calls will be again authoritatively renewed during the Calcutta season.

We foresters, philosophers of the jungle, to quote a phrase used by a departing Lieutenant-Governor to epitomize all his sylvan knowledge, were soon out of the reach of telegrams and coloured slips, on the road to Chakráta, with the pleasant prospect of leaving it at an early date; for this is a path of unnecessary gradients and of unexpected heats, and on it there will be born no novel or inspiring thought, for it winds amongst the hills and valleys just a frequented and common highway. It is good to leave the lofty Chhor Peak, a landmark from Simla and the resort of meteorologists, and turn northwards towards still higher elevations, the little town of Taroch being the last considerable human habitation that will be met for some days. Here the Raja comes to call, and brings the inevitable sheep that accompanies the camp in its future wanderings, and whose confiding familiarity prevents even a reference to mutton; and the return visit affords an opportunity to inspect an example of an old hill-fort, with its square citadel and picturesque high-pitched roof. To cross the ridge and descend to Chagpur requires an early start, else there may be trouble when the evening frosts convert the road into a slippery track where the mules flounder helplessly, and loads are scattered, in spite of the torches lit to show the way; there will be scant leisure even to admire the dancing shadows under the silent pines when every effort is necessary to reach shelter for the night.

Some twenty marches may be made through the mountain forests of Jaunsár-Bawár, at almost any elevation that the traveller may prefer. He may wander above the tree-level in the Harki-doon, and enjoy the open air of the upland meadows; or he may hide in the recesses of the cedar and fir forests at Deota, where stands the little and ancient stone temple in its silent glade; or he may descend to the forests of long-leaved pine, on the banks of the Tons River at Thadiar, and admire the swift stream, with its waters the colour of grey-green jade, as it flows cold from the glaciers. And when at last he arrives at Deoban, the forest house that looks down on the military station of Chakráta and on the plains, he will feel regretful that a happy and peaceful time is over, and that he must descend some 8,000 feet before the time when the snow and storms of winter create a longing for the warmth of the lowlands.

Jaunsár is especially interesting to the forester, because here the coniferous forests of the Himalaya have been most carefully exploited and protected. They afford evidence of what may be and should be done over more extensive areas, not only for the growth of timber, but in order to regulate the water-supply in the plains below. The word "inaccessible," once so common in the forester's vocabulary, has now almost disappeared from it; in the past it was applied to those areas whence there were no exits for timber; to-day it would be difficult to find localities where exits have not or cannot be made. Winding paths through precipices, tramways and ropeways, sledge-roads and water-slides, all testify to the energy of the Englishman when living in a good climate where no physical exertion is too strenuous; and of these the water-slides are particularly fascinating Imagine a trough the width of a railway sleeper that runs round precipices, and, supported on trestles, hangs over abysses, and stretches sinuously from the heights above to the river beneath; at the upper end stands a man, who places sleepers one by one in the trough, at the same time watching that the water-supply shall be sufficient to cover its floor. The sleeper hurtles down the incline at first with prodigious speed; then, collecting the water in front till it forms a cushion, its velocity is checked, and a curve of sparkling foam streams from either side till this automatic brake removes itself, allowing speed to be again gathered, and after a time again checked.

It is fascinating to watch the thin line of trough curving away into the distance, and adorned at intervals with the brilliant waterspouts that mark the position of each descending sleeper, and then at the end of the trip to see these leap from the slide into the river, and rise from a prolonged dive to take the way to the Jamna River and to the waiting railway. On the farther journey they encounter many adventures: some are gripped by whirlpools, where they helplessly revolve; others are jammed between rocks, to be gradually ground to fibre; others, again, remain stranded on the banks or heap themselves on islands in midstream. And then come the salvage men, naked save for a scanty loin-cloth, under their arm an inflated goatskin, who cross the fiercest current to reach the straying individuals of their flock. They are safe in the water so long as they keep fast hold of the life-buoy, but danger is before them if they lay it aside when landing on some rock in order to relieve a jam of piled-up timber; for it may happen that the key-stone of the obstruction gives way without sufficient warning, and the man, helpless without his float, is overwhelmed in a jarring mass of sleepers as the flood carries them away.

There is some shooting to be had in Jaunsár and a useful spaniel will find many pheasants in the course of a march through the forest, where also there are barking-deer and panthers. But, since the great man-eater was killed many years ago by Mr. Osmaston, tigers have not been found in these forests. Many blood-curdling tales are yet told of this monster, some of them, no doubt, mellowed by time; but the simple facts attending his death are in themselves quite unusual enough to merit record. Mr. Osmaston was taking an evening walk with a companion in search of sport, and the two separated to command opposite sides of a small ravine, in the hope that some animal might be hiding there. Their expectations were not unfounded, save that the animal was the man-eater, who promptly seized on Mr. Osmaston's companion. The youth's cry for assistance was answered by Mr. Osmaston with two shots that killed the tiger on the spot, and, fortunately, his victim recovered in course of time, though severely mauled in the head. The scene of the occurrence is pointed out to this day by the people of the neighbourhood, who are still grateful for their timely deliverance from this tyrant of the forest.

From Jaunsár to the Sundarbans, from the sources of the Jamna to where its waters, mingled with those of the Ganges, flow into the sea, is a long cry, for it includes a railway journey of nearly thirty-six hours, and a descent of several thousand feet, before the launch lying in the canal at Calcutta is reached. For the tidal waters, which are often rough with cyclonic storms, a stiffer, more powerful boat is required than in the fresh-water highways of India; and here again the Chittagonian Mohammedan is in charge, and the chant of the leadsman sounds strangely familiar. No beauty of architecture or of boat design need be expected in the Sundarbans; the people live in huge beehives thatched with palm-leaves, and their boats do not show, as in the farther East, any signs of artistic skill. The well-to-do Bengali is seldom attractive to his visitors; his assumption of European dress and of a knowledge of the English language lays him open to criticism which is perhaps undeserved; for how should he believe that he appears to our eyes more charming when he takes a proper pride in his national costume and in the soft language of his country?

The Bengali of the Sundarbans, however, does not follow Western fashions; a scanty loin-cloth is ample covering to his perspiring body, for such a dress is adapted to his severe climate and arduous work. He is engaged in supplying Calcutta with timber and fuel, with matting, and with palm-leaves for thatching; he is the slave of winds and tides, and awaits their pleasure. If he lands, he must be on the look-out for tigers, for in these forests some seventy or eighty human beings are annually killed for food; and as the narrow creeks fringed to the water's edge with mangroves are passed, you may see the melancholy records, bushes hung with scraps of many coloured cloths, that serve to mark, not so much the death of a companion, as votive offerings from the survivors.

It is a pity that this hard-working people should be also such adepts at illicit timber-trading. At that time the forest had practically been depleted of mature timber by raiders from hundreds of boats that lay secretly up the innumerable creeks, and hid their booty under a covering of innocent fuel and palm-leaves; while the forest subordinates, sitting at the receipt of custom, grew rich on their share of the spoil. To check the trade in timber and fuel of a district where the people depend for their livelihood to a great extent on the forest, and on whom also depended in a great measure the supply of these commodities to the capital of India, was a delicate task, and its accomplishment reflects credit on those that carried it to completion. To-day there are few thieves, because the risk of detection is too great, and perhaps fewer wealthy subordinates, because a source of income has been removed; the fellings are confined to one area, and their produce leaves the forest marked and paid for; the registered and numbered boats have fixed trade routes, and the Forest Officers are provided with more comforts and better pay in their lonely and arduous lives.

The Sundarbans serve as watering-places to the residents of Calcutta, but to explore them a private launch is a necessity; it is impossible to do so from a passenger steamer running to fixed times. From such a launch all the beauties of the misty sunrise and of the vivid sunsets can be enjoyed, and a run taken to the sea-face, and thence a walk along the sandy stretch, with its line of refuges for shipwrecked mariners, or through the dry forests that fringe the coast. This will be found more enjoyable than ploughing knee-deep amongst the spiky roots of the "sundri" trees, armed to the teeth in case of a sudden assault from a hungry tiger, and especially is the breeze blown from the sullen Bay of Bengal preferable to the hot silence of the tidal forests.

The creeks are full of fish, and of fishermen who use nets with skill and success. They have a curious custom of training otters to their service; these animals are secured by a girth to a boom projecting over the gunwale, so that they rest on the surface of the water and can be released so soon as occasion arises. The pack then, after the manner of otters, extend in line across the creek, and drive the frightened fish headlong into the nets, when the otters are again tethered and rewarded with some savoury morsel. In open dugouts may be seen rows of lugubrious cormorants sitting awaiting the order of the paddler, and this is conveyed with emphasis as each bird is pushed into the water, to return after a time with a fish in his beak. A ring on the neck prevents the bird from swallowing his prey, so that he receives for his labour only a fixed wage, and, however skilful he may be, he must go hungry till the fishing is over. There is a great fish-market at Khulna, the chief town of the district, and baskets of fish of assorted sizes, of huge prawns, and of crabs, are daily despatched in the fish-mail to Calcutta. The inhabitants are to have a fresh-water supply of their own at some future day; at present low ebb-tide is marked by the arrival of hundreds of women on the river-bank, who bear away in earthen pots the sweet muddy waters of the Ganges before the return of the salt water from the sea. To live in a boat in the Sundarbans is charming, for you have the means of escape under your feet; to live on land must be horrible in the extreme, and from this fate at least the Forest Officer is spared.

Everyone who has been to India knows Darjeeling; thousands visit it yearly if only to catch a glimpse in the far distance of the highest mountain in the world, though of course Kinchinjunga is infinitely more striking on account of its proximity. But it is perhaps not altogether to be regretted that the frequent clouds at Darjeeling clothe this magnificent mountain with mystery, and even at times hide it from view; for were it otherwise familiarity might breed contempt in some, and in others a painful sense of inferiority under the calm stare of this majestic hill. During ten days of a clear, frosty Christmas we enjoyed an uninterrupted view of the Himalaya, most charming, perhaps, when framed in the evergreen foliage along some forest road, or when the precipitous mountain-sides were barred with many colours at evening.

As is frequent in European hill-settlements, the forestry question was of importance. In Simla it is the fuel-supply that gives trouble; in Darjeeling the milk-supply adds to the difficulty. It is the primitive custom of the East to turn into the forest herds of cattle of mixed sexes, and abstract from them on their return such milk as may be available. The habit is a cheap and nasty form of dairy-farming.

The cost of upkeep of a cow reaches to about one shilling a year, the animals are unclean and half starved, and from unsupervised interbreeding they are of inferior quality, so that it would be a good cow of this description that would yield 3 quarts of milk a day; while milking-time is a revelation in insanitary practices to those who are acquainted only with European dairy procedure.

The stall-feeding of cows and the disposal of their milk under municipal direction is no doubt what the residents of European settlements in the hills should insist upon in their own interests, and this system, too, is what the forester ardently desires. He wishes to be rid of the herds of cattle which prevent the natural regeneration of the forests; which tread the open slopes into innumerable tracks, each becoming in the rains a small torrent that in course of time washes away the soil to the bare rock; which browse on the shrubs that hold together the loose soil on the landslips: for he is responsible for the sylvan amenities of the settlement, and it is his duty to point out any dangers that may be menacing it from neglect of silvicultural rules. A glance at the northern slopes near Darjeeling, and at the records of disasters in the past, will show what sort of dangers may result from cattle grazing on unsuitable ground, and unbiassed opinions may be formed as to whether a cheap supply of milk of questionable purity is worth the damage that it may entail.

The whole question of grazing in India is one of vast importance, for the progress of any country may be estimated by the treatment of its cattle, and land must be almost valueless if its best use is to supply unregulated grazing to inferior animals. At first in any country, when population is scarce, there are large areas available where half-wild herds may roam harmlessly; gradually their range is restricted, and eventually a larger population find a more remunerative use for the land, while more careful breeding and stall-feeding provide a better return from the cattle. India is in the middle stage of restriction of area; the best breeds, which it is desired to maintain pure, are even now no longer forest-fed, and Nature intervenes to wipe out by scarcity and pestilence millions of the others whose chief value is the supply of hides of a vastly inferior description, and bones that serve for manure. In times of scarcity the forests are indeed thrown open for the grazing of these miserable beasts, but only those in the neighbourhood benefit; for how shall the others, already weakened by hunger, complete the march through a desert country, and how recruit their strength on the coarse grasses the forest provides? It will be well when the third stage of cattle-breeding is reached, when the Indian peasant devotes his attention to the well-being of a few animals, and attempts to provide for them within the homestead: for now in famine times he tries to save all, and loses all; while even the efforts made by the Government to supply fodder are often rendered futile by the vast numbers of animals it is attempted to save.

Below Darjeeling extends the Tarai, and the tea-gardens of the hills look down on those of the plains. The country is one of watercourses, which often display unexpected violence at flood-time, when much damage is done to railway bridges and embankments, and silt and stones are deposited, to the detriment of the hardly-won gardens. These disasters have their origin in the hills of Sikhim, and a recent examination of the forests of that country showed that up to a level of about 7,000 feet the forests had been much cut over, so that the silt and boulders that descended to British territory represented, to some extent, the surface soil and the underlying stratum of Sikhim fields. It would be well both for the Sikhim peasantry and for the tea-planters if this evil could be remedied. But the same difficulty presents itself farther west, where Bhutan has encouraged Nepalese settlers who destroy the forest without providing any adequate protection to the exposed soil by terracing or draining; it is, in fact, prominent in all Provinces where the sources of the water-supply are outside the control of the British Government, and that, unfortunately, is but too frequently the case.

In the olden days we possessed ourselves of the fertile plains, and refrained from following the defeated foe to his fastnesses in the hills; we did not comprehend that the fertility of the land we took possession of depended, to a great extent, on the control of the water-supply exercised by the forest above, nor did we anticipate that the quietude that followed our rule would so shortly lead to an increase in population, and that this population would find vent for its energies, on the one hand in destroying the forest, so as to permit of extended cultivation, on the other in the inauguration of industries whose estimates of profit would be based on a continuation of the physical conditions that their promoters were acquainted with. It has taken a generation and more to open our eyes to the necessity of protecting the catchment areas of our watercourses, and we find ourselves now in the predicament that we are bound to further the interests of the industries we have encouraged, while at the same time we demur to interference with the rights of those native States that possess the key to the position. A way out of the difficulty will surely be found as time goes on ; it would more speedily be discovered were British capital attracted to industrial enterprises in India: for then the water-power that now runs to waste would become a most valuable asset, and no doubt the native Princes would find it worth their while to permit the regulation of its supply where this is most easy to accomplish—namely, at its source.

There are rhinoceros and bison in the Bengal Tarai, but at the time of our visit these had become so scarce that shooting was prohibited. The Máhárájá of Kuch Behar, whose palatial residence and estate adjoins the Government reserves, was an ardent and hospitable sportsman, and the head of game had become insufficient to afford diversion both to himself and to his guests; the planting community had also, in self-defence, thinned down these animals considerably, and, as it is the unexpected that happens most frequently in the forest, it was hardly surprising that we should meet these beasts when quite unprepared for an encounter. We had the pleasure of watching for some time a bison, who in the absence of prohibition would probably never have been seen, and certainly would not have been so accommodating; and we for a time awaited the pleasure of a rhinoceros whose bulk appeared to block the width of the forest path, but who ultimately decided to permit our escape, though our elephants had already fled, their drivers taking full advantage of the well-known distaste of elephants for rhinoceros. That dislike, however, is not so pronounced as to cause the elephant to flee when none pursueth, and we formed no good opinion of the mahouts of Bengal, in comparison with those of Northern India, after this occurrence; for we knew from experience that, though the latter might on very rare occasions demur to taking the sportsman into danger, they would never leave him there alone to save their own skins.

There is excellent fishing on the river boundary between Bengal and Assam, and in other streams, and enthusiasts would have no difficulty in getting good sport. For shooting, a stanch elephant is a desideratum, but a great deal might be done on foot or on horseback. Tigers are frequent, but the grasslands extend over so wide an area that in the winter months tracking is almost impossible, save in the wide stretch of sandy watercourses, where in the early morning tigers are sometimes found basking in the warm rays of the sun. The ideas of the Bengali with regard to shooting over a bait are distinctly amusing. We entrusted ourselves to an aged "shikari," who placed us in a leafy bower, so large that a bridge-party might have been accommodated. The staircase by which we approached was in itself enough to frighten any domestic animal, but we said nothing that might hurt the feelings of one who had done all he knew to provide sport in a manner suitable to our dignity. At any rate, this attempt was better than another we were shown some days later. This was a permanent erection with a wooden roof, perched some 30 feet above the ground, and reached by a rickety ladder; it seemed adapted for the lookout of a fire-guard, but it was not conceivable that there was an animal in the forest who did not know of its existence and give it a wide berth.

CHAPTER X

THE SUTLEJ VALLEY; THE CENTRAL PROVINCES AND OUDH

THE season of 1904 was spent in Simla, as were those of the two following years. The question of the improvement of conditions of service in the Forest Department still occupied attention, and various minute calculations were carried out with the object of comparing the pay and prospects of Forest Officers with those of other Indian public departments recruited in England, excepting always, of course, the Indian Civil Service. It would be wearisome to attempt to follow even generally the course of this inquiry; it will suffice to say that to the late Sir Denzil Ibbetson was due one of the most important changes ultimately made, that of substituting personal or incremental pay for the grade promotion hitherto in force. The acceptance of this system removed the inequality of remuneration caused by the varying casualty rates in each Province; it enabled an officer to look ahead with a certainty of promotion, and it did away with the too eager desire for the departure of colleagues that would result in a perhaps too long deferred rise in salary.

But the work was not completed with the acceptance of a system—it required the filling in of details; and this caused reference to Local Governments, and prolonged correspondence that was not completed till the issue of the Secretary of State's orders in 1906. The result was a marked improvement in prospects, but not contentment; for though the pay was raised so that each officer attained a salary of £1,000 a year in the twentieth year of his service, while his average pay amounted to about £600 during that period, yet administrative officers were not placed on an equality with those of corresponding responsibility in other departments, while the head of the department received no increase of his maximum salary. Such matters, together with those affecting pension, will no doubt be righted when future representations are sympathetically considered. The fact that the rules of the so-called "Uncovenanted" Services were originally drafted with the intention of recruiting these services in India from Indians, and that they are now for the most part manned by officers appointed under covenant in England, who possess as good an education and attainments as any in the country, must some day be more fully acknowledged; in short, it is not so much equality in emoluments that is aimed at, but adequate payment for the higher attainments now insisted upon, and thereby a more practical distinction between the men for whom the "Uncovenanted" Service rules were drafted and those who are now invited to enter that service from Universities, colleges, and other institutions, in England.

It was inevitable that great improvements should

have been already made in this direction in the past, and the law of supply and demand will probably continue to compel further improvements in the future. Meanwhile the young Englishman, provided that he is prepared to forego all ambition, may now enter the Forest Department with a certainty of receiving a salary that will allow him to live in comfort, and he may enjoy a pleasant existence if he is fond of his profession and takes an interest in any science cognate to forestry or in any sport that the country affords—provided also that he escapes the attacks of those tropical disorders that are particularly common in his calling. Against such risks there can be precautions, but not immunity, for malaria and dysentery do not appear either to be deterred by the stronger physique or invited by the weaker.

In the autumn of 1904 we started to visit the forests of the Sutlej Valley. The rather dreary road to Narkanda may be negotiated in a rickshaw, two sets of coolies covering the forty miles in about seven to eight hours; and the next march to Bághi can be completed the same day if desired, landing the traveller, fifty miles from Simla, in one of the most beautiful forests of the hills. Beyond Bághi few Europeans are met, and the forest and district houses are usually unoccupied; but tents sometimes prove convenient, and are, if the main-road is left, indispensable. The road is badly graded and rough, and in some places too narrow for the flocks of laden sheep that are met in the autumn; for at this time the dwellers on the Roof of the World bring down their produce, to return later on with goods from the plains.

There is an annual fair at Rámpur, the capital of Bashahr, which is opened by the Rájá in state, and here the specialities of Kulu, Thibet, and Ladákh, may be purchased, chiefly woollen cloths and rugs, heavy and warm. The Rájá is an aged man who speaks English well, and was a great sportsman in his day; he has no son, and has, in common with many Indian Princes, the unhappiness of seeing in his heir, not a direct descendant, but a relative from the neighbouring State of Tehri. The Bashahris are a stupid people who cannot realize that events are happening around them. They have once of late years broken out into an absurd revolt that yielded to the presence of a few police; and a short time ago they ambushed a Forest Officer, and succeeded in shooting his dog. They appear to imagine that by such misdeeds they will overawe the British Government, and the punishment that is meted out to them no doubt takes their innate foolishness into account.

The Hindustan-Thibet road is known to all who travel in the Panjab hills, and is not of much interest either as regards scenery or sport, but it is of the greatest importance as regards the forests on either side of it. These control the watershed of the Sutlej River, and are leased from the Raja for about £650 a year. Under scientific treatment they bring in a large revenue, a fair proportion of which is now spent on improving the roads and bridges in the State, and thus facilitating intercourse with the surrounding countries. The forests consist principally of cedar and pine, the former being of great size and beauty, especially in the temple groves, where they are protected as sacred. It is sad when

The Baspa Valley.

such noble stems have to be felled to make way for the regeneration of their kind, for one knows that the commercial instincts of the present day will never permit the growth, through future ages, of similar giants of 20 feet in girth or more; their successors will be allowed to attain only a measurement of about one third of that circumference, and will be cut off in their early maturity at the age of about a century and a half.

Above Kilba, the Baspa River flows into the Sutlej, and the traveller will be well advised to follow its course into the mountains, for he will be rewarded with a glimpse of a high-level village perched on the mountain slopes below the black rocks, and almost darker oaks and firs. At its feet a narrow valley twists through meadow-lands, dotted with walnut-trees, and the river loses itself in rugged forests ending in precipices and snow. We contemplated crossing the watershed between the Ganges and Sutlej Rivers, but the weather forbade; a cyclone descended on our tents and snowed us in for three days, while the villagers kept us from freezing by supplying braziers of live charcoal; then, as the skies cleared, we fled to the south, were overtaken by another storm, and finally drove in rickshaws into Simla, over fifty miles of snow, in two days, our men's feet paddling in the freezing slush until we ached to hear them. During this trip we lost two mules, killed by a panther; another was seriously injured by a falling rock; while one man was killed by falling through the flimsy balustrade of a wooden bridge. It is a six weeks' journey from Simla to see the Sutlej

Valley at all in detail, and during that time about 400 miles may be walked, even only when changing camp; the inspection of forests and the pursuit of partridge and pheasant may easily lead to double that distance being traversed.

To spend Christmas and the New Year in camp in the Central Provinces, as we did in 1904, and again in 1906, affords unqualified pleasure. At that season the country is dry, while in the Tarai it is still damp; and the chilly nights are followed by balmy warmth. On our first tour we explored the Bálaghát forests, where Mr. Percival was then the officer in charge, and he knew the country as only a good sportsman would. The forests of the Central Provinces, extending over more than 20,000 square miles, are too vast for any but a superficial acquaintance by means of short visits; but those who have spent their lives in them speak of the country with an enthusiasm that finds an echo in the heart of any listener who appreciates the freedom that is implied by endless wooded hills, and by Nature unhampered by the pressure of population. But even here it will not always be so. The Province has long since been circumscribed by railways, which are now commencing to throw out feeders towards its centre; and when there are outlets for the immense supply of forest produce to those adjoining territories that have already consumed their own, when there is cheap carriage for the mineral wealth of the country to the seaboard, when the wasted water-power has been harnessed for industrial purposes, and, lastly, when population increases as a natural consequence of a demand for more men, then will follow restrictions in the areas open to the wanderer, and the prosperity of civilization will, doubtless, take the place of the content due to the infinitely small requirements of the jungle people.

The forests have suffered in the past from frosts and from fires. The former evil can only be mitigated by the encouragement of a healthy stock, and care against unduly opening it out. The latter has been overcome by the personal influence and efforts of the Forest Officers, and in response thereto the hills are thickly covered with a regrowth of "ṣál" trees that is almost visibly improving the soil by means of the protection offered against sun and rain—at least, where the grazing of cattle can be regulated or excluded. The interesting question now sometimes arises, how this existing stock may be harvested so as to make way for the improved crop of the future, and the reply remains dependent on the demand that exists for the material of the fellings. It cannot all be sold, for there is no use for it; even the alternative of giving it away does not provide sufficient inducement to anyone to undertake the expense of removal; and so it happens that in places the forester may have to wait for progress because he is ahead of his market, consoling himself with the knowledge that if in the East he happened to be behind it he would have found even greater difficulty, and have, perhaps, encountered the risk of having to retire from a position that he was not able remuneratively to fill. There is as yet, however, no land pressure in the Central Provinces; hundreds of square miles of forest lie ready for the entry of the future agriculturist, and the increase of population and the diminution of the forest area will make the residue doubly valuable in the future.

An inspecting officer has no jurisdiction and no territorial charge, and such shooting as he obtains is given to him by the courtesy of those he visits. In this, as in many of my journeys, much hospitality of this description was shown. Mr. Percival had tigers driven up for us, and some were duly bagged; one tigress in particular furnishing a lively scrap with the two inferior elephants at our disposal, for neither would face her, and both were bitten in the hind-quarters, when they pranced about so that the ground was littered with various impedimenta of the chase, and it was a marvel that Mr. Percival at last managed to kill her. On another occasion we had the satisfaction of seeing a heavy tiger charge across the open and fall dead at the foot of the "machán," a most fascinating and invigorating spectacle.

I was also out for three days after bison, tracking on foot with Gonds, the cheery aboriginals of this part of the Province; and I enjoyed the early start before dawn, and the day spent in their company, learning what they had to teach of woodcraft. I have never seen any European who could compete with the Indian tracker in the forest, and most of us, surfeited with civilization, cannot detect even what is pointed out; while as to a sense of direction, we have it not, and it is good sometimes to feel inferiority to a savage who will strike a bee-line for home through the pathless jungle, and arrive without a mistake, for such feelings tend to bring us once more on to the common level of human nature. The forest was so dense at this time of year that it was difficult to distinguish the sex of the bison even at short range. The trackers would not venture any assertion lest they should lose their reputation; they would swear to the footprint, but not to one animal amongst several. Luckily, my victim was a male, and I escaped the fine that one Forest Officer had to pay as a result of failure to recognize sex. But the bison is almost too good an animal to kill; he is charming to hunt, but his size and his beauty are such that he presents an almost irresistible appeal for mercy from the hunter.

On the second trip we proceeded to the Raipur District, then in charge of Mr. A. Lowrie, a gentleman who possessed the fullest confidence of the jungle people and an unrivalled knowledge of their ways, so that the tour was of special interest. Mr. Lowrie was in addition an accomplished sportsman who knew every mile of his large charge, and how to bring driven tigers up to the guns. Our party shot several, and missed perhaps as many, but the regret at allowing a tiger to escape from a line of guns can never be so acute as that felt by the solitary sportsman at the failure of his individual efforts; in the former case such a contretemps may only cause amusement, and I have even known unrestrained laughter to follow on the discomfiture of the sportsman who has failed to take advantage of undeniable chances.

Mr. Lowrie was also kind enough to send his trackers with me after buffalo, and I had many an interesting walk through the forest on the trail. More than once a bull was suddenly detected, standing morosely in thick cover, only to dash away with a snort before the rifle could be raised; for these beasts are wary and have keen scent and hearing, and the cunning displayed in doubling back on their trail, so as to keep it within view, is a well-known attribute that increases the danger in tracking a wounded animal. Yet ultimately the hunter's luck again descended. I was following a trail on an open plain covered with knee-high grass and shrubs, when we heard a sound as if of the approach of a cavalry squadron at full gallop, and in a few seconds a procession of three bulls came in sight. As usual, the smallest was leading, and the heaviest bringing up the rear; they passed at about 30 yards distance, so close that a neck shot was easy, and one stumbled on to his head, shaking the earth with his fall. The second bullet struck the next largest in the body, but two days' tracking failed to recover him, and it appeared probable that he soon recovered from the wound, as it did not seem to hamper his movements in any way.

The forests of Raipur have a great future before them; they are exceptional in the value of their stock and in the facilities they will enjoy from future railway construction; but what was of most interest was the attempt that was being made to establish the cultivation of lac as a forest industry. As is well known, the lac of commerce in its various forms is the production of a minute insect which in very early infancy fixes its proboscis into the tender twig of a suitable tree, and thenceforward passes its life in the same position, occupied in the absorption of savoury saps and in the excretion of valuable resin. With this resin a cell is formed in which is a solitary but willing prisoner, and in this cell, too, the insect dies, after having given birth to a numerous progeny that repeat the life-history of their ancestor. In former days it was the lac dye that was of value, and the memory of these times is still perpetuated in the colour called "lake" by artists; at present it is the resin that is sought after, and the elimination of the crimson dye, which consists really of the mortal remains of the mother insect, is a problem that has not been quite successfully solved.

The period of swarming of the young insects is for them a time of stress: some are killed by sun or rain; some are devoured by insects or birds; others, again, may not survive the painful march to a proper food-supply. And here it is that man may intervene by breaking off the lac-laden twigs before the exit of the young has commenced, and tying these in the tender shoots of suitable trees, by watching the new crop, and by affording protection against the enemies of the helpless insects. It was, of course, also well known to the forester that the best lac grows on certain species of forest trees, but the difficulty was how to control its cultivation on such trees, that grow scattered throughout a large area. In open village lands this problem presented no such difficulty, for the trees were under constant observation, yet the increasing value of the commodity, that now leaves India to a yearly value of hundreds of thousands of pounds sterling, justified every attempt made to increase its yield. Mr. Lowrie was able to solve the difficulty by the establishment of forest villages, each with a large area of forest set aside for its use; and within this area the settlers made their own arrangements for individual ownership of numbered trees, for the sowing of the insect crop and reaping of the resin harvest, and received in remuneration a proportion of the lac they had gathered. It is a system that, when perfected by experience, will have laid the foundation of a new forest industry over a large tract of country hitherto unexploited for this purpose, and thus conduce both to increased prosperity in the country-side and to a considerable improvement in the forest revenues.

From Raipur we went to Biláspur, a most fascinating district, where was most vividly exemplified the effect of well-wooded hills upon the perennial streams that rippled through the country, and also the results that might follow on excessive grazing. Fortunately, here the cattle of the agriculturist do not require to enter save in times of stress, but the professional grazier and breeder asserts his claims to ruining the forest for his convenience or profit; it is, happily, easier to deal effectively with such commercial enterprises than with legitimate demands for agricultural requirements, even when these are excessive, else were the State forests but grazing-grounds for the benefit of the members of a lucrative profession.

The Biláspur forests are ideal as a resort for the sportsman who leads the simple life; there are many tigers and panthers and some bison. The swamp-deer here grow immense antlers, while their habits approximate so closely to those of the sámbhar, and their hides and horns bear so striking resemblance to those of that deer, that the question arises whether there did not exist hybrids between the two species. In Northern India, where the swamp-deer live in the localities indicated by their name, the type is quite different in many noticeable ways, and the subject would repay further investigation. The broken and hilly ground renders it possible for much foot-work to be done in Biláspur, and the beauty of the sylvan scenery is another recommendation in its favour. We shot two tigers under the careful supervision of Mr. Morgan, the Forest Officer, and on three mornings and evenings endeavoured to come to terms with a large male, who proved too cunning, but who afforded much more interest than if he had been driven out to a line of guns. There are also memories of a bear that visited the camp, and retired amidst a hail of ineffective bullets and much laughter, as well as of a phantom panther that ran the gauntlet of two shots in the dusk. A most enjoyable forest, and one that would be revisited with pleasure.

From the Central Provinces we went to Oudh, where there was much interest in revisiting the forests after some years' absence; for it is only thus that progress can be fully recognized, and it is astonishing how little those who live year after year with the same trees will notice their growth. At a place in the neighbourhood of Chorgalia stood a sál forest of quite remarkable vitality, where yearly measurements of numbered stems were taken, showing a girth increment of nearly three-quarters of an inch; there a venerable and able administrator once said to me that I was wasting my time in such investigation, for he had seen the trees for forty years, and there had been no change during that period! The average age in that forest was fifty years, and the gradual change from, say, 12 to 70 feet in height had made no impression on a brain that could recall faces and incidents with startling accuracy, but took no useful notice of the vegetable life around. The thought could not be repressed that administrators responsible for the forest wealth of a Province, but incapable of recognizing the growth of its woodlands, were unlikely to be able to check their disappearance; and again was vividly presented the difference between individual trees and the community of which they form part. Even a Viceroy, burdened with the responsibility of both foreign and home politics, will notice the removal of some favourite tree under which his camp of idleness has been pitched, and will pause to mete out condign punishment to the offender; but it seemingly requires a trained eye to remark the sequence of forest maltreatment that has terminated, perhaps, in a landslip wiping out fertile fields, and setting a landmark for the next score years on the country-side.

But the forests of Oudh were flourishing; they had almost passed through their period of weeding and cleaning, and were ready for the selection treatment that was to follow. The "sál" tree is all-powerful in its natural habitat, perhaps chiefly by its forceful growth in favourable conditions; it covers the soil with vigorous celerity, its seeds are blown, ripe for germination, whirling in the monsoon winds, to alight on any open spot, and hide it with seedling growth. There, once settled, the plants die down annually to earth level while the root system is engaged in seeking to perfect itself by reaching permanent moisture, till success is proved by the sudden vigorous growth of stems many feet in height and of sturdy girth. Then at once begins in the even aged groups the struggle towards the light; those individuals that are passed in the race remain alive, but quiescent; the victors spring up to rapid maturity, and so, though the groups are of the same age, the trees are of varying sizes, the place of the larger as they disappear being taken by their brethren, just as the gaps formed by the fall of each giant of the forest are at once either carpeted with eager seedlings, or filled up by plants that have been waiting their turn, perhaps, for a generation.

It may be that there is a better way of treating such a forest than by anticipating with the axe the selective process of Nature, and it is right that experiments should be made in this direction; for it is no doubt inconvenient that regeneration should be going on over the whole of a forest area at one and the same time, and it is evident that a better restriction of the various size-classes to various areas would be more business-like. It is in such investigations that the interest of Indian forestry asserts itself, and such interest is inexhaustible; for we have not only a few species to deal with, as in Europe, nor have we a forest literature compiled by generations of able observers whose attention has been concentrated in relatively small areas; nor (and this is most important of all) had we till recent years any central institution where the results of the investigations of zealous foresters might be recorded for the use of their colleagues. Often such knowledge lies hidden in reports or note-books, or has been even more deeply buried in the brain of those who had learnt from Nature some of her secrets—so much so that it has happened that experiments long since carried out have again been proposed as necessary novelties years after, showing that there has been no record of knowledge gained, and therefore no full utilization of the work of our predecessors.

In 1904 and during the next two years I had the pleasure of a yearly visit in April to the Pátli Doon, where Mr. L. Mercer was then Conservator of Forests. The few days spent in these well-known jungles were always a delight, occurring as they did at the pleasantest springtime, when in Northern India the overpowering vitality of the forest was awakening. Good sport, too, we enjoyed, roaming with rod or rifle in early morning and late evening along the river-banks or at the foot of the hills; and I shall always cherish memories of a tussle with one big tiger in the Shishamkáta Forest, and of meeting another at earliest dawn over his kill, when the silence of the forest gave no cause for suspicion on the part of even the wariest of its inhabitants. Here, too, I met with pleasure many old friends, subordinates and contractors, who came to visit me, and compliment me on my promotion, and chatter about former days; for it is one of the greatest compliments to the officer, who is soon to sever his active connection with his life's work in India, to be assured that he has the respect and the good-will of those over whom he has ruled in the early days of his career.

On April 4, 1905, the great Kángra earthquake occurred, which is credited with the death of some 20,000 human beings. On arrival at Simla, I found that, not unnaturally, great nervousness prevailed, and this was intensified by the frequent recurrence of earth tremors. Our house, Kennedy Lodge, one of the oldest in the station, and now pulled down to make room for public offices, had received rather severe damage, necessitating the rebuilding of party walls and chimney-stacks, and seemed withal very responsive to surface movements. At Boxar, where I had experienced it, the earthquake had no such intensity; the shock was merely sufficient to loosen the plaster from the walls of the old mill, but it was remarked that both birds and animals expressed great terror at the unusual occurrence; the former flew, widely circling in the air, and the elephants, always most sensitive to any insecurity under their ponderous weight, could with difficulty be restrained from flight; we had, however, at the time no idea that such widespread devastation had occurred elsewhere. Many, no doubt, were the sleepless nights passed at Simla during that season, but this did not outwardly affect either the normal gaiety of the settlement or its normal labours.

The question of forest education was, as I have before indicated, one now demanding considerable attention. Assuming it to be admitted that the object of State forestry in India is to further the welfare of the inhabitants, and also the industrial development of the country, and that the attainment of those ends is dependent to a large extent on the personal influence of the forester on the people, on his knowledge of their requirements and of the systems of silviculture by which they may be met, it is evident that the forester's training is worthy of the most careful consideration, so that it may be suitable to the fulfilment of the important duties entrusted to him.

For nearly a quarter of a century a forest school had existed at Dehra Dun, whence issued yearly some thirty to fifty subordinate officers trained in the theory, and also, to the limited extent that the course of two years permitted, in the local practice of forestry. From these men were drawn, after many years' service, recruits for the executive and territorial posts in the Provincial Service, but these recruits received no special supplemental education; they were, indeed, supposed to have added to their knowledge by the practical experience of some eighteen years in the subordinate grades, but too often promotion found them more ignorant professionally than when they had left school, and ill equipped to wield the larger authority that was now given to them. And, as it is to indigenous agency that India must in the future look for the expansion of her executive establishments, it became urgently necessary to train the men who were to fill such posts so that they might efficiently carry out the duties that were to be imposed on them.

Again, the lowest subordinates, such as Forest Guards and Foresters, were those in the most intimate connection with the "toiling millions" of India, and as in the East a misconception of the aims and objects of the Government is the most potent cause of discontent, and is, moreover, the weapon that lies easiest to the hand of professional agitators, each such subordinate Forest Officer when instructed in the rudiments of his profession might be of great assistance in imparting to an ignorant population the true reasons for the practice of State forestry. Finally, there could be no professional progress without a systematic record of results of investigations, and these investigations themselves could not be successful unless conducted by men who were given leisure from routine work, and time to increase their knowledge by special study and experiment. Such were some of the considerations that led to the creation of a Forest Research Institute, with a separate staff of selected officers; to raising the Forest School to the status of a college; to inaugurating elementary forest schools in each Province; and to providing education and opportunities for early entry into the Provincial Service for young men of a suitable social standing.

It was objected, at the time when these proposals were first made, that the Forest Department could comprise no officers who were competent to specialize in botany, zoology, chemistry, and economics, and that it would be necessary to procure professors from England in these subjects; but we required these sciences in their application to Indian forestry, and none would serve our purpose save those who had a practical knowledge of that branch of their profession. And so opportunity was given to men like Messrs. Haines, Stebbing, Hole, and Troup, to prove that the department was not deficient in scientific attainment or incapable of imparting special knowledge to others. They found no difficulty in doing so. Then, too, began the publication of forest manuals, wherein was set forth in simple language such knowledge of silviculture and its cognate sciences as would serve to take Indian students of forestry on the road to higher attainments in their profession; while at the same time series of pamphlets, records, and memoirs, were first started to form an Indian forest literature that should serve both for public information and for the use of succeeding generations of foresters. The time had, in short, fully arrived when the necessity of utilizing the knowledge that was available, and of increasing it, was amply acknowledged.

The result of raising the standard of education, in answer to the demand for work of a better class from the forest establishment, was inevitable. The best material, even at its lowest price, must be more costly than an inferior article, and therefore it followed that, in order to attract a superior class of recruit, better terms had to be offered, both as regarded salaries and other labour conditions; and in consequence a reorganization of the establishments of each Province, both as regards their strength and remuneration, had to be undertaken. Such an investigation, affecting the welfare of over 15,000 subordinates, was, in spite of the extra labour involved, peculiarly congenial to at least one of those engaged therein, who was firmly convinced of the disadvantages under which many of his colleagues laboured. It occupied several years to bring this work even within view of completion, but the results were eminently satisfactory, for the minimum wage of the subordinates was raised by about 40 per cent., and the establishments were regraded so as to afford earlier promotion; while numberless small concessions were granted, such as free uniforms, local allowances, etc., that did much to raise the status of the subordinate, and so encourage the recruitment of a better class of men. One portion of the Service was, however, still left without relief, the most important provincial branch; its claims had not been overlooked, but unforeseen hindrances arose in the final issue of the orders that were designed to ameliorate the lot of these hard-worked officers. This delay was most regrettable in every way, but here, too, matters have since been satisfactorily settled.

In thus writing of the interests of an Inspector-General of Forests at Simla and Calcutta, it must be understood that he is entrusted with no powers of administration; his duty is to advise when called upon to do so, and, though he may be permitted to make suggestions on his own initiative, the fate of such advice or suggestions rests entirely with the Government of India. Thus, though an inspecting officer may enjoy the satisfaction of working in accordance with his own convictions, and on lines that he personally ardently desires to follow, this may be due rather to good fortune than to merit; he may, for instance, be both enthusiastic in his profession and persuasive in argument, yet have little opportunity of using these important administrative talents. For myself, I had the good fortune to be associated with members of the Council of India, such as Sir Denzil Ibbetson, Sir Lewis Tupper, Sir John Hewitt, and the Hon. Mr. Miller; with Secretaries to Government, such as Sir James Wilson and Mr. Carlyle—all men of influence who recognized the value of State forestry in India, and appreciated the good work that had been accomplished during the last half-century, and who therefore were glad of the opportunity afforded by the then favourable financial conditions of the country to further the interests of forestry in the present, and to equip it for yet more useful work in the future.

It is needless to say that a change had come over public opinion in the matter of State forestry since the time of my early service, so much so that the description already given of the official attitude of those days would be hardly credible in these. Now the question was being more accurately judged by the Indian educated classes, and even the peasantry understood the direction in which their interests lay; while the Indian Press took a living interest in the aims of forestry, in its management, in its present and prospective value to the Empire, and did not hesitate to criticize and give advice when in its opinion matters were proceeding too slowly. Almost every native State and Principality also had its own forest service, and managed its forests on principles either prescribed or approved of by Western foresters; the large landowners were rapidly following suit, convinced of the importance of forests under business-like management; while the revenue officials had not only accepted the policy laid down for their guidance, but numbers of them took an enthusiastic interest in the practice of the science. Thus, when the day at last arrived when the forests of India were mentioned in the Budget debate at Simla, and their statistics were quoted by a Secretary of State in England, it became safe to assert that the administration for nearly half a century of one-fifth of the area of British India had been carried out by the Forest Department to the benefit of the public interests, and to anticipate that the future progress of the work depended solely on the knowledge and enthusiasm of the department, and on a continuance of the sympathetic consideration now accorded by the Government.

CHAPTER XI

KASHMIR AND ASSAM

In the autumn of 1905 we started for a tour in the forests of Kashmir. I have already indicated in general terms the position that the rulers of native States in India occupy as regards the catchment area of its main rivers; and, in fact, the upper catchment areas of the Indus, Jhelam, and Chenáb, lie in Kashmir territory, that of the Beás in British India, and that of the Sutlej in the native State of Bashahr. Thus, though the Panjab is watered by five rivers, as its name denotes, and though it bears on its provincial arms a primitive rendering of this fact, only one of these streams is controlled by its Government. Farther east, the Jumna and the Ganges flow in the earlier portion of their courses through the native State of Tehri-Garhwál, and from thence onwards to the most easterly boundary of India the rivers that flow from the north have their origin, with few exceptions, in foreign territory. Towards the centre and south of the Peninsula the same conditions prevail to some extent; for instance, the Cauvery River rises in Mysore, and there are many others whose names any suitable modern atlas will disclose, the result being that British enterprise, whether this includes irrigation, agriculture, plant-

On the Dal Lake, Kashmir.

ing, or other industrial investments, remains to some extent at the mercy of those who have the power to regulate the flow of water between the hills and the plains.

The method adopted by Nature for the purposes of holding up the water-supply, and of preventing surface flow and consequent erosion, is well understood in France and other European countries, where large sums are now being spent in reboisement and other protective works to remedy the neglect of the past. It is there admitted that, if the soil is permitted to clothe itself with vegetation, with trees, shrubs, or grass, not only are the immediate effects of heavy aqueous precipitation mitigated, but that time is afforded for absorption of moisture into the surface covering, and thence into the soil itself, from whence it is given off in perennial streams that maintain the water-level of the country below at a suitable height. If, on the contrary, the soil is exposed to a rainfall that is allowed to flow rapidly away from the mountain-slopes, first deep channels are cut in the soil, till ultimately the bedrock is exposed, and later the force of unchecked torrents forms deep ravines that carry stones, sand, and boulders, depositing them in the country below, to the inconvenience or danger of its inhabitants. If such things happen in France, in Switzerland, in Germany, where climatic influences are not so powerful, it is reasonable to infer that in India much more rapid and drastic results may be expected; for though the Indian climate may not always come under the classification of tropical, yet the rainfall, limited as it is to restricted periods, may generally be qualified by a term that implies both violence and quantity. Probably the heaviest rainfall occurs in India between the plains and an elevation of 7,000 feet. Above that height it diminishes gradually, till the region of perpetual snow is reached. The yearly average rainfall in the plains districts is, therefore, much less than on the higher ground, from whence, however, both the surface and the subterranean water flows.

The importance, therefore, of restricting the evil effects of heavy rainfall, more especially in the area from the foot of the mountains up to the tree limit, is undoubted, and, moreover, Nature has from time immemorial busied herself in affording this necessary protection without the approval—sometimes without even the knowledge—of man. Her work is arduous, for so well counterbalanced are her forces that a moment's inattention to any one of them is followed by the preponderance of another, and thus when, in the struggle between water and vegetation, man, interferes with wasteful grazing, firing, and felling, Nature retires defeated from the struggle; nor will she without much coaxing again furnish her powerful aid at the time when, experienced through disaster, man returns to replant the waste places, and to re-erect the only permanent defence that can be devised against alternate floods and drought.

In a country where agriculture is the staple industry, the preservation of hill forests becomes a necessity; but there is also a secondary reason for their protection, for water not only provides the medium to dissolve the plant food in the soil and permit of its circulation to the growing crops, but also possesses a power the most economical that man can employ, whether he be engaged in simple industries that supply the necessaries of life, or in more important manufactures that add to the national wealth. Yet it is not until the supply of this power can be regulated that its full employment becomes possible, and in India most of the rivers are at present so uncertain in the volume of water they carry that hydro-electric works seem to be secure only when a portion of the minimum off-flow is depended upon, and it will need much careful work before in India, as in France, every jet of water capable of driving a sewing-machine is harnessed for the benefit of an industrious population.

The forests of Kashmir have for long been in charge of an officer of the Indian Forest Service, who worked under the orders of the Durbar, and received his salary from that body. He was therefore not free to introduce such reforms as he considered advisable, and, indeed, was frequently hampered professionally—for instance, by the distaste of Hindu rulers to interfere with the grazing of cattle, or by their desire to sacrifice too much to the collection of a large revenue; yet in spite of these drawbacks much good work had been done in protecting the forests and bringing them under regular working.

The deodar cedar is the most striking tree of the Kashmir hills, as the plane and poplar are of its valley. The former is first met with on the drive along the Jhelam road, some marches out of Baramula, and it extends across the watershed of the

Chenab River. No tree, perhaps, is so beautiful either in close-grown ranks, when it rises straight and branchless for many score feet towards the sky, or when, standing alone on some steep precipice, it extends enormous lateral branches, and, ceasing from upward growth, displays a flattened crown like a soft bed of greenery. Where the deodar flourishes there is a climate where the white man may also dwell in comfort. It thrives from an elevation of 4,000 feet above the sea, and single stunted specimens may be seen even at three times that height. It yields timber that remains scented for years, resisting the attacks of insects and fungi, and were there sufficient for the regular supply of an export market, the wood might find a better fate than carrying the burning rails of a North-Western train.

The deodar-forests of the Jhelam and of its affluents have been sadly ill-treated by axe, fire, and cattle. Looking at them from a distance, they give good promise of pleasant growth ; but enter them, and you will find scarce a sound mature tree, while the sad stumps of those that have been felled above the winter snow-level bear piteous shoots that will never serve any useful purpose. And yet the tree responds generously to any care or attention bestowed upon it. Its natural regeneration or artificial reproduction by sowing or planting is easy, and it is even asserted that it will grow from suckers. All it requests is a porous soil and a modicum of light and moisture. All that it insists on is that its young brood shall not be eaten by cattle or burnt by fire. Then, if these simple demands are granted, it will give in return sound fragrant wood of great strength, that will float buoyantly on the waterways that lead to its destination.

We went up the Lolab Valley when the deodar pollen was ripe, and found Nature was taking no chances in the fructification of the tiny cones that lay nestled on the outer branchlets of the deodar; the air was full of golden dust, and, as the wind blew in fitful gusts, great billows of pollen were wafted across the forest, so that the trees were hidden in mist, to emerge gaily decorated with colour, while the roads, the fences, the houses, were covered with the yellow film. Then from this sunny valley, where the black bears watch the ripening maize, we turned towards the Sinthan Pass, and climbed its foot through the "sable, silent, solemn forest" of fir. Here were mighty trees that only stood on sufferance and because they had no present value, for the pulp-maker had not yet reached these parts; and here we camped for two days in blinding snow and sleet till the mountains above bore no trace of road and no footstep of man. When we reached the summit, on the one side lay the forest of birch, fir, pine, and deodar, extending in their appointed order till they joined with the deciduous trees in the valley below, where the muddy Jhelam River masqueraded as a silver thread; on the other side stretched the bare hills and rocks of the Chenáb Valley, dotted with the melancholy remnants of forests secure in their impenetrable precipices.

We visited Kishtwar, and saw the ancient polo-ground with goal-posts of solid stone, and admired the ruins of the paved road that once led to this ancient capital; along the length of this path were a multitude of stone waterspouts, now dry and filled with earth, and we questioned the oldest inhabitant, who claimed to remember when running water was plentiful, "before," he said, "the forests were cut down." There were none there now, and we shot chikor partridge in a thorny scrub that now clung to crevices in the rocks, where once the shade of the forest had yielded coolness and moisture to a larger population; then onwards, to find the march from Kishtwar to Jaunmu a toilsome nightmare of atrocious paths and much fatigue. It is recommended that no one should go this road save for penitential purposes, nor does Jaunmu present any attractions, save when the Máhárájá dispenses princely hospitality to the great.

Kashmir is now commencing its industrial career in earnest by harnessing the Jhelam to supply many thousand horse-power to the city of Srinagar and to the industries in the neighbourhood. But, though not a tithe of the available force is yet utilized, the better regulation of the flow of the Jhelam has had to come under consideration, the wild floods that yearly spread devastation in the valley have to be controlled, and engineers are already engaged in dredging the bed of the river, so that the Woolar Lake may be drained and defined limits assigned to the flow of the river. Later on attention may be turned to its catchment area in the hills, and in the interests of this new enterprise careful protection will be afforded to the forests above. There is already a precedent on a small scale for such a scheme, for the source of the water-supply of Srinagar is fully protected from man and beast, to the great benefit of the sanitary conditions of the city, where in former days cholera was too frequent.

Shooting in Kashmir has arrived at the stage when it is chiefly for the elect. The days are past when the sportsman could roam the hills as he willed in search of the noble Kashmir stag and of the red-bear, and bring back many a trophy after a delightful tour in the wilds. Here, as elsewhere in India, there is not enough game to go round: red-bear are scarce, and the deer resort to the Máhá-rájá's preserves, which are watched jealously by a competent staff commanded by European officers. Stags may still be obtained as they cross the passes in their seasonal change from one locality to another; but many are killed in the preserves in drives organized for the pastime of the mighty, who have no time to spare to enjoy the pleasures of the stalk on the open mountain, or to listen by the camp-fire to the belling of the stags.

In the spring of 1907 we again went to Kashmir on leave, and found the valley in the throes of a cholera epidemic that precluded all enjoyment in marching; so an inferior side of Kashmir life was tried—the indolent existence in a roomy house-boat on the clear waters of the Dal Lake, within reach of the iron water-pipes of civilization. The beauty of poplar and plane, of the iris and water-lily, of the orchards white with blossom, of the blue hills barred with mist and capped with snow, afforded luxurious enjoyment after many years of continual work, though the journey back to India in the heat and discomfort of a pause in the monsoon did much to efface the feeling of quiet ease that had been enjoyed.

Kashmir possesses, surely, many industries that may be developed now that hydro-electric power is available. Connected with forestry is that of paper-pulp manufacture, which may some day prove remunerative to the State, for it would afford some means of utilizing the inferior stock of timber that now crowds the forest at low elevations, and prevents the progress of a better crop; it might even lead to the exploitation of the spruce and fir forests, and give an impetus to the planting of poplar and willow, that grow like any weed in the damp, fertile lands of the valley. And the more valuable the products of the forest area, the better will certainly be the protection afforded to the forests, for they provide a source of State revenue that would be badly missed if it was allowed to fall off through want of proper supervision.

About the valley of Kashmir many books have been written, and everything is known; those who go there may enjoy the finest scenery in the world in all its variations of fertile plains, wooded mountains, and rocky desert heights, all beautified by the finest colouring that Nature can supply; and at the same time they will have before their eyes the squalor, filth, and the misery of endemic diseases, which are more common in the temperate countries of the East than where burning sun and burning winds cleanse the land as if by fire. For enjoyment in Kashmir the traveller must fix his mind and his eyes on the landscape, and forget the trivialities of common daily life; yet it would be well to make a competent person responsible that during such abstraction these trivialities be not entirely forgotten, lest cholera, typhoid, or smallpox, spoil his holiday, and maybe ruin his constitution.

In the beginning of 1906 a visit was paid to Assam. Though it is possible to obtain some idea of the forestry conditions of a Province from a study of reports and other literature, such knowledge is not an adequate equipment for an advisory officer, who should have a good insight into the customs and requirements of the population, and some acquaintance with local conditions of labour and commerce. It is only by visiting the country concerned that he can form opinions useful for future guidance or offer advice based on experience gathered elsewhere; he is a student as well as a professor, and in learning he is more likely to be helped by an executive officer, who is intimately acquainted with the locality, than by an administrative officer, who perhaps has only lately taken over a new post, and who may be too apt to lay stress on knowledge gained under quite different conditions. I owe acknowledgment to many earnest executive Forest Officers, both for affording information and making suggestions for improvements the introduction of which we have had the satisfaction of witnessing.

Mr. P. Coventry was then in charge of the Government rubber plantations of *Ficus elastica* in the Province; these were then coming into bearing, and he has since compiled an able monograph which affords the fullest information on a subject that is becoming of considerable commercial importance in India, even though it is not likely that this particular species will ever be extensively cultivated, for there are others that promise to provide a more remunerative investment.

The importation of wild rubber from the territories beyond Assam and Burma afforded at one time a considerable revenue to the British Government, but wasteful utilization has led to the usual result of shortening the supply; and it seems certain that in the future plantation rubber will entirely control the world's market, as it perhaps already does to a great extent. The *Ficus elastica* is a light-loving plant, and occurs naturally as an epiphyte growing on the tallest forest trees, whose stems it encircles till the host is hidden and forgotten. The enormous height of the wild tree therefore is due to the host selected, and is not apparent in an artificial plantation originating from seed or from cuttings; there the tree is forced to itself form a trunk for the support of its heavy crown; it does not desire to do this, nor has it, when surrounded by stems of similar age, any special impulse towards height growth so long as it secures its due share of illumination. The tree has also in close-growing plantations little use for the development of aerial roots; but, on the other hand, the underground root system coalesces, so that no tree can be termed entirely independent. It is probably due to the unnatural position of the tree, and to neglect to force its upward growth in early youth, that somewhat unsatisfactory results have been obtained in Assam from the *Ficus elastica* as compared with those recorded from other species; yet it seems certain that even under rather adverse conditions the Assam plantations will yield a good return on the capital expended, while they have served the purpose for which they were designed, that of showing the way to the establishment of a new industry in the Province, and thus Government intrusion into an industrial enterprise has been justified.

The Province of Assam is as regards its forests in a backward condition. The work of creating a permanent forest estate from public waste land has been approached on a different system from that followed in the Central Provinces. There the whole area comes under Forest Law as a State Reserve, and portions are from time to time handed over to the agriculturist as demand arises. In Assam reserves are cut out of the public waste whenever extension of State forests is deemed desirable. This is an inferior method in a Province where, though the river connections are good, railways have yet much scope for extension, because no protection is available for the waste-land forests pending a decision as to their future; while all kinds of rights and interests may grow up within the area that subsequently interfere with the formation of large blocks of forest for national use. Up to the present the forests of Assam are far from being exploited to their full extent, and in one instance it was almost ludicrous to observe the importation from a distance of articles manufactured from a timber that grows profusely in the Province itself. The large area of evergreen forest is also not worked for the valuable timber it holds, and it was only in the district of Goalpara that forest commercial activity appeared to be developing; here the fellings of "sál," the tramways, and the roads, all presented a forecast of what might later on be imitated in other parts of the Province.

A visit was next paid to the Garo Hills, an isolated mountain district inhabited by a somewhat truculent tribe who practise shifting cultivation in the forests. No book on India, certainly none that refers to its forests, can be complete without reference to this most wasteful form of cultivation, which has had, and to some extent is still having, so marked an influence on the country. Primitive man when struggling for existence in the virgin forests that once covered mountains and plains had but few weapons at his disposal; his axe, his spear, and his bow, may have conferred some equality with the animal and vegetable life around him, but it was through fire that he asserted his superiority; and to-day the record of his victory is visible on every hill in India. To fell the forest and to burn the timber, so that food grains might be sown broadcast amongst the fertilizing ashes, to watch the seedlings flourish in the monsoon rains and the harvest ripen in the winter, was a method of cultivation suitable to those who possessed neither agricultural implements nor domestic cattle, and who, to a great extent dependent like the monkeys on the wild products of the forest, like them were forced to roam as soon as local supplies were exhausted. And thus it is that the mountains are scarred where the soil has slipped from the underlying rock, or where torrents have cut deep into their slopes, and that, even where such pronounced effects of erosion are not fully manifest, the forest is honeycombed with patches of dense grass and shrubs that are useless to man, and yet prevent the germination of any more valuable vegetation.

Such a system, excusable in the stress of the past, admits of no defence in the present, when there is no vital conflict with the forces of Nature, and when there is a Government ready to assist with the gift or loan of plough-cattle and seed towards the establishment of a permanent home. But custom will not be denied: on the one hand, the creed that what the fathers have done that also must the sons practise could not be discredited by argument alone; on the other, the Government would not intervene in practice before it had ocular and contemporary proof of the effects of shifting cultivation in the loss of fertile lands above, in damage to agriculture below, and in danger to the permanent water-supply of the country. The steps that have been taken to regulate the potato industry in Kumaon, and the inquiries instituted in Upper Burma, offer interesting evidence that the British Government is reluctant enough to interfere actively with established habits, and that action, when ultimately inevitable, often involves greater expense and fiercer criticism than if earlier steps had been taken in the same direction.

Interference with shifting cultivation, even though unduly delayed, is still of a mild nature; it consists in allotting areas for the practice of this pernicious custom, at the same time prohibiting the entry of new settlers into these areas; and this policy has been successful, especially in Burma, where the Karens doubtless owe to it that they have hitherto escaped the fate that overtakes most savage tribes in India, that of absorption with the mixed races of Hindustan. In the Central Provinces the practice is fast dying out; in other parts of India it remains under altered conditions; for instance, in Bombay the people laboriously strip the forest trees of their green shoots, and convey them to their fields to burn on the seed-beds, when they can have any quantity of similar material ready cut in the annual felling areas, thereby indicating a blind trust in the hidden wisdom of their ancestors that is both humorous and pathetic. In Assam, too, there should be no difficulty in gradually checking this evil, if no lapses are permitted from the constant supervision that is required to effect the object in view. The Garos claim that in their hills there is no waste land, that it is all their own property, and forestry, pending a consideration of this unusual claim, has made but slight progress; but the people are already mixing with the outside population, and in a few more years will probably be less suspicious, and more eager to exploit to the full the products of their wild country.

In the Garo Hills are earthquakes and elephants: the former occur frequently, with strange rumblings that terrify the unaccustomed traveller; the latter are easily avoided in this hilly country, and perhaps as easily evade their hunters, for they grow to a great size, and a pair of tusks, each 6 feet long and fairly symmetrical, was eagerly purchased in Calcutta, on its written description alone, for 60 guineas. This elephant had been killed in self-defence by forest guards armed with antiquated Snider rifles. Personally I saw no elephants during my toúr, and I did not regret it. We lived in shanties made of bamboo, the staircase being a notched stick, and an elephant of the size of those whose footprints we inspected could have flattened the whole outfit without even being aware that there were human beings inside.

From thence the Goalpara district was visited, a Tarai country of grass and swamps, where rhinoceros, elephants, bison, buffalo, and tiger, still roamed in comfort, and where every stream held mahseer eager to take the most primitive bait. Mr. W. Perree was the officer in charge, and what he did not know about these beasts, dead or alive, was hardly worth further study. In the search for rhinoceros, in which we were unsuccessful owing to the heavy grass of winter, we saw many elephants and bison; and the start before dawn, in the chilly darkness, was amply rewarded by the weirdness of the landscape as the grey light crept up, revealing herds of bison still grazing in the open country. There were bulls and cows and calves feeding in peaceful confidence, nor did we fire a shot to alarm them as they trundled away into the forest; but to be seen at his best the bison should be on firm ground on a steep hillside, when the agility and speed of so ponderous an animal inspires amazement. But though we shot nothing we saw much of the life of the forest: we observed how the evergreen trees, aided by fire protection, were ousting the more valuable trees of the deciduous forest, and we laid plans for the assistance of the latter; we noticed how the "sál" trees on the alluvial deposits were making good growth, promising dividends much superior to those anticipated by our predecessors; how on the grasslands the cotton-trees were covering the ground and preparing the way for the arrival of superior species; how luxuriantly grew the "shisham" and "khair" on the islands of the clear, flowing rivers, so that we were sorry to come again to the muddy stream of the Brahmaputra, flowing through solitudes of grass and sand.

This is perhaps a mightier river than the Irrawadi, but without its charm. The great Assam waterway seems deserted by the habitations of man. As one emerges from the gloom of a night spent in a stranded steamer on a dank sand-bank, one may see a few fever-stricken wretches waiting on a dreary wharf; but on the great Burmese river the steamer carries the market-stalls for the inhabitants of a country-side who live on the banks of the stream; the people, well dressed and eager, crowd around, cheapening their purchases and praising their own wares, and the livelong day is an endless repetition of such social enjoyments. Assam is a sad place in comparison with Burma, but perhaps more congenial to the lover of Nature and sport, and our abiding impressions of the country will be, first, of the starry nights as seen through the thin grassy roofs of the sleeping-huts when wakened by the sounds of the forest around ; and next, of an English lady and her little girl in a bamboo shanty on a swampy plain, living open to the assaults of tigers, wild-elephants, and wild-men, but who subsequently escaped and lived happily ever after.

CHAPTER XII

KULU; MADRAS; BOMBAY AND CEYLON

IN the autumn of 1906 we visited the district of Kulu. We were prepared for the best by the tales of the travellers and residents, who were sometimes almost inarticulate in their praises; it was therefore but natural that we should have been disappointed. The valley of Kulu is warm after the hill-tops of Simla, nor is the climate bracing; and to reach it an uninteresting march has to be undertaken, even before the summit of the Jalori Pass is reached, and the Beás River becomes visible in the distance. There is perhaps another reason for depression in the fact that there are many European residents in the valley; but such a feeling is referable entirely to personal sentiments.

The attempt to make an English home in India is almost always a failure, because India should represent for the Englishman work in exile; and if he has no work, and repudiates the idea of exile, he assumes a difficult and unnatural position. He will find that the attitude of his Indian fellow-subjects alters from the moment that he doffs the authority of office, and that at the same time his interest in official life is removed, while officialdom has no further interest in him; thus he is left to make out with such other occupations as the locality will afford, while he is cut off from all those artistic, political, and the rest, of his own country. To dwell in a fruit-garden without getting into mischief was beyond the power of the first man—his successors have far greater temptation ; and even the excitements of the apple-market, that in Kulu are added to those of the first garden of Eden, only provide a transient interest that cannot entirely stifle the call of the West. Therefore, when one of the rulers of the country settles amongst the ruled, there is a pity or regret that his health or other circumstance have prevented the fulfilment of a desire to return to his native land, a desire that must surely at one time have been an incentive to his manhood's work.

The scenery of the Kulu Valley is pleasant, but not beautiful. The alder groves on the Beás River are characteristic of the country; the tree stands with its feet in the water, with foliage overhanging the rippling river, whose course it stays within the low banks. The mountains rise on either side from terraced fields or from the orchards of the residents. It is believed that the native of Kulu is a poor sort of person; he will not willingly work, nor will he even take the trouble to grow the superior fruit and maize that is offered to him for the purpose. Field cultivation has declined in the valley, and pastoral pursuits have increased, for it is easier to watch the sheep and goats destroying the forests than to bend the back over ploughing and irrigation. And yet without the protection of the forests this fertile country would soon be desolate. The chief tree is the blue-pine, that grows profusely wherever the attention of man is temporarily diverted from its progress; but the time of respite is generally short, for the tree is lopped till only a ridiculous tuft of needles is left to carry on its growth, and the branches are used for stable litter and for charcoal-burning, so that whole hillsides are covered with rows of upright spindles that once were trees. The Forest Officers labour against men, sheep, and goats, with varying success, but the conditions have not been so favourable as, for instance, in the Sutlej Valley, where forestry has a firm hold on the country.

Altogether it is pleasant to turn aside from the main valley of Kulu, and ascend the course of the Parbati River, passing the hot springs at Manikarn—where a bath is guaranteed to bring all internal aches to the surface, and leave them there for some time—and so reach the pleasant forest-house at Phulga. On the way are fine forests of long-leaved pine, blue-pine, and deodar, and above are the snowy slopes where ibex, "burhel," and red-bear, are still to be found; while "chikor" are plentiful in the late autumn, when the first snowfall drives the birds to lower elevations; there are also at that season many woodcock in the marshes that are still unfrozen. Thus, the resident in Kulu lives sumptuously at a phenomenally low cost, for he adds excellent mutton to his bill of fare; and this he buys by live-weight, being careful to keep the sheep under observation, lest it should be dosed with salt and then encouraged to drink, so that mutton price may be obtained for inferior brine. On the whole, Kulu offers no special attractions that cannot be better obtained in many places in the Himalaya; it is a place to visit once if the tourist happens to be in the neighbourhood, but does not repay the long march that separates it from Simla unless the traveller has a special interest in the question of forest protection against man and goats.

In July, 1907, I attained the age when officers appointed by the Secretary of State to Indian Services other than the Indian Civil Service may claim to retire or be ordered to do so. I then asked for and received an extension of fifteen months' service, and as soon as the Simla season had passed away turned towards Madras, on an invitation from the Government of that Province, where, under the kindly guidance of the Conservators, Messrs. Lushington, Lodge, and Peete, a most interesting forest tour was made.

Forestry in Madras presents some difficult problems. There are about forty millions of inhabitants and only 20,000 square miles of forest. It appears that formerly this area was considerably larger, but that a portion was handed over to the unregulated use of the people in settlement of all claims on the remainder. The statesmen who conceived this arrangement were certainly signally ignorant of the requirements of the forest and of the attitude of the people towards it. For the maintenance of a forest requires a knowledge which was characteristic neither of the revenue officers nor of the people, and where a multitude possess a collective claim to a valuable property it is contrary to human nature that the individual should not strive for his full share. In these circumstances the yield of the seceded area was certain to rapidly fall off, and as certainly, when both capital and interest had been eaten up, the people again clamoured for further similar concessions.

It is, I have heard, impossible to divide the wealth of individuals amongst a community so that each member thereof shall be independent of his surroundings, and in the same way it is impracticable to distribute the produce from 20,000 square miles of tropical forest among forty million persons, so that each individual may have his actual share. Such an attempt is bound to end in the destruction of the forest, and the loss to the public of what might remain a most valuable asset to the general prosperity. For instance, in the small area of 1,200 square miles of State forest in Oudh no attempt is made to distribute its harvest amongst a population that is in places as dense as that of Belgium; there the policy is adopted of permitting those in the vicinity of the forest to reap considerable advantages in cheap or free produce, or in the offer of work in return for the responsibility imposed on them by law for its protection; while the rest of the population must be content to profit by the supply of timber and other produce at a cheaper rate than would be possible were it not for the maintenance of a State forest in the Province, and by such relaxation of taxation as the profits of its management may justify. That is to say, the vast majority can profit only indirectly by the presence of the forest, and wherever this axiom is ignored trouble is certain to continue.

There can be no effective protection of forests in India until the people themselves afford it, and they

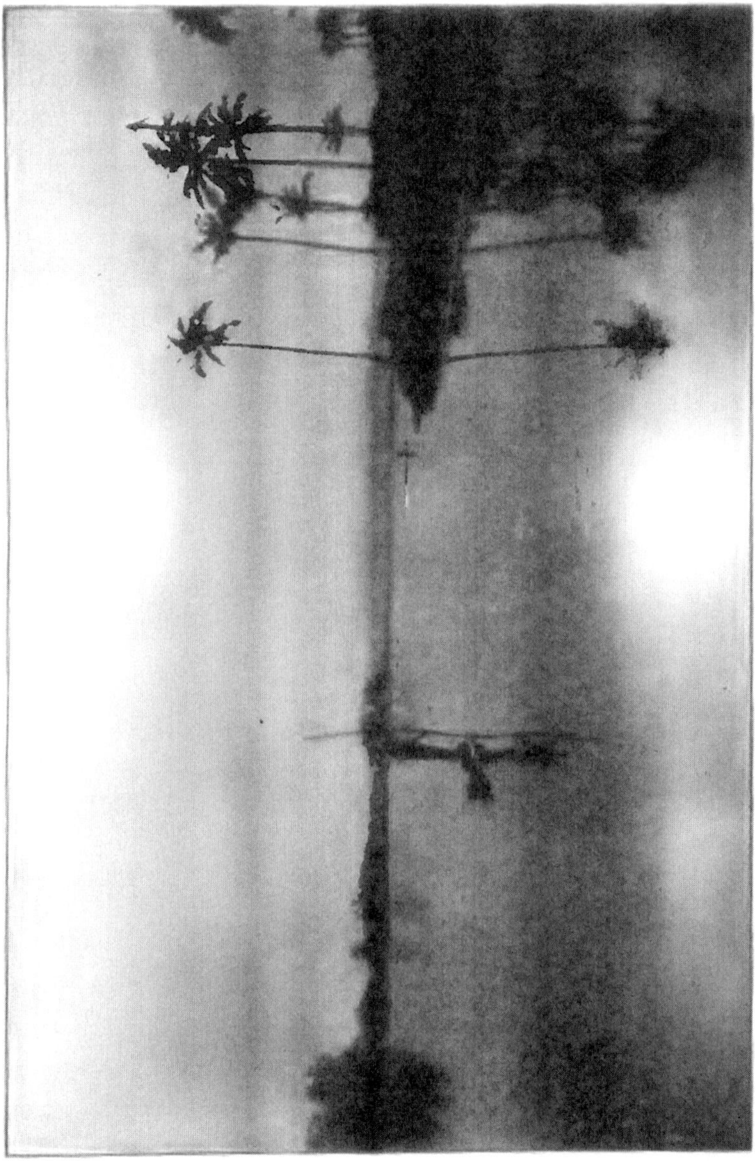

will not afford it unless they have a personal interest in doing so; if the whole population of a Province is given the rights of entry to, and removal of produce from, State reserves, then the interest of the local population will be confined to securing, during the scramble that ensues, a good share of the spoil before all disappears. The work of the Forest Officer cannot in such circumstances be successful; he may wander over the rocky slopes, inserting seeds from forest trees in each pitiful pocket of earth that he may discover in the clefts. He may do all in his power to minimize the evils he cannot prevent, but success will ultimately be with the herds of goat, sheep, and cattle, whose owners, coming from a distance, may not have the slightest claim to the soil, and for whose profit agriculture will pay in the future as soon as the forests are no longer in a condition to do so.

But not all, even of the few forests of Madras that I had an opportunity of visiting, are ruined by the ill-regulated demands of the people; some there are on the slopes of the mountains, or in secluded places, where grow excellent rosewood, blackwood, and teak, which bring in a good revenue to the State because they can be worked in a rational manner. But the area of such forests is not so large as it should be, or, indeed, might be, if the policy above indicated controlled the forest management more fully.

At Nilambur is a famous teak plantation, already a great financial success and superior to anything of the kind in Burma—well situated, too, on a floating stream for the removal of the harvest. But here the dangers of pure plantations are already exemplified in the attacks of a moth that defoliates the stems sometimes twice in one year, so that they can pay little attention to increasing their growth, because always occupied in the struggle to replace their leaves. It is improbable that plantation work of this description will be extended, for the Forest Officer has enough to do in looking after the natural forests in his charge. At Nilambur one looks over a wide stretch of wooded hills, restful to the eye and giving promise of good sport; and, indeed, bison and elephant are frequent in these parts, but we had arrived at the wrong season of the year, and, moreover, could not stay in our hurried march, where so much of interest was to be seen.

From Calicut, a place of mosquitoes and Arab traders, we visited the Nallamallai Hills, where the interesting work of teaching the jungle tribes to aid in forestry was in progress under the guidance of Mr. Wood, the Forest Officer. The Nallamallai forests extend over an area of about 2,000 square miles, forming an undulating plateau at an elevation of from 1,000 to 3,000 feet above the sea. The forest has been yearly burnt over by the Chenchus, who number about 4,000 souls, and, though the average rainfall is over 40 inches, few of the streams are perennial—a fact indicating the devastation that may be wrought on so large an area by so small a population. The Chenchus possess to a more marked extent than most others some of the worst characteristics of a forest tribe when surrounded by comparative civilization; they are drunkards and thieves, and do not always abstain from murder.

But this should arouse sympathy, for it indicates rather the discontent of an unhappy people than a preference for evil ways. It is so easy to be good when in easy circumstances; but these men were oppressed by money-lenders, who made cash advances against payment in forest products, and, keeping no accounts that their clients could understand, were able to swindle with impunity. Moreover, a good crop of such products only occurs about once in three years, so that there was recurring distress which could not be alleviated by the scanty crops of maize, or even by working for timber contractors, who also had it in their power to underpay or even refuse payment.

The British Government has one duty in India even greater than that of abstaining from oppression, and that is, to intervene to prevent it; for Heaven help the helpless Hindustani when he comes under the power of a fellow-countryman who has not been converted to a belief in the disinterested justice of the West. In this instance intervention between the spoiler and the spoiled took the shape of asserting a pre-emptive right to forest produce in the Nallamallais, so that the Chenchus now trade direct with Government, and receive value for their work. Next came the question of providing suitable labour for the tribe, and this was found in plantation work near the permanent springs, where their chief villages are situated; and for this work they are given credit at Government shops, so as to prevent their wages being taken to the nearest grog-shop, a proceeding that formerly often resulted in wasting their earnings, and also in other trouble, for a drunken

Chenchu thinks nothing of firing the forest, and, if the thought struck him, would not hesitate to start out to rob or to put an arrow through his special enemy.

Mr. Wood writes that, as an example of the characteristics of this tribe, one man, an outlaw for murder, only visits his village at night for food; while another, after suffering six months' imprisonment for an assault on a Forest Officer, visited a temple festival in the neighbourhood, and returned with enough loot to purchase six milch buffaloes, so that he is now wealthy and contented. He adds that the plantation work is a great success, and that the forest now being created by the labour of these men will be a valuable property in the future; while the Chenchus, who at first would only work when they wanted to, are now keen to obtain regular employment that is honestly paid for, and afford the greatest assistance in protecting the forest from fire, which was previously an impossible task.

The future of these tribes is thus assured, provided that the officers who have charge of them from time to time continue to treat them as children, in a sympathetic manner. For instance, much harm may be done by Indian Excise officers hunting for private stills amongst jungle tribes who cannot withstand the inroads of malaria and dysentery if deprived of alcohol or opium. The rigid application of Excise laws in the case of Thárus, who could not understand why they should be haled to prison for brewing rice when there were licensed shops for the retail of inferior liquor in their neighbourhood, has before now proved most unsettling to the community;

and so it was good to hear that the collection of "mohwa" flower, that is chiefly used in the Nallamallais for distillation, is now entrusted to the Chenchus, who can earn a good wage by bringing it into the Government depots, and are allowed to retain a certain quantity for home consumption: for by this means they are able to maintain their health and avoid the temptation of drinking to excess in the licensed distilleries in their neighbourhood.

The history of the treatment of Chenchus has been given at length, so that some idea may be formed of the work of the Forest Officer in reference to wild tribes. Throughout the length and breadth of the Peninsula may be found these jungle men, to whom the approach of civilization has brought stress and trouble hitherto unknown; for their customs must be interfered with, and their liberty to some extent restricted, so soon as permanent settlements are made in the vicinity of the forests they look upon as their own. To make these changes bear less hardly on these simple people, to encourage them to accept the advantages that are offered in exchange, is not a difficult task when confidence has been won and sympathy practically proved. The Forest Officer has always excelled in successful dealings with the men of the forest, to whom he is often the best-known representative of a distant Government; and if it stood alone to the credit of the department that it has been the means of saving from misery some of these wild tribes, that record would be sufficient to justify its existence, without writing of the vast forest estate that has been saved to the Empire by its exertions.

After a second visit to Madras, we returned to Calcutta towards the end of January. Christmas had meanwhile been passed at Ootacamund. The settlement was empty save of its permanent residents and a few visitors, but nevertheless the walks across the breezy downs and through the plantations of eucalyptus and wattle were most enjoyable. It was years since we had seen the hoar-frost on such English-looking hedges, and the long sprays of whitened bramble sparkling over the narrow lanes, and the change from the plains and their hot forests to the open country and brisk cold of Ootacamund was all the more enjoyable in that there was some reminiscence of the West in the air. Perhaps the giant heliotrope and fuchsias, or perhaps the scent of the fragrant eucalyptus firewood, called to remembrance Cornwall or the South of Europe.

To the forester the acclimatization of the eucalyptus was most interesting. The tree grows and coppices freely, providing a full and cheap supply of fuel that must be most convenient. The fuel question is one that is particularly prominent in all hill-stations in India, and causes the forester endless thought and trouble. In Simla the problem is nothing short of acute, when good wood fuel is valued at over £1 a ton, and coal is sold at double that price, and yet fails to meet the requirements of the native inhabitants, whose simple meals necessitate the use of a clear fire that will at once give out heat. The reboisement of the bare hills around Simla with eucalyptus and wattle is a matter that has received a passing consideration, but the undertaking will need care in the selection of species that will bear the ranges of temperature prevalent at 7,000 feet elevation in Northern India. At Ootacamund fuel costs one-tenth of what is charged at Simla, and the tree may find extended use in replanting the "sholas," or spinneys of evergreen forest, that guard the springs on the downs of the Nilgherry Hills.

Those averse from the practice of forestry in Madras declare that these remnants of the forest are not decreasing in size, and they point to isolated stems now standing in the open as proof of their assertion. But those who know the habits of evergreen trees are aware that such stems are only the survivors of those that once covered large areas with their heavy shade, and have been left solitary when the forest receded under the attacks of cattle and fire. In open country, especially where a heavy rainfall obtains, erosion presents some danger even if the watercourses are protected; but when these are being laid bare of vegetation it will proceed with a rapidity that will cause both astonishment and annoyance to those interested in the hill-settlements of Madras. It would have been delightful to have camped on these high downs of Southern India, for it must be charming to roam at these elevations, where also tiger, panther, bison, and the Nilgherry goat, are to be found; but we had no leisure for pastime—little time, indeed, to see as much as was desirable in so large a country as Madras.

On return to Calcutta, the question of forest education in reference to the recruitment of officers of the Imperial Forest Service was under consideration by the Government of India. Attention had been attracted to this subject by the absence of competition at the yearly examinations held in London, and this difficulty was thought to be traceable to the expense of preparation, and to the inferior conditions of the service in India as compared with those offered in other departments. The latter drawback had, as already described, been to some extent remedied, and it remained to devise a suitable system of training at home that should not involve parents and guardians in excessive expenditure. Forest students had for twenty years or so been training at Cooper's Hill College, and on the closure of that institution had been transferred under the charge of Dr. (now Sir William) Schlich and Mr. W. R. Fisher to Oxford, where for the past three years new probationers had also been directed to prosecute their studies. To my mind, the chief points were to provide a University training, so that Forest Officers might have the same educational advantages as recruits for the Indian Civil Service; to shorten the term of probation so as to reduce its expense, and to aid this object by granting a suitable stipend to probationers; to do away with residence in the forests of Germany, prescribing only visits to Continental forests during the vacations; to throw open the training of probationers to all suitably equipped British Universities; and, lastly, to insist that there should be a probationary period in India on a suitable salary, so that the recruit should have sufficient time to adapt his Western theories of forestry to actual practice in the East, and for an introduction to the language, manners, and customs, of a people he was to be brought into intimate contact with during the whole of his service.

The Committee I travelled to London to attend, as the member representing the views of the Government of India, comprised gentlemen whose names afforded assurance that the subject of forestry education would be most thoroughly dealt with; they were Sir John Edge, Sir William Thiselton-Dyer, Mr. (now Sir Stafford) Howard, with Mr. Munro-Ferguson as President, and a unanimous report was drawn up after the examination of many witnesses. But as that report has not yet been published, the views of the Government of India and of the Committee appointed by the Secretary of State—interesting as they would be to all who have the progress of forestry at heart—are not available to the public, and inquirers must draw their own inferences from a comparison of the Regulations for Indian Forest Probationers issued for the year before, and for the years following, the sitting of the Committee, and also from the increase in the number of candidates who now appear before the Selection Board for Forest Probationers that sits yearly at the India Office. There were, it is said, seventy-six candidates for twelve vacancies on the last occasion, so that the efforts to insure a larger selection from amongst the youth of England who desire to take up forestry as their life's work have not been unavailing.

I returned to Simla in May, 1908, and was engaged in labours similar to those I have endeavoured to describe in previous pages until November 9, when I handed over charge of my duties, and received the cordial thanks of the Government of India for the work of thirty-five years. But that work was not quite completed. Six weeks we had promised ourselves to revisit some of the show-places of Central and Northern India, and to bid farewell to the forests that had for so long been our home; and after taking a last look at Agra, Delhi, and Udaipur, we joined our friend, Mr. R. Burns, I.C.S., at Bankatwa in the Gonda district, where for ten days he placed his camp and all the best "shikaris" of the district at our service.

From thence we went to spend a last Christmas in camp at Bijrani, near the Ramnagar railway-station, where Mr. E. F. Winter, I.C.S., then Commissioner of Kumaon, had pitched his camp. It was a spot I was intimately acquainted with, of broken hills and stony streams, and there a most pleasant time was passed. When we arrived, the tigers were roaring a welcome, and we did our best to charm them; but there were counter-attractions in the shape of a versatile tigress who possessed superior claims, so that we had to be content with the good fortune of seeing much more than we killed, which is as it should be. One tiger there was who for long could not choose between the pleasures of the table and the invitation of the fair sex. Twice I watched him walking through the forest intent on the meal that lay below me, and twice he was recalled by the insistent cries of his mate. On the third evening he came again in the red glow of the setting winter sun, his hide shining like burnished copper as he stole through the yellow grass; then he stood erect over his kill, to fall a few feet from it just in the moment of the proud assertion of his strength.

From Bijrani we went to Amángarh, where also there were tigers; but they, too, would have none of our baits, nor should we have seen more than their tracks had they not killed a stray buffalo from the village. The victim lay on the sand of a deep watercourse ; the dense forest came to the edge of the perpendicular banks, here cut into fantastic ridges by the action of the rains. On one of these, scarce three feet wide, was a bare tree that overlooked both the kill and the ravines below on either side, and here I took an unstable seat in the sunlight, intending that the tiger should come along the watercourse and be seen before he could notice this very evident ambush ; but it fell out otherwise. The buffalo was covered with feeding vultures, and so torn and defiled that no clean tiger would touch it, and the scent from these offensive birds was so strong as to be hardly supportable ; what interest there was consisted in watching the peevishness of these fowls, and their brutal and unprovoked attacks on each other, till suddenly a crow uttered the danger-cry, and the obscene crowd flapped heavily away in every direction. No tiger could be observed in the ravines, where first my glances were directed, but, looking nearer home, he was seen standing on the narrow ridge, contemplating with savage earnestness the ruins of his repast ; his head was sunk low between his shoulders, and from time to time he jerked it forward as if gulping down his wrath. He detected something unusual in the surroundings immediately the rifle was raised to guard the narrow passage to my tree. It was not convenient that he should come along that path, and when I fired he bounded down the cliff, and disappeared at a gallop in the long grass quite unscathed, as subsequent tracking proved. And so ended my tiger-shooting in India with a most interesting episode, for I had not before seen a tiger express his disgust and wrath so unmistakably as had this one, and I had not often witnessed such a clever and speedy departure in precipitous ground.

From Amángarh we went to Chila, and spent some days with Mr. B. Osmaston, bidding adieu to the forests on the Ganges, where there was not a walk but recalled some recollection of early days of hunting with horse, dog, and rifle, of man-eating tigers and wild-elephants, so that sometimes time was put back for a quarter of a century, when the memory of olden days revived with the sight of some familiar spot. Elephants and tigers there were still sufficient, but the former were not aggressive, and the latter were too polite to feed in the company of man; however, we shot a panther that sat coolly regarding our progress through the forest, and two days after our departure Mr. Osmaston met and slew the ten-foot tiger that had afforded us a week's amusement on his trail. And so we finally left the forests of Northern India, and took train to Bombay on special deputation to report on forest establishments there before leaving the country for good.

The forests of Bombay are diverse; there are the riparian forests of Scinde, the desert forests of the

Deccan, and the evergreen forests of Kanara, with many varying types distributed between these extremes, as well there may be when 15,000 square miles, or 12 per cent. of the area of the Province, is concerned. But there was little time afforded for silviculture—indeed, none to spare from an examination of the methods of exploitation and of the supply of produce to the villagers, the two subjects which were responsible for the large staff that was maintained. In Bombay the forests are maintained for the use of the people, but those who live near them are they who reap the direct benefits therefrom, and who are held to be to some extent responsible for their welfare; and in result the forests are not disappearing, but improving—though, as regards the yield of the larger portion of the area, this is naturally not in large timber, but in the small stuff that the Indian agriculturist uses. For large timber the 4,000 square miles of the Kanara forests are available, and these present a pleasant change from the dry rocks characteristic of the Deccan, though even the latter fascinate by the weird forms and colours assumed in the evening glow or during the short twilight.

It will be remembered that the Province of Bombay has been during many years subjected to the stress of plague and scarcity, from which recovery can be but slow; also that the industrial development of the country has drawn many of the able-bodied of both sexes to the towns, so that at the present time there is little pressure on the land, and no necessity to settle on the less profitable or less fertile areas. Such conditions have an immediate effect on the forests in diminishing the demand for such produce as is locally consumed, and in reducing the amount of labour available for the extraction of timber and other products for export. It is no doubt sad for a Government to contemplate an area of several thousands of square miles under forest, especially if it is considered that a part of it might preferably be occupied by happy homesteads surrounded by flourishing fields; but, if there is still room for such homesteads in areas where the initial labour of preparing the land for permanent cultivation has already been supplied, the sole remedy is to wait till a larger population shall increase the demand for arable land beyond that which is already available.

To convert large forests into fruitful fields, a regular plan of campaign must be devised and followed. It is useless to encourage the settlement of small isolated villages which are unable to clear more than trivial areas of jungle in their immediate vicinity; for small communities have not the strength to fight against the disadvantages of the forest, and ultimately succumb to the inroads of vegetation, of wild beasts, and of sickness. Large forest areas must therefore be attacked from the outside in a regular sequence of operations, on the principle of sending column after column of invaders to the assault; and so though at present there is no demand for Kanara forest land, yet with returning prosperity and increase of population the land will be ready, when the time arrives, to yield very considerable areas for cultivation, and the Government of Bombay may be pleased to feel that they have at their disposal the means to meet the expansion of this industry in the future, for not all Provinces are equally favourably situated. The forests as they exist yield a considerable revenue to the State, and would afford a larger one if sufficient labour were available for their working. In this matter a difficulty exists, not only in Bombay, but in other parts of India, as has already been indicated; for the native of the country considers that the word "jungle" is as synonymous with "desolation" as "gurkháli" is with "oppression." To him forest life means a resignation of all the social amenities, and withal the certainty of the inroads of disease; so that, while he fully recognizes the claim to future reward possessed by hermits and other holy men who sit in penance or meditation, he himself is not capable of such sacrifices, and finds his delight in the busy haunts of men, where incessant conversation passes for proof of superior intellect.

The only present remedy for the lack of forest labour in Bombay seems to lie in its importation; there are other places in India, not so fertile, where the population is in excess of the demands of the land, and is therefore willing to make winter visits to Burma, or even to spend years in the West Indies. And it might be that persuasive offers of land and of other initial help would attract visitors, and even tempt them to remain, and in time to replace the worn-out inhabitants of the Kanara forests, over whom the jungle is asserting its supremacy. All forest folk eat heartily, take opium or alcohol, and are well sheltered against the climate; and this they contrive, not exclusively by their own efforts in raising food and other crops, for the forest supplies them with flesh and fish, with a thousand articles of domestic use, while the sale of surplus forest products affords them the means of purchasing those necessaries or luxuries which are otherwise out of reach of the community. A village that cannot live on the forest cannot expect to live long in it under conditions that would soon kill the European of much stronger constitution, and therefore all the greater reason why colonization of forest areas should proceed from outside, where the base of operations rests securely on the settled lands.

Another burning question in Bombay was that of cattle-grazing in the Deccan, where the rainfall is so small that tree growth survives with difficulty, and where it is of much importance that the soil covering should be maintained so far as it is possible to do so. It may be imagined that the rocky and infertile soil of this area does not afford much food for cattle, that these will devour with the avidity born of starvation almost any green thing that may be found, and that thus forest conservation and cattle-grazing are impossible within the same area. Consistent protection of such forests during twenty or thirty years merely encourages a growth of small trees and shrubs that are, it is true, enriching the soil, and will doubtless prepare the way for better growth centuries hence; and the question arises whether it is worth while to risk the discontent of the people during a lengthy period, when at its close no appreciable benefit may result to their descendants. The answer probably will be found in relinquishing all the small areas that cost much in protection, and also cause much irritation to the people, and in retaining the larger that are situated on the summit of ridges; for these will have good effect in improving the water-supply in this arid country, and are as a rule less accessible from the villages below.

The Kanara forests contain bison and tiger and other big game. The former are driven to sportsmen perched on the top of high ladders, though it is somewhat astonishing that it should be possible to fire a heavy rifle while still retaining a seat on a slippery plank. The heavy grass of the Tarai forests of Northern India, in which tiger and elephant are swallowed up, is not frequent here, so that driving game with coolies and tracking it on foot are feasible. But there was no time for sport during my short visit; I accompanied my kindly hosts, Messrs. Talbot, Murray and Millett, to Bombay, whence, after meeting in conference, I returned to Calcutta to prepare my report for the Bombay Government.

My two last tours in Madras and Bombay had given opportunity to compare forest conditions there with those in the Provinces under the more direct control of the Government of India, and the result of such comparisons seemed to afford proof that the system of government did not affect the progress of State forestry, but solely the attitude of the Government towards it. In all Provinces the rules for the subservience of the Forest to the Revenue Department were theoretically identical, but their application was widely different; and in those Provinces where there was deemed to be no practical necessity to enforce these rules literally—that is, where the

Revenue officer was glad to be allowed to stick to his last, and permitted the forester to do the same —there were to be found the best progress in forestry and the most contentment in its regard amongst the population. The *impasse* that State forestry was approaching on one side of the Peninsula, and its success on the other, afforded striking examples of the results of the two methods. On the one side, the Senior Conservator was a member of the Provincial Council, and was consulted by the Government in all forest matters; on the other, the forest administration was carried out by a member of the Board of Revenue, who, even if he possessed transcendent ability and was at the same time eaten up with zeal for silviculture, yet had not the time either to inspect his forests or to become acquainted with his staff.

The subject of the respective merits of exotic and indigenous Governors is not one that may be lightly approached by a layman, nor, now that both are to govern with the aid of an official minority, is there much interest in doing so; and the most that can be said is that, on the face of it, it would appear that an officer who possessed experience acquired in another part of the Empire, and was furnished with the best advice on local matters, would be in a better position than another who only had the latter of these advantages. For the rest, success must depend to a great extent on good fortune in selection. On the one hand, too much attention may be paid to the claims of seniority in the Indian Civil Service; on the other, party considerations at home may influence the choice. In any case, a man who has made a reputation, whose judgment can be depended upon in an emergency, and not one who is on his trial, is indicated for the control of an Indian Province: for, in present conditions of unrest, experiments that may affect the passions of thirty or forty millions of people may turn out to be a too costly method of gauging the abilities of the most promising of statesmen.

Both Sir George Clarke and Sir H. Lawley showed great interest in the management of the forests of their Provinces, and brought to bear on the subject the wide experience they had gained in foreign lands; and especially they realized the importance of popularizing forest education, and in consequence it appears probable that Forest Schools will be established in connection with the Agricultural Colleges both at Poona and Coimbatoire, whereby both sciences will benefit. For as yet it has hardly become established in the mind of the peasant that he owes a not unimportant proportion of his prosperity to forest influences, nor has the Forest Guard realized the bearing of these influences on agriculture. At Coimbatoire is a Forest Museum that will well repay a visit as teaching the importance of forest products to the people, and also as providing a better acquaintance with certain products that are familiar through export to Europe.

Having completed my work in Calcutta, we sailed for Ceylon, and spent a fortnight visiting the forests of that island through the courtesy of the Conservator, Mr. Campbell, formerly of the Indian Forest Service. The area of Ceylon is about 25,500 square miles, comprised within a length of about 270 miles, by a breadth of about 140; so that a fortnight's tour, even with the advantages of a Government motor-car and the excellent roads of the island, could convey but a slight impression of the forests and their working. I have often envied the ability of those who after a few weeks' trip, covering a much vaster area, are able to decide with the assurance of first-hand knowledge all of the social as well as many of the political problems that face Government servants in the East, and have wondered why such phenomenal perspicacity is not taken more advantage of in selections for the higher appointments that control the home and foreign policies of the Empire. For the ordinary individual, painstaking and enthusiastic as he may be, too often leaves some Imperial dependency, where he has passed half a lifetime, with a feeling of how little he knows even of the special work to which he has devoted himself, and how little he has learnt of the people amongst whom he has lived, though he may be aware that mutual trust, and even affection, has made that work interesting and successful.

Of the 25,500 square miles of Ceylon, some 4,000 square miles comprise the mountains, which consist of a series of ridges running in a general direction from south-east to north-west, while rising to a maximum altitude of 8,300 feet above sea-level. Thus these mountain ridges lie across the track of the two monsoon currents, and have a marked effect on the occurrence of the wet and dry seasons on the east and west sides of the island. The rainfall, so important a consideration in the constitution and growth of the forest, varies from 150 to 45 inches, according to locality, and the mean temperature between 79° and 82° F., air moisture being constant at from 80° to 85°. It may be inferred, therefore, that the forests are evergreen, and that the crops and other vegetation grow with marvellous rapidity. There are over 500 different kinds of marketable trees, the most valuable being satinwood and ebony, so that forestry might be deemed to be a profitable undertaking; but here again the forester has arrived too late, and must occupy himself with saving a remnant for the State.

It is probable that in no other country in the world can so large a continuous area of shifting cultivation be found as in Ceylon, and it is more than probable that the vast areas of poor scrub jungle that are everywhere noticeable consist but of the secondary growth of the magnificent evergreen forest whose huge stems may now and again be observed in those places that have escaped the axe and fire of the wandering cultivator. Nor was it till comparatively recent years that the Government, recognizing at last the value of the forest, desisted from selling the best portions thereof at prices often much less than the value of the standing timber, and without reference to climatic and economic considerations; so that since 1883, when systematic forestry was introduced, the work of the forester has been hampered by the want of an adequate staff, by the wasteful customs of the country, by opposition from vested interests that had been allowed to spring up, and in consequence little progress has been made towards the object in view.

Even now there are less than 1,000 square miles of reserved forest in the island, though some 3,000 more are under consideration for reservation; and this is obviously too small a proportion of the total area in a land where the habits of the people and the interests of the planting community both tend to encourage the denudation of the soil, with the results that have already been touched upon elsewhere. Already a prohibition of forest clearances above the 5,000-feet line has been issued, but this, though a good beginning, is not sufficient to guard against possible danger to the garden and field cultivation of the island. More stringent regulations for the protection of both public and private lands (as is done in France and Switzerland) are required, and more attention is necessary to restocking the areas left blank by shifting cultivation.

From a forester's point of view, a tour in Ceylon is interesting in enabling some idea to be formed of what these forests were like in the days before they were recklessly destroyed, and of what they might be like should forestry be fostered by the Government in the future. In such circumstances the ridges would again be well wooded, and the catchment areas would again be filled with valuable timber trees; while perennial streams would run clear to the sea, instead of, as now, forming muddy torrents that intermittently convey thousands upon thousands of tons of valuable soil yearly into the ocean. Tea, rubber, cocoa, citronelles, etc., are the valuable products of Ceylon at the present time, as coffee and cinchona were in the past. The two latter have disappeared, perhaps aided by too intensive cultivation; and some of the dangers that threaten the continuance of the others may perhaps be found, first, in the attacks of insects and fungi that in the tropics almost invariably follow on the adoption of a system of pure plantation; and, second, in the erosion of the fertile soil that may be hastened by the destruction of a protective forest belt, and by the method employed in planting commercial products in vertical rows on the hillside—a system whereby the off-flow of torrential rains is able to produce the greatest damage.

As these remarks are being written, rubber is booming in the City, and the Forest Officer is frequently asked for his advice in the matter of investment. He can give none unless he is personally acquainted with the local conditions of the plantation, for there are many circumstances which insure success or foretell failure. The suitability of the climate, rainfall, and soil, for the selected species, the configuration of the ground and the conveniences of carriage, the supply and price of labour, and the efficiency and energy of the management, are all important factors. The investor must in the majority of cases trust to information at second-hand, and he will do well to ascertain that this is reliable and disinterested. If he has satisfied himself on these points, there are yet other influences to be taken into account; for instance, will the increase in production of rubber plantation keep pace with or exceed the increased demand for the raw material? and will present inflated prices for rubber, which, it is claimed, can be produced at a shilling per pound or a little over, be permitted to continue? Finally there remains the consideration of the probability of the deterioration of the stock of standing trees, and of the possibility that the soil may not respond to a second rotation of the same species without expensive preparations, or that insect and fungus damage, so frequent in pure plantations in the tropics, may work havoc, as was the case, for example, with coffee. Of the rubber industry it can be said, as of many others, that it is perfectly sound in itself, and it will ultimately rest on a firm basis, but that individual enterprises of the present day may vary, as regards their future, between those that can be classified as hopeless and others that possess all the attributes of unqualified success.

And so we left for England, having visited the forests of every Province of British India, and seen something of those of an adjacent colony; but there was still regret that, though opportunity had been afforded by the courtesy of Political Residents, there had not been time to gain a knowledge of the forests of native States in the centre and south of the Peninsula better than that possible to a railway traveller through these territories; and thus, though during the past thirty-five years, save when absent on leave, some seven months of each year had been spent in laying up stores of experience and local knowledge, one result of this labour was to prove how very much more was left to learn.

CHAPTER XIII

CONCLUSION

THE forests of India, vast as they are, will have but little effect in solving the difficulty that is already beginning to be felt in supplying the demand for timber in the British Isles, because they have first to meet the demands of a yet vaster population. They will continue to yield teak and ornamental woods, because India cannot yet fully utilize these expensive products; and there will be an increasing supply of lac, tanning material, and other forest products, available for export, as the exploitation of the forests continues to develop. There may also spring up in the future other industries of some magnitude, such as the manufacture of paper pulp and tannin extracts, but this will probably not take place until the prices of these commodities rise; for it is impossible at present to compete against the advantages possessed by factories in other countries which are located in the midst of dense coniferous forests, or in virgin mangrove swamps, that are both treated on the system of clear felling, often without any provision for a marketable regrowth, when in India much larger areas would have to be worked over in the search for material of suitable quality, and arrangements made for effective natural reproduction.

In the difficulties that are likely to be experienced from a shortage of the timber-supply of the world, England would be well advised to remember the old adage about self-help; for she will get but little from outside, as yearly those countries become fewer that possess enough timber for export as well as for home consumption. As population and prosperity progress, so does also the demand for forest products, so that even those countries that now possess a surplus stock may not in the future have enough even for their own requirements. In some European countries, where there are large areas of both public and private forests that have been under scientific management for centuries, the demand of the population for timber is already in excess of supply, while both to the east and to the west of these islands difficulties before unknown are beginning to make themselves felt. For instance, the combined forest area of France and Germany and Switzerland approaches some 100,000 square miles, yet each of these countries imports timber from abroad, and can better afford to do so by reason of the profit derived from the careful management of their own forests. Denmark, Italy, Spain, and Portugal, are in a worse plight; for their forests neither yield sufficient produce for the inhabitants, nor, apparently, any large revenue to the State.

Russia, Scandinavia, and Austria-Hungary, are still exporters of timber, but the amount that will continue to be available from thence must depend on the demands of the population of these countries, and on the answer to the question whether the forest capital or only the interest therefrom is now being used; while the price of the material that these countries export will rise if it should happen that those nearer the source of supply than England have in the future a larger use for the surplus available. For instance, Continental countries absorb the excess forest harvest of Austria and Hungary, and will probably intercept that of Russia and Scandinavia as soon as any pressing need for it arises; and thus England might easily occupy a worse position in the timber market in the future than she does at present.

In America the needs of the future have been recognized, and within a comparatively few years a State Forest Department has been created, with the intention of supplying later on the needs of the population; but trees do not grow in a day, and if the Americans want Canadian timber they can get it cheaper than we can. In the East, Japan is an instance of a country that has foreseen the importance of forest conservation, and is taking steps to make it effective; while China has hitherto paid little attention to the matter, so that now there are places of which it is said that, so great is the scarcity of wood, there is neither fuel for the living nor coffins for the dead.

All these countries are forced to maintain forests to protect the water-supply and to prevent erosion in the hills, and in proportion to the timely recognition of these indirect benefits, has been that of the direct benefits that have been conferred by the forests. England, on the other hand, is in a position to ignore to some extent the indirect influences of the forest, and will certainly suffer in the future from the absence of the direct benefits they confer; for she has preferred to place entire dependence upon the forest resources of other countries, although she has before her eyes examples of how State forestry not only aids in meeting an ever-increasing industrial demand, but, while bringing profit to the Treasury, also provides remunerative employment to the inhabitants of the country. In the case of an European war, the starvation, not only of the timber market, but also of all those trades that depend on forest material, either in its raw or converted form, would probably deal a severe blow to very many important industrial concerns in England.

The arguments that are adduced against the introduction of State forestry in England appear to be, chiefly, that it will not pay, and that, if it does, a long period must be passed before any return is received on the capital expended. The first objection is based on the current price of timber, which will probably rise in the future much more rapidly than it has in the past, and, moreover, it takes only cash returns into consideration, leaving out others that may become of equal or even greater importance; the second is based on the assumption that it is not the duty of a Government to make provision for the future welfare of the nation; and both appear to have their foundation in errors, either commercial or political.

Meanwhile India has prepared for the future as regards the direct benefits the forests afford to its population, and is commencing to understand that their indirect influences may also affect the industrial progress of the country, not only as regards agriculture, which is, of course, of paramount interest, but also as regards those manufactures for which only the raw material is at present exported. With regard to the former, the yearly yield of five million tons of timber and fuel, of two hundred millions of bamboos, of half a million sterling of minor produce, as well as the grazing afforded to thirteen million cattle, shows what the local demand is at present; and to this may be added produce amounting in value to a quarter of a million sterling that is given freely away to the people. The forest, however, is not exploited even for the amount of produce it can supply at present, nor probably for a tithe of what it could supply if a larger demand justified the expense of more extensive working; but that demand will come in time with the increase of population, and with the construction of railways and their feeder roads that provide cheap and sure carriage; for without such communications the moving of material bulky in proportion to its value must always be hindered by an expenditure incommensurate with the probable profit on its delivery.

The object of State forestry in India is therefore to supply the requirements of its population in forest products, to protect the water-supply of the country, and to afford help in its industrial development. As is the case in European countries, the forest management should, as it always has, result in profit, but this profit should be subsidiary to the main objects in view; it should be a consequence of, and not a reason for, a forest policy. The financial success of State forestry as a whole is now assured in India, but even so it is not possible that the forests of each district should produce a profit until they have been so organized as to discount the ill-treatment of the past; and it is certain that, at the introduction of scientific forestry in any locality, reasonable liberality in expenditure pays far more in the results attained than rigid economy merely for the sake of saving, and equally is it sure that any system that restricts expenditure in a fixed proportion to the revenue of the past years must result in limiting the expansion of the income of the future. The estimates of reliable and experienced experts are vain if it is insisted on that an increased revenue should precede an increased expenditure; nor is this believed to be the mode of business adopted by progressive commercial firms in any country in the world.

The growing importance of forestry in India has demanded a proportionate increase in professional knowledge and in the strength of establishments. It has been shown how during the past few years these matters have received practical consideration involving somewhat expensive improvements in conditions of service and recruitment. There remains one other, perhaps the most important, attribute of the Forest Officer that should be fostered, and that is enthusiasm, a virtue that may spread by contagion through all classes, from the jungle savage to the head of the Government. Without enthusiasm persuasion and personal influence are ineffective, but enthusiasm is difficult without contentment.

Of all the Indian public Services, the Forest Department acknowledges no superior in loyalty to its employers and in self-abnegation, however trying the conditions of the work. All the more is it a pity that there should have existed an almost chronic state of agitation for concessions to this Service. Such a state is probably not peculiar to one department of the Uncovenanted Services more than to another, and the concessions that have been granted from time to time during the past generation prove that agitation has been based on legitimate demands. There can be no disloyalty in the presentation of such demands by men who in early youth have signed a lifelong contract; the regret is rather that the demands were not conceded as of voluntary gift, whereby generosity would have been imputed instead of pressure from difficulty of recruitment.

But there remains yet opportunity for a trial of what may be termed original munificence, by removing some remnants of the ancient Uncovenanted Service rules that appear to be either obnoxious or unsuitable to present conditions. For instance, differentiation between the age of retirement of Englishmen recruited from the same public schools, colleges and Universities of England; and limitation of the pension of certain branches of the public Service to a small maximum sum, ignoring either length of service or amount of salary, and thus fixing the pension at a much lower sum than can be earned by Englishmen who serve the Empire either at home or in the colonies. Were such concessions made, the time and talent freed from the public Service, by obviating the necessity of the preparation of arguments that shall insure the ultimate success of organized protest, would be a considerable asset in any department that has already more than its full tale of work to perform, without taking into consideration the gain in the harmonious relations of employer and employed.

Finally, as to sport in India, in so far as the forest is concerned, the time has already arrived when bitterness and jealousies are not uncommon, as a perusal of correspondence in the daily press will show. And this is but natural when the Government has been forced to interfere to protect from promiscuous slaughter the interesting fauna of the country. At present no one can shoot in Government forests without first purchasing a licence that defines the area placed at the sportsman's disposal, the number and kind of animals he may kill, and the close seasons that have been fixed; and in the midst of the eager applications for these licences the Forest Officer may find himself entirely cut off from sport in the area under his charge, or be afraid to fire a shot, lest he should be encroaching on territory leased to another. So much is this the case that more than one Forest Officer has laid aside gun and rifle entirely, so as to have a freer hand in the issue of licences and in the decision of disputes that may arise amongst others—a distinctly humorous result of game laws that add to the duties of the forester that of gamekeeper, and deprive him of one of the most popular incentives to a forester's career.

As a rule, the man who passes his life amongst the big game attacks it in his youth, with the ferocity born of primeval instincts and of novelty. As he grows older he becomes more merciful, till at last intimate acquaintance conduces to sympathetic affection. He may still feel his blood boil with the excitement of a tiger-hunt, for here is a pastime that never stales with its monotony, provided that man and tiger meet with some pretence of equality ; but, for the rest, the wild beasts afford a companionship that is fully recognized in the feeling of solitude experienced when living in a forest devoid of animal life. To read by day on the ground the circumstances and occupations of his neighbours, to interpret by night the cries that tell of their passions and dangers, supplies that added interest which brings vigour to the continuous labour of the forester. For that labour he will find his reward in the generous response of the forest to his fostering care, and in results that will endure for generations after he has completed the short work of a lifetime.

INDEX